Amy looked lovely — & indeed I knew her &

HOW LOVELY Y... *yesterday*

O my ...

e all now ...

...ly — ...G 2005 ... somel...

... / ...

U LOOKED *yesterday —*

... love you with a larger heart

— & somel... Amy looked lovely — &

LOOKED *yested. O my first how /*

... larger heart / See all now with

A PROFOUND SECRET

www.**booksattransworld**.co.uk

A PROFOUND SECRET

MAY GASKELL, HER DAUGHTER AMY,
AND EDWARD BURNE-JONES

JOSCELINE DIMBLEBY

Doubleday

LONDON · NEW YORK · TORONTO · SYDNEY · AUCKLAND

TRANSWORLD PUBLISHERS
61–63 Uxbridge Road, London W5 5SA
a division of The Random House Group Ltd

RANDOM HOUSE AUSTRALIA (PTY) LTD
20 Alfred Street, Milsons Point, Sydney,
New South Wales 2061, Australia

RANDOM HOUSE NEW ZEALAND LTD
18 Poland Road, Glenfield, Auckland 10, New Zealand

RANDOM HOUSE SOUTH AFRICA (PTY) LTD
Endulini, 5a Jubilee Road, Parktown 2193, South Africa

Published 2004 by Doubleday
a division of Transworld Publishers

A catalogue record for this book is available from the British Library.
ISBN 0385 603231

Typeset in 11.5/14pt Granjon by
Falcon Oast Graphic Art Ltd.

Printed in Great Britain by
Mackays of Chatham plc, Chatham, Kent

1 3 5 7 9 10 8 6 4 2

Papers used by Transworld Publishers are natural, recyclable products made from wood grown in sustainable
forests. The manufacturing processes conform to the environmental regulations of the country of origin.

To my wonderful aunt Diana,
without whom this story might never
have been told.

CONTENTS

ACKNOWLEDGEMENTS

WRITING IS NECESSARILY A SOLITARY OCCUPATION; IT CAN BE LONELY. However, with this book I felt I was not alone, but in the fascinating company of men and women who had come back from the past. I also came into contact with many more living people than I would normally, all of whom helped me on my way. I am indebted to them for giving me advice, information and encouragement. My special thanks go to my editor, Marianne Velmans, who has been painstaking, sympathetic and confidence inspiring, as well as Kate Samano and Sheila Lee at Transworld. I am also very grateful to my agent, Araminta Witley, together with Peta Nightingale and Celia Hayley at LAW, and to Emma Rogers.

Equally important have been Andrew Lloyd Webber, my brother Ben Gaskell, Victoria Glendinning, Antony and Harriet Granville, Heather Holden Brown, Julian Rose, my sister Joanna Gaskell, Helen Sutchbury, Elizabeth Rose, the late Phoebe Rose, John Christian, Bill Waters, Caroline Dakers, Hugh and Mirabel Cecil, Andrew Lycett, David Fraser Jenkins, Judith Flanders, Tim Jeal, Michael Holroyd, Selina Hastings, Angela Huth, Caroline Moorehead, Valerie Grove, Katie Hickman, John Julius Norwich, Philip Stevens, Sir Anthony Bonham, and Lord Tweedsmuir.

Valued contributions have been made by Peter Nahum, Godfrey Pilkington, Peyton Skipwith, Jane Abdy, Angelo Hornak, Nicky Gaskell, Tom Lindsay, the Earl of Crawford and Balcarres, Suzanne Fagence Cooper at the V&A, Pam Roberts of the Royal Photographic Society, Peter Faulkner of the William Morris Society, the Red Cross and the Order of St John of Jerusalem, Captain Mason of the Grenadier Guards archives, Dr David Robinson at the Surrey History Centre and Pamela Clark of the Royal Archives.

Further afield, I have been kindly helped by Maurice and Chloe Robson at Kiddington Hall, Dorothy Hunt in Kiddington village, Susie Bagot at Levens Hall, Ruth Butler in Worcestershire, Canon Ian Mackenzie and David Mason of Worcester cathedral, Arthur Moyes of Hatfield College, Durham, Mr and Mrs Chapman of The Old Rectory at Witley, Mary Oaten at Holdhurst, Lord Oxford at Mells, Ismeth Ibraheem in Sri Lanka, Lavinia Keene and Nicholas Kennard in Argentina, Sofka Zinovieff in Rome, Dr Lynda Dryden in Edinburgh, Colin Harrison at the Ashmolean Museum in Oxford and Colin Harris and Hilary Clare at the Bodleian Library.

I greatly appreciate the patience of certain close friends and relations, who have heard me talk far too much about my voyage of discovery during the last three years but have remained supportive; above all, my friend Johnny Culme-Seymour, my children Liza, Henry and Kate, their father David Dimbleby and my son-in-law Rupert Howe, followed by Robin and Hannerle Sligh, Kay and Nicholas Dimbleby, Joe Dimbleby, Jonathan and Bel Dimbleby, Sally Dimbleby, Dil and Ron Travers, Penny and Bill Curry, Erik and Priscilla Smith, Christina and Bamber Gascoigne, Elizabeth McKay, Terence and Vivien Griffin, Jon Swain, Virginia Ironside, Sukie Paravacini, Jessica Douglas Home and Romana McEwen.

I am grateful to the Warden and Fellows of New College, Oxford, for their permission to quote from the letters written by May Gaskell to Lord Milner. I must also thank the Earl of Crawford and Balcarres for his permission to quote from letters which his father, David Balneil, wrote to May Gaskell, and also the Earl of Oxford and Asquith for letting me use a short quote from a letter his grandmother, Frances Homer, wrote to May.

The verse from Rudyard Kipling's 'The Native Born', which he wrote out in Amy Gaskell's birthday book, is reproduced by permission of AP Watt Ltd on behalf of The National Trust for Places of Historical Interest or Natural Beauty.

Finally, I am very grateful to the descendants of Edward Burne-Jones for their kind permission to quote from his unpublished letters to May Gaskell.

I have searched thoroughly for a copyright holder for Loyd Haberly's writings, but have found none.

PICTURE CREDITS

The photographs in the text and in the plate section have been supplied by the author, except for the following:

xii: courtesy of the Fine Art Society PLC, London; 81: ©Chrisite's Images (2004); 78, 95, 228, 306: ©The National Portrait Gallery Picture Library; 216: photo 644/3 by permission of the British Library; 149, 231: ©Hulton-Deutsch Collection/CORBIS.

Picture section:

Edward Burne-Jones, *Amy Gaskell*, 1894, Collection of Lord Lloyd-Webber. Photograph courtesy of Sotheby's Picture Library, London.

Edward Burne-Jones, *The Briar Wood* and *The Rose Bower*, from 'The Briar Rose' Series 1870–90. Farindgon Collecton, Buscot, Oxon, UK/Bridgeman Art Library.

Edward Burne-Jones, *The Last Sleep of Arthur in Avalon* (detail), 1881–98. Museo de Arte, Ponce, Puerto Rico, West Indies/Bridgeman Art Library.

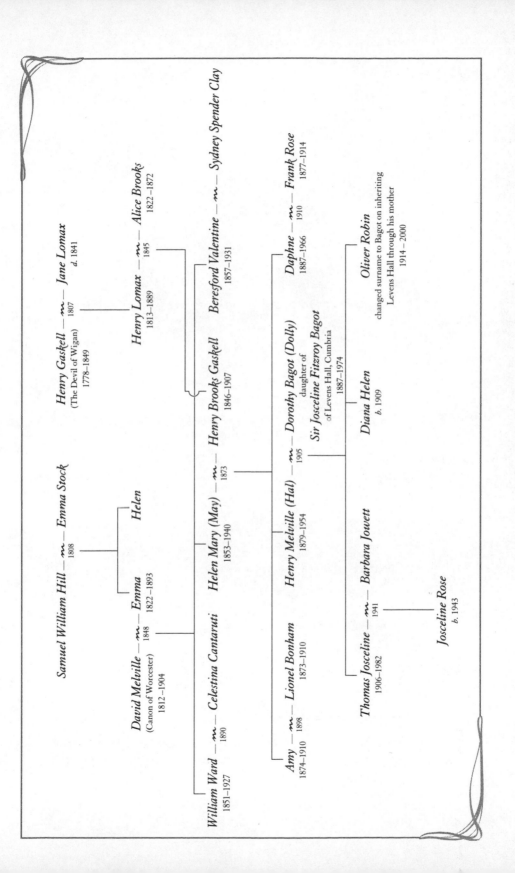

Samuel William Hill —m— Emma Stock
1808
1812–1904

Henry Gaskell —m— Jane Lomax
(The Devil of Wigan)   1807
1778–1849   d. 1841

Henry Lomax —m— Alice Brooks
1813–1889   1845   1822–1872

Beresford Valentine —m— Sydney Spender Clay
1857–1931

David Melville —m— Emma
(Canon of Worcester) 1848 1822–1893
1812–1904

Helen

Helen Mary (May) —m— Henry Brooks Gaskell
1853–1940   1873   1846–1907

William Ward —m— Celestina Cantaruti
1851–1927   1890

Henry Melville (Hal) —m— Dorothy Bagot (Dolly)
1879–1954   1905   daughter of
Sir Josceline Fitzroy Bagot
of Levens Hall, Cumbria
1887–1974

Daphne —m— Frank Rose
1887–1966 1910 1877–1914

Amy —m— Lionel Bonham
1874–1910 1898 1873–1910

Diana Helen
b. 1909

Oliver Robin
changed surname to Bagot on inheriting
Levens Hall through his mother
1914–2000

Thomas Josceline —m— Barbara Jowett
1906–1982   1941

Josceline Rose
b. 1943

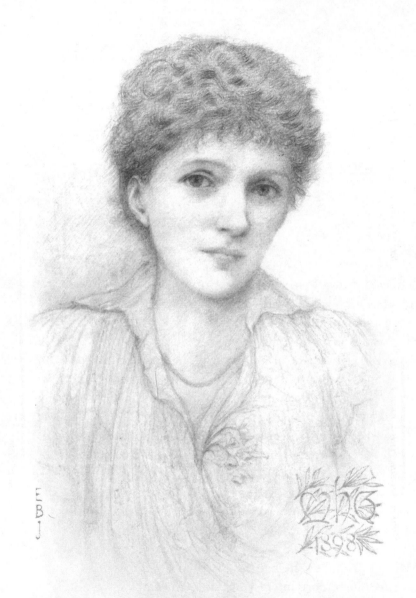

Edward Burne-Jones's last drawing of May Gaskell, 1898, which first made me curious about her and her daughter Amy.

PROLOGUE

HALFWAY DOWN THE STAIRS OF MY FATHER'S HOUSE AN ENCHANTING picture hung on the wall. Dated 1898, it was a drawing of a pretty young woman. She had curly hair, which framed a heart-shaped face. Her head was slightly inclined to one side, and her lovely eyes, which looked straight at the artist, had an intelligent yet tender expression. Her lips were almost parted. She wore a single string of beads round her neck, and an open-necked, muslin blouse with a little bunch of lilies of the valley pinned at the bosom. I always stopped when I passed her on the stairs; she seemed alive, watching me, as if she were about to tell me something. But for some years I did not think to ask my father who she was.

One school holidays, when I was in my early teens, my father told me that the drawing was of my great-grandmother and that the artist had been a leading Pre-Raphaelite painter, Sir Edward Burne-Jones, who he said had been a close friend of hers. Her name was Helen Mary Gaskell, but she had always been known as May. After this, I became much more interested in the old family photograph albums, which were piled up in the drawing room beside my father's jazz records. As I looked through them I began to form an impression of my great-grandmother's surroundings, and of her family life. I was fascinated by those pictures. It dawned on me that this picturesque late-Victorian family were my direct blood relations. I shared their genes; part of what I was came from them. As I studied the pictures I could see that my father, his father, and his grandfather, May's husband, were in many ways physically alike. They all shared an eccentric appearance, as does my own brother, and an exceptionally large, bony nose.

The women in the albums seemed part of a much more distant era. They wore long dresses that never showed a naked arm or ankle, and their hair was elaborately arranged, often under large and spectacular hats. Their figures were so tightly corseted that it made me feel breathless just looking at them. Nevertheless I searched for a hint of myself in them. May's beautiful oldest daughter, Amy, had dark hair like mine, but with her ivory skin, large dreamy eyes and air of calm confidence she really did not look like me. Romantically posed photographs of Amy dominated the albums. The most striking images showed her in a punt on a glassy lake set in landscaped grounds. She stood alone, dressed completely in white, pushing the punt away from an ivy-covered boathouse. Her dress showed off a tiny waist, and you could see thick dark hair drawn up under a huge, floppy white hat that shielded her pale skin from the sun. These photographs, often in large panoramic form and perfectly in focus, were remarkable by any standards. They were artistically composed pictures, not snapshots. Throughout the albums it was obvious that the photographer was someone who had an acute eye for light and form.

In most of the photographs Amy was posed in an extremely self-aware manner, and I wondered what she could have been like. She clearly wanted to show off the swirling arrangement of her abundant hair, her graceful neck, and her shapely figure. Her large eyes, which sloped downwards at the corner, had a slightly mournful expression. But in some pictures she looked almost arrogant. She seemed to have a penchant for white dresses. I was intrigued by her, and became even more so when my father, leaning over me as I looked at the albums, said, 'She died of a broken heart.'

I looked up at him in surprise. 'What do you mean?'

'That's all Granny told us,' replied my father. 'She was only thirty-five. I was too young at the time to remember her.'

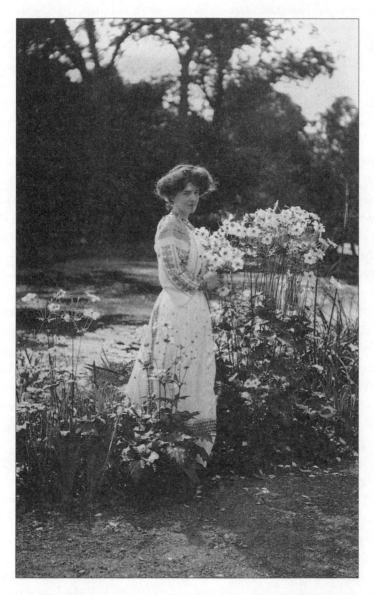

One of the many self-portraits of Amy. She is standing by the
lake at Kiddington in a dress which was clearly a favourite as
she wore it often. Many of her dresses look rather Bohemian in
style, and were perhaps brought back from her travels abroad.

Soon after learning about Amy's death, I noticed an uncannily prophetic self-portrait in one of her own albums. She was about twenty years old and had posed herself lying on her canopied bed. Her dark hair was loose, and fell back over the pillows; her eyes were closed. Underneath the picture she had written in her round, youthful handwriting: 'Self "dead"' (see photograph on p. 178). Much later I would be startled to find that Amy had indeed died in the same pose, in her own bed.

The lake on which Amy punted, the setting for many of the photographs, was familiar to me, for the pictures were taken at Kiddington Hall, a late-eighteenth-century house in Oxfordshire where I had often stayed with my grandparents when I was a little girl. In the cold winter of 1943, my mother had been staying there the day before I was born. When I was a child the house still lacked heating or electricity, so the intense cold and darkness of Kiddington was familiar to me. Nevertheless I found the house fascinating, and I have happy memories of sunny days spent in the garden. Occasionally, my eccentric grandfather, Hal Gaskell, would collect me at Hanborough station himself and drive very slowly, never speaking, through the Oxfordshire lanes. Finally we would creep up a drive of moss-covered pebbles with an arch of branches overhead like a long green tunnel until we reached the house. I did not realize then, of course, that this had once been the home of my great-grandmother May, whose portrait I would come to know much later on the stairs of my father's house.

It was a chance meeting at a party in London that started my investigation into an intriguing family legend and led to a totally new venture after twenty-five years of writing about food. I had known for some time that May Gaskell had been given paintings and drawings by her friend the artist Edward Burne-Jones, and that they had, sadly, been sold out of the family in 1981. I was told that the most remarkable painting in the collection had been a portrait of Amy Gaskell, May's lovely young daughter. Amy was the girl in the punt, the one who had died 'of a broken heart'.

Amy was nineteen years old when Burne-Jones painted her portrait as a present for her mother May. Even in photographs the picture is arresting. Amy's thick dark-brown hair is simply drawn back from her smooth-skinned, pale face. Flawlessly pretty, she is wearing a long-sleeved, high-necked, black silk dress and sits in half-profile, one hand lightly holding the thumb of the other as if to reassure herself. The background is as black as her dress. Her eyes are gentle but her expression tentative; she looks very young in an old setting, and slightly sad. I had pinned an auction-catalogue photograph of the picture on a board above my desk years ago and come to know it well, always wishing I could see the picture 'in the flesh'. I did not know where it was until I heard that it had recently been sold again. The new owner was the well-known composer Andrew Lloyd Webber, a passionate collector of Pre-Raphaelite and Victorian art. I resolved to write to him and ask if I could possibly come and see the painting of my lost relation.

But before I had done so, as I stood outside in the chattering crowd of a summer party in London, I saw Andrew Lloyd Webber across the garden. I had never met him, but I recognized him from photographs. I squeezed my way through the other guests and asked him bluntly if I could come and see the portrait he had of my great-aunt.

'Ah, that wonderful dark picture,' he said. 'Yes, please come. I'll give you my secretary's number and you can arrange a time.'

I told him we had always thought the portrait looked like my younger sister.

'Well, I think she looks rather like you,' Andrew replied.

I found this deeply flattering; after all, he was talking about a ravishing nineteen-year-old girl and I am now a woman of more than 'a certain age'.

'Did you know that she died young?' I asked him. 'Of a broken heart, we were always told.'

He looked surprised. 'No, I don't know anything about her.'

'And Burne-Jones did some lovely drawings of her mother, whom he was very close to – in love with, I think,' I added.

As I said this I suddenly remembered that the year before, at a family funeral, a cousin I had not met before had told me that he had some long-forgotten family papers and books, which included quantities of love-letters from Burne-Jones to May Gaskell, as well as letters, notes and sketches which the artist had sent to May's daughter Amy when he was working on her portrait in the early 1890s. The cousin, who lived in the country, had invited me to come and look at what he had at any time. Impulsively, as I moved away from Andrew Lloyd Webber, I continued: 'If you like, I'll try and find out more – it's always good knowing the background to a picture, and in any case I'm becoming increasingly intrigued by the story.'

I had no idea then, in the throng of that smart summer party, just how gripped I would become by my research, and what a sad, romantic and mysterious story would start to unfold. Nor could I have guessed that in trying to find out about Amy Gaskell I would begin to be equally fascinated by her mother, my remarkable great-grandmother May.

The following week I drove down to my cousin's house in the country, where he had told me I could look at the papers and letters which related to May Gaskell. It was a large, gabled house of red brick and flint. My cousin opened the door and took me straight to the library, which felt rather cold, and looked as if it had not been used for decades. In the middle of the room was a large chest of drawers of inlaid veneer. He opened two exceptionally deep, heavy drawers in which I could see leather volumes and paper folders full of letters.

'I'll leave you to it now,' said my cousin as he left the room. Through the window I could see smooth green lawns and an avenue of tall lime trees whose branches waved slightly in the wind. In the library the stillness and silence were unearthly.

There was so much material that I did not know where to begin. But almost at once I came across something that captivated me. It was a letter written by May Gaskell when she was in her eighties, addressed to her younger daughter Daphne. There were instructions on the envelope that it should be opened only after May's death, together with a parcel, which turned out to contain a large collection of Burne-Jones's most private letters to her. Some of these letters were beautifully bound in leather volumes, but many were loose, slipped into paper folders. On one of the leather-bound volumes, engraved in gold, were the words: 'TIME WILL HASTE AND WASTE, THESE WILL LAST'.

And last they have, lying untouched in the house where Daphne lived for over sixty years of her adult life. The envelope I held in my hand was crisp and pristine, as was the sheet of paper inside. It was as if it had been read only once, in 1940, when Daphne opened it after her mother died.

The letter was dated November 1937; the year, I was to discover, when May began to prepare herself for her death.

'Dear one,' it begins, 'I shall have passed out of your life when you read this.' May explains that she has kept these letters from Burne-Jones separate from the ones his trustees had insisted she should leave to the British Museum.

> *You who knew and loved him will understand that they are so precious and tender and wise and witty – but not for the eye of the scoffer, or for the eye of the casual reader. His friendship to me was like a benediction through the storms of life – his love a safeguard – his influence a continual help to the present hour. And so I leave you these treasures my darling in the hope that in your life they may be a help and comfort and delight as they have been to me. I cannot tell you my child what you have been to me these last years. God bless you for all your care and give you happiness and peace. Good bye, Mother.*

As I began to read the first letter from Burne-Jones to my great-grandmother, I felt privileged but a little guilty as well. This was soon followed by amazement. The letter could have lit a fire in the cold drawer where it had lain unread for so many years:

> *O my God how I love you – it's terrible that one creature should have such power over any other – and I lie under your feet – and have no will or strength against you. Why did I leave you today – I left all my happiness with you – a poor thing came back here, a poor shell, and my heart was away – my heart nestles under your feet, so tread softly . . . I shall lie and think of you and wake and think of you and of the sweet comfort we shall be to each other over our life days – you are not to mind if I have been hurt – it is such sweet pain and it's all for you.*

I shivered slightly in the dark room as I digested these wild proclamations of passion and devotion. But the next letter made me smile, and begin to wish that I had met this emotional but engaging man:

Going to town today, at the day's end, to order a top coat – so as to walk
out with you and not bring ridicule or disgrace upon you – for you once
upbraided me a little for not dressing like other people and I have never
forgotten it – but I can't – if my hat is right, my coat is amiss, or
otherwise is not as it should be – I should look right if I were dressed like
Giotto – or like a crusader – or like Buffalo Bill – pyjamas look all right
– if I might be permitted to say anything so intimate – but I can't look
right somehow in London – and so I am going today to tell the tailor he
must make me look ordinary and unnoticeable – he must.

The letter was illustrated with a cartoon-like drawing of himself as a
little old man with a long thin beard, a few wisps of hair on his bald
head, and a pathetic expression on his face.

I soon noticed a repeated instruction to May to burn the letters – an
instruction that she had evidently ignored: 'Don't let my letters
accumulate, when a new one comes burn the old one, as I do.'

May obviously could not bring herself to do this, and re-reading the
words that Burne-Jones had written to her clearly remained a comfort
to the end of her life. Later, finding no trace of May's letters to him, I
had to assume that by contrast he did indeed burn her letters. This
was a great disappointment to me, as I knew from May's other
writings that she wrote sensitively and at length; her letters would
have told me so much more about their unusual friendship.

In one of Burne-Jones's first letters, in the early spring of 1892, he
responds to a clear anxiety on May's part by reassuring her that he too
feels discretion is important, and stressing that their friendship shall
be 'a profound secret'.

'The least murmur or rumour of questioning jars and vulgarizes
whoever it is who asks – I want this to be a most holy compact,' he
writes, and tells her she will 'bless the day when you opened your
heart to me – it was a week ago today', and that 'none shall hear the
faintest whisper of this friendship which is a real heavenly friendship
for you, to help you and sustain you and make you want to live'.

But why, I wondered, did May so need to confide in him? And why
did he think she didn't want to live? What could her secret have been?

May was clever and cultivated. She was the beautiful wife of a rich
man, and a devoted mother. She had three handsome houses, an

interesting social life and many close friends. You would have thought she'd have had everything to live for. As I continued to read Burne-Jones's letters to her, I tried to imagine what the nature of her friendship with this famous painter, twenty years her senior, could possibly have been. He managed to find time to write her up to five letters a day, and I could see at first glance that many of these letters contained perhaps the most passionate outpourings I had ever come across. Any woman would have been flattered. But with her other commitments and loyalties, how deeply would May have wanted to become involved?

It has always been supposed by Burne-Jones's biographers that, although he adored a series of women, the only extra-marital relationship that was physically consummated was with the young Greek sculptress Maria Zambaco. This affair was ultimately disastrous, and it had been over for twenty-five years by the time he met May. But when my eldest daughter saw some of the letters I had deciphered and typed out lying on my desk, she challenged me: 'Mum, I thought you said this was a platonic friendship!'

Her disbelief was understandable. If someone wrote such declarations of passion today, it would be inconceivable that their relationship was not a physical one. However, this was the Victorian era, when people loved romance and sentimentality, when emotions were either wallowed in or kept painfully secret. But even if Burne-Jones believed in pure and spiritual love, as the historian Bill Waters told me, it is hard not to detect an underlying physical longing in many of his letters to May. He sometimes betrays at the very least a demand for his love to be reciprocated:

> . . . *from the very first I said to myself that all that matters was that I should help you – and my heart in those days was innocent of any other thought than wanting to make your life days prettier for you – I want to go back to those days when I cared nothing for myself.*

As I began to discover numerous references to May's adored daughter Amy, and several letters addressed to her, I wondered how she fitted into their friendship. When Burne-Jones was painting nineteen-year-old Amy's portrait, he wrote touchingly to her, trying to help when she too appeared to be unhappy. It was becoming more and more puzzling to me. Why did both mother and daughter need comfort from Burne-Jones? And would I be able to discover any clue to the mystery of Amy's 'broken heart' and early death?

During that first visit to my cousin's silent library, I realized that I wanted to find out much more about Amy than the little information I had promised Andrew Lloyd Webber. Rather like the Victorians themselves, I have always had a weakness for stories of romance, mystery and tragedy. This promised to be one. It was also a compelling chronicle about people whose genes I shared, who would have recognizable family traits; a story which had been all but forgotten, and which my generation, who were now fast becoming the oldest generation, knew little of. In addition, through Burne-Jones's intimate words, I would gain insight into the more personal side of a famous artist.

May clearly wanted to pass on family history to her descendants. Towards the end of her life she wrote several discerning and heartfelt accounts of what she knew of her own family, the Melvilles, and her husband's, the Gaskells of Kiddington Hall, during the previous two generations. My father gave me photocopies of these writings about two years after I had discovered the old photograph albums. I read them without much concentration, and soon put them away. By that time, I was turning from a child into a young adult; it was the present and myself I was interested in, not the past and other people.

Shortly after starting to research this book, I read May's words again, and far more carefully this time. Now that I was a middle-aged woman, with experience of my own family life, its joys and sadnesses, its gains and losses, of watching my children grow and develop, I suddenly found the document engrossing. May's acute observations on the characters and fates of members of our family riveted me. I came to the last page, which I could not remember reading before. May concluded:

It is for those who come after me to add to these remarks. I have mentioned dates, and a few facts that might be lost in the passing of years, or be of use to those who come after – As I write the words 'to those who come after' a vision rises of the children who are yet to be born, and will hold in their bodies and minds the inheritance of our strength and weakness, our virtues and failings, our intellectual and artistic gifts; and our dullness and narrowness. May the best conquer the faults and build up men and women in the future for the help of Man and for the glory of God.

Well, I thought, I know I shall never be the perfect descendant May had hoped for, nor do I think I have ever done anything for the glory of God. I did not even marry in church, or have my children christened when they were babies. May herself, I was to learn, had many admirable qualities which would be hard to match. But rediscovering these words now made me even more convinced that investigating the story of May and Amy Gaskell and Edward Burne-Jones, although such completely new territory for me, was something I had to do. I am, after all, I thought, one of 'those who come after'. May would have been pleased that I was acting on her words; of this I felt sure.

'You'll become a driven woman,' said a friend of mine who had also written a book which delved into her family's past. And she was right.

I soon went back to spend another day in my cousin's library, poring over Burne-Jones's letters and deciphering his difficult handwriting, often written in the faintest pencil. At the end of a long day it was completely quiet in the house. No sound of anyone around. I gathered up my things and prepared to go home. As I replaced the folders of letters I had been working on in one of the deep drawers of the veneered chest, I noticed a package wrapped in discoloured white paper, just discernible in the darkness at the back. I brought it out. The bundle was tied up with dusty string and had a grey-blue luggage label attached to it. On this I could recognize May's neat handwriting in the blue-black ink she always used. I could hardly believe what I read: 'Paintbrushes given to Helen Mary Gaskell by Edward Burne-Jones.'

My heart thumped as I undid the string – the first time it had been untied, I felt sure, since the 1930s, or perhaps well before. As I unwrapped the parcel carefully, the paper crackled with the brittleness of age. Then suddenly, there in front of me, were at least twenty brushes of different sizes; all of them were well used, the handles smudged with colour. Some had flakes of paint still sticking to the bristles. In another small package were Burne-Jones's gesso tools. I took up a brush and held it as if I was about to put it to a canvas. I could almost feel the artist's hand on the brush and then May's, as she must have held it thoughtfully after the death of this dearest friend, who had made such a great impact on her life. Then, glancing in the drawer again, I noticed another label, which must have dropped off the package; on this one May had written that these very brushes had been used to paint the darkly beautiful portrait of her daughter Amy.

Now I felt I had truly travelled back in time and reached what I was looking for. I had touched the living world of my great-grandmother and of Burne-Jones, perhaps almost in the same way that art historians such as John Christian and Bill Waters say that Burne-Jones lived in the ancient, legendary world of his paintings. In one letter to May he told her that he 'lived inside the pictures and from the inside of them looked out upon a world less real than they'. To me, this new world I had entered seemed as magical.

I could hardly bear to leave, to go back into the unreal world. Unwillingly I wrapped up the brushes again and placed them at the far end of the drawer where I had found them. For a moment I was tempted to take one with me so that I could continue, physically, to touch the past. I saw no one when I walked out of the house, and as I drove away my heart was still beating strongly. I felt like the lucky child in a fairy story who has discovered a door that leads into some secret, enchanted place. And I knew that whenever I wanted to be taken back into the world of May, Amy and Burne-Jones, all I had to do was to touch those brushes once more.

CHAPTER ONE

ROMANCE IN OXFORD

IN 1840, TWO YOUNG IRISH SISTERS LEFT THEIR STRICT PROTESTANT home in County Down for the first time. Their father, Captain Samuel Hill, was agent to Lord Roden's estates. Lord Roden was a staunch Orangeman, who had been made Grand Master of the Orange Order in 1837. Helen and Emma Hill crossed the Irish Sea and arrived in Oxford by coach to stay for six months with their uncle, who was a don at the university. They were unsophisticated but very pretty girls, sweet natured and musical. With well-trained, beautiful voices, they used to sing traditional Irish duets together. Both girls were petite, with delicate features; but Emma, the younger sister, had a striking combination of rich brown hair and eyes of the palest blue, made even more remarkable by a dark-blue rim round the pupils. Her complexion was creamy smooth, her neck graceful, and her pretty figure and tiny feet were envied by other women, and admired by men.

It was not long before the Hill sisters were noticed in Oxford. One day their uncle took his nieces to a commemorative ceremony in one of the college halls. The girls wore new blue bonnets, which their mother had given them before they left Ireland. While they waited for the ceremony to begin, the rumbustious undergraduates in the upper gallery called out the names of young women they recognized in the hall below and then cheered or blew kisses as they felt inclined. Finally, a voice from the gallery called out 'The two blue bonnets,' which prompted a storm of applause. From then on the pair of sisters captivated many hearts in Oxford.

Decades later, this story was told to my great-grandmother, May Gaskell, by her mother, who had been the young Emma Hill. Emma had blushed as she remembered it. Shortly after the incident in the college hall, Emma told her daughter, she was taken to see the gardens of Worcester College.

'Look,' said her companion, 'there is Long Melville rolling down the walk.'

Emma saw an extremely tall, thin man coming towards her, with dark-brown, wavy hair, a high, strong brow and clear-cut features. 'Who is Long Melville?' she asked.

'One of the most agreeable, charming and clever men in Oxford,' was the reply.

As he came nearer, Emma noticed Long Melville's large grey eyes with heavy lids within deep eye sockets, and his distinguished aquiline nose. She remarked that his hands were 'most beautiful', and that though his mouth was mobile, his chin remained firm when he talked. She would later tell May that he had 'a brilliant and ever-changing expression'. His remarkably mellifluous voice made him all the more mesmerizing. Emma soon learnt that David Melville was already known in Oxford as a stimulating speaker, with an entertaining and satirical view on men and events.

This notable man was to become May's father.

David Melville had studied theology at Oxford on a scholarship to Brasenose College. After graduating, penniless due to his father's bankruptcy, he was ordained as a clergyman and became a don at the university. He was tutor, among others, to Lord Ward, the young heir to the immense wealth of the industrialist Dudley family; it was said years later in an obituary of David Melville that Lord Ward had been 'erratic, clever, wild and fascinating'. William Humble Ward was charmed by his scintillating tutor and an intimate and lifelong friendship ensued between the two men. Later, as David Melville's patron, William was to shape his life. And when David Melville's first son was born, he named him William Ward.

During her time in Oxford, Emma Hill saw Long Melville regularly. They used to walk together through the historic streets and along the river. They must have looked an unlikely couple; at six foot three, Melville would, in those days, have seemed like a giant, and tiny Emma was barely five foot tall. To Emma, who had been brought up to be deeply religious, the fact that such a handsome, clever man was also an ordained clergyman must have made him irresistible. Apart from being attracted by Emma's prettiness and gentle nature, David Melville was clearly struck by her 'intellectual turn of mind' and wit, as May Gaskell recorded later when she wrote about her mother. But even after many weeks of friendship he had 'said no words of love' to Emma.

Eventually, back in Ireland, Captain and Mrs Hill heard reports of their daughters' social success in Oxford. Anxious about the possibility of influences they would not approve of, they recalled them at once. So on a cold March morning the two Irish girls, who had made such an impression on the university circle, left Oxford by coach. David Melville was there to say goodbye, and wrapped little Emma Hill up in a fine tartan rug he had thoughtfully brought for her.

At first I had no photograph of Emma, so it was from May's writings that I learnt about her appearance: the delicacy of her features, the smoothness of her brown hair, and those clear eyes of baby blue with their dark outer rim. Then one day my brother produced four small, flat leather boxes which had been left to him. They were lined on one side with soft red velvet. On the opposite side, within a gold embossed mount, was a daguerreotype portrait. The Frenchman Louis Daguerre had perfected his secret process of taking photographic portraits in 1839. They were achieved by projecting light through a camera lens onto iodized silver plates. Colour was added by scratching in powdered pigment and gold leaf.

Decades later, May Gaskell had inserted labels into the leather boxes, naming the sitters for future generations. There was Samuel Hill, Emma's father, with a very stern expression; there was her sister Helen, who had travelled with her to Oxford; and there was a strong-looking dark beauty called Isabella Melville, who May told us was married to David Melville's brother Beresford, a devastatingly handsome hero of the first Afghan War.

But one name was missing. 'Do you know who this one is?' my brother Ben asked me, handing me the fourth leather box. The fragile-looking woman was at once familiar; and when I looked at her through a magnifying glass I was certain. There were the neat features, the sleek brown hair and the creamy skin; but above all, there were those pale, clear-blue eyes with their dark-blue rim, painted on the metal with unbelievable precision. The gold of her necklace stood out in raised gold leaf and the pearls set on it were a glowing white. In this early mixture of photography and art, the young Emma Hill, as she was when David Melville fell in love with her, came alive for me.

Although no love had been declared, it was not long before David Melville set out for Bryansford, set in a beautiful mountainous area in the south of County Down, where the Hill family lived. A friend of Melville, another Oxford don, who had fallen in love with Emma's older sister Helen, accompanied him.

The purpose of David Melville's visit was to ask Captain and Mrs Hill for the hand of their daughter Emma in marriage. But he was to be disappointed. I learnt from May's writings that the two young dons found that the Hills believed in 'the narrowest evangelical form of religion'. They disliked what they called the 'worldly surroundings' of Oxford. They particularly distrusted the 'brilliant, broadminded Mr Melville', with his intellect and life of strenuous work. They told him that although he was a clergyman, according to their beliefs 'they could not look upon him as a converted Christian'. When he asked for Emma's hand, they refused.

David Melville was a clear-thinking, fair man; he would never have followed Emma to Ireland if he had not been sure that it was the right thing to do. He was to be described in an obituary as a man of 'exceedingly wise judgement'. Deeply wounded by the Hills' reaction to his request, David Melville returned at once to Oxford and dropped all contact. Poor little Emma was 'left to weep'.

Before long, a parcel arrived in Oxford addressed to David Melville. In it was the tartan rug he had given Emma when she left Oxford on that cold March morning. There was also a note; Emma wrote that she would 'pray for his conversion' – which in modern terms would probably mean becoming 'born again' – so that he could 'cherish her devoted love'.

*

Five years passed, and David Melville's life and career widened. He moved from Oxford to Durham, where he was instrumental in establishing a new theological college at the university, Bishop Hatfield Hall, and became its first principal. He was also primarily responsible for the rapid development of Durham as an active and popular centre of higher education. His aim was to make it as well regarded as Oxford. In establishing Hatfield, David Melville conducted a social experiment that, with hindsight, was revolutionary. He was determined that less fortunate students should be able to benefit from high academic standards, and arranged for Hatfield, as a residential college, to let its rooms for students fully furnished, to provide all their meals in Hall, and keep the fees fixed and affordable. Thus, at Durham in 1846, David Melville instigated what later became the norm in universities worldwide.

One of the young men from the country who applied for admission to the college was one William Griffiths, who remembered later: 'I had been led to think of college dons as being almost superhuman; and he, the first I had ever seen, was so much taller than I had imagined even a don to be that I almost shook with awe. But he took me kindly into his room, setting me at ease with one of his little jocularities.' According to Griffiths, Melville was 'a severe disciplinarian, but rigidly just, and withal full of tenderness'. Some students were, however, 'hugely afraid of him', particularly those who smoked, as he strongly disapproved of 'that bad weed' and when he smelt 'the odour of a recent cigar' on a student, he would say sternly, 'Stand a little farther away, sir.'

When I rang Hatfield College to see if they had any records of David Melville, I met with an immediate and enthusiastic response.

'He's still revered here,' said Arthur Moyes, who has written a history of Hatfield. 'His portrait is the first thing you see in the main hall, and we have the Melville Room, so he'll always be remembered.' In the 1960s, he explained, there was even a Melville Society, which consisted of a group of thirty men who met to wine, dine and debate, wearing black tie and dress suit. 'Not quite in keeping with David Melville's philosophy,' commented Arthur Moyes, 'but at least it was a tribute to him.'

I told Arthur about May Gaskell's strength of character and determination in her later years, and he commented that it sounded as if she had inherited some of her father's characteristics. May had also been known in London for her fashionable soirées. At Durham in the 1840s David Melville's brilliant mind, exceptional social gifts and witty conversation made him sought after both at the university and in country society. His striking good looks attracted women and men alike. When I saw the college portrait, painted when he was thirty-five, I could understand why. I wondered what May meant when she wrote later that at this time 'many friendships with women and extended social relationships had come into his life'.

Years later, May's father would reminisce to his daughter about those days at Durham, when 'every canon had ten thousand pounds a year and the Dean not less than twenty or thirty thousand'. This was an absolute fortune by modern standards. Each canon in residence, David Melville told May, would have one hundred pounds a month for entertaining, and the use of a gold-plate dinner service. When May returned to Durham in the early 1900s she asked to see the gold-plate services she had heard about from her father. Only two or three pieces remained, she was told, the rest having mysteriously disappeared the year the Ecclesiastical Commissioners took the funds in hand.

It was while he was at Durham, working hard during the day but dining out night after night on 'portentuous feasts', that David Melville finally heard from Ireland again. Captain and Mrs Hill wrote that 'the strain of bearing the absence of the man she loved' had told on their daughter's 'simple, lovely mind and body' and that she had 'utterly broken down in nerves'. May was later to write that she felt her mother Emma's upbringing in the 'hothouse, spiritual atmosphere' of the Hill household had accentuated her 'naturally morbid mind' and 'highly sensitive nervous system'. Emma's worried parents now asked David Melville if he still cared for their daughter, as they felt her health depended upon his feelings for her. They would therefore withdraw their objections to the marriage, they added.

David Melville did not hesitate. He went straight to Ireland, wrote May, and 'gave the pure and perfect heart he had won a faithful tenderness that remained to the end'. He and Emma were married on 28 July 1848 in the parish church of Kilcoo, near Emma's home at

Bryansford. The officiating priest was a friend of David Melville's, the Rev. Thomas Claughton. Only Emma's grandfather, John Hill, and her brother Valentine signed the register. Perhaps her parents had not felt able to attend because of their reservations about the marriage. But Emma never faltered. 'My mother worshipped him to the last hour of her life with a most perfect love,' wrote May.

As I pursued my quest, I heard that another of my newly discovered relations had found a Victorian japanned tin box in his attic. It turned out to contain Irish and Flemish lace from Emma Hill's trousseau, which she brought when she came back to England as David Melville's bride. Her grandparents had been lace makers, and in the box I found little caps, inner bodices for low dresses, lace borders, embroidered lace scarves, fingerless long gloves of fine crochet work, and a lace cape worn by Emma at her wedding. The work was unbelievably fine; as I gently fingered it I felt sure that no machine could achieve anything like this nowadays. I unwrapped more and more tissue-paper bundles, labelled by May long after her mother had died. At the bottom there was an ancient lavender bag and underneath this a tiny envelope on which May had written 'Strip of lace which I found in Amy's bag on the day she died.' I wonder still if Amy carried that little strip of Waterford lace about with her to remind her of her gentle Irish grandmother.

So David Melville, considered the most scintillating figure in Durham society, brought his shy little bride from the simple life of an Irish evangelical home to what May later described as 'this overfed, overpaid, aristocratic and autocratic milieu'. It was hard to imagine her in this setting, May wrote, but 'she won everyone's love and interest by her simplicity and charm'. Only the warden of Durham University, Charles Thorp, had reservations: he had stipulated that the Principal of Bishop Hatfield Hall should remain unmarried. David Melville had now brought his wife to live with him in college, and, to add insult to injury, soon a son, William, was born to them there. But this was not the only way in which Warden Thorp and Principal Melville did not see eye to eye. Their bickering continued for two more years. In his *History of Hatfield*, Arthur Moyes suggests that as a vigorous reformer with strong ideas, subservience did not come naturally to David Melville. 'He was a determined and stubborn

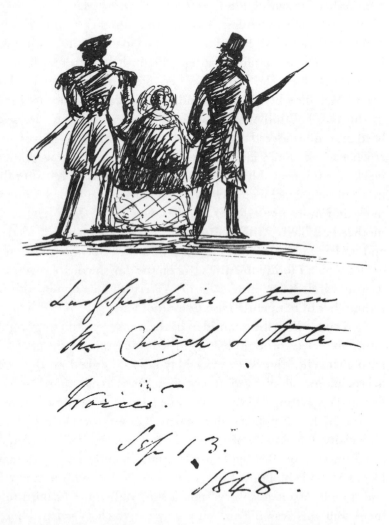

Tiny Emma Melville, just married, walks between two giants: her husband David Melville, 'Church', on the right and his patron and former pupil Lord Ward, 'State', on the left. The drawing is by David Melville.

young man in opposition to an equally determined and stubborn old man,' he writes. Finally, in 1850, Warden Thorp could take no more, and David Melville's career at Durham came to an abrupt end.

By coincidence, it was at this moment that David Melville's old friend and ex-pupil Lord Ward asked his advice on what to do about the recently vacated living of Shelsley Beauchamp, which formed part of his Worcestershire estates. David Melville told him to consult Psalm cxxxii, the first three words of which would give him guidance. The words were 'Lord, remember David'. William Ward was a keen appreciator of his friend's wit and replied by quoting from II Samuel xii 7. 'And Nathan said unto David: thou art the man.'

Soon after this, David and Emma Melville moved from the grand halls and gold-plated tables of Durham to a small rectory in the remote village of Shelsley Beauchamp, in the beautiful valley of the Teme. There they found what could hardly have been a more contrasting life and surroundings. The best description I could find of it came from David Melville himself, and the humour shown in his writing made me long to have known him:

> It was a lovely but very primitive place. Letters came twice a week, generally in the hat of a carrier. The rector who preceded me spent his days at the side of the river, with an old servant sitting by him to bait his hooks, but who always fell asleep when wanted. The church was a ruin, and everything else a memorial of better days. The one service on Sundays had a very limited congregation. Through the doorway in the tower a bass and flageolet emerged and accompanied a hymn, seeking their retreat when the service was over with much cider . . . Among my earliest visitations was one to the dying representative of an old family, who lived on his property, such as it was. He had had a wretched life, never having been to church, and neither able to read or write. He was a thorough reprobate. I found a circle of old women gathered round the corpse with clasped hands, so that, they said, they might keep the devil from his sure prey.

David Melville rebuilt the church and the school, restored village life at Shelsley and founded a reformatory for boys. In the timeworn rectory, on 18 March 1853, David and Emma's daughter May was born. It was an exceptionally cold March, and on that morning there was a severe frost. Then snow fell.

May did not remember much about her first years at Shelsley Beauchamp, but she was to tell her grandchildren about the old village of only six cottages, and the ancient black and white half-timbered house where they lived. She described her mischievous older brother Willie telling her to shut her eyes and open her mouth, and popping in a wriggling worm. She remembered the tiny early English church set in an orchard, with its beautiful carved pews and screen. And she talked of the complete peace in that isolated valley. This contrasted with May's earliest memory of all, however, which was far from peaceful. May wrote of staying with her Hill grandparents in Ireland when she was very little, and 'being hastily lifted down from my nursery window at which bloody fists were being shaken, and a crowd was roaring curses because a vase of orange lilies stood on the sill while a Roman Catholic funeral passed by'.

However idyllic that sylvan valley, life at Shelsley Beauchamp was too quiet for an active man of ideas like David Melville. 'I think the years at Shelsley were a severe trial to my father,' wrote May. But before too long, Lord Ward, who had recently been created the First Earl of Dudley, came to his friend's aid once more. He offered him a much more prominent parish, seven miles away at Great Witley, where he himself lived in the palatial Witley Court, which adjoined the beautiful and historic baroque church.

Witley was in one of the loveliest parts of Worcestershire; there were fern-covered hills, woods, rivers, hop fields and orchards. The rectory was set between the Abberley and Woodbury Hills; a fine redbrick house which had been built at the beginning of the nineteenth century. When the Melville family arrived it was covered with ivy, but the moulded stone architraves could still be seen above ten windows on the two upper floors. Tall Doric columns flanked the central front door, and there was one deep stone step in front. The floor of the hall and an elegant staircase rising from it were made of polished English oak. Large landings on the two upper floors led into large, light bedrooms. May, her two brothers and their nurse, Augusta, had rooms on the top floor. It was poor Augusta who dropped May's younger

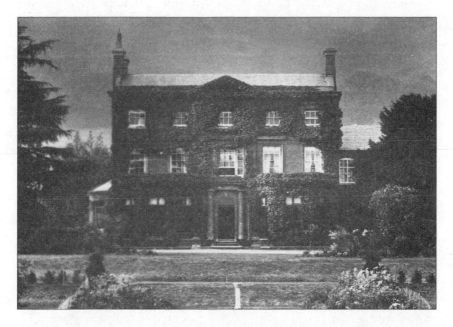

The rectory at Great Whitley in Worcestershire, where May and her
elder brother Willie spent happy childhood days together.

brother Beresford when he was two years old, an accident which resulted in one partly paralysed leg, which remained slightly shorter than the other. The children's rooms had the best views over the garden and large grounds, which stretched down to a lake, and across to Woodbury Hill on the other side of the valley.

May Melville's early days at Witley Rectory revolved around her brother Willie, who was two years older; a tall, good-looking boy with dark hair. 'Our childhood was very happy, we were so free,' May wrote. 'Willie became my adored master and I his willing slave.' Animals and birds fascinated Willie Melville. He kept ferrets in his pockets, and white mice in his bedroom. He could call birds and animals to him by imitating their notes and noises, and he would be seen walking home, hooting, with an owl following him. Together, Willie and May collected birds' eggs and butterflies. One day Willie nearly lost his eye when he tried to get a white owl from a nest in a hollow trunk of the cedar tree. As he was peering inside, a large owl swooped at his face with a rush of wings, missing his eye by a hair's breadth and wounding his cheek.

One of May and Willie's greatest excitements was their secret fishing expeditions. May wrote:

We used to rush out of the house together with shouts of joy and oh how I loved him and how he loved me. There was a deep, dark pool in a large wood belonging to Lord Dudley, which we thought of as our own secret pool. It was a haunted place to us – the sun never touched it as the trees grew round so thickly, but very big perch and roach lived in it. We never told anyone about our secret place, but on half-holidays we begged for sandwiches and milk and stole away to it. It was two miles away from our home, through woods and down the stream that fed the pool. I think we always felt a little afraid and awed by the gloom of it. It was a great adventure, and in the evening, when the large fish were served for tea, our parents would say, 'Where did you catch such fine perch?' We would look at each other mysteriously and answer 'Oh, in one of the pools.'

But when it came to lessons, which they had at home in David Melville's book-lined study, it was May who was far quicker than

Willie, and who became her learned father's favourite. In the way little girls often do, she found it easy to get down to school work. With Willie, David was impatient and frequently showed his annoyance; he would catch his son glancing out of the window, yearning to get back to his animals, the garden, the fields and the woods, instead of doing his sums. While their father wrote solemnly at his desk, May remembered that her brother's face opposite her at the work table would be miserable, dreading the moment when he would have to show his father the work he had not been able to do.

Education was one of David Melville's lifelong interests; he was a strenuous advocate of public education long before it was thought to be of general importance. He had known William Gladstone since the beginning of the 1850s, and the two men communicated frequently on the subject of education when Gladstone's government passed the 1870 Education Act to provide elementary education for all. Melville was also an adviser to Robert Lowe, who, as Vice-President of the Education Board, had announced a revised code for education in 1862, and became Gladstone's Chancellor of the Exchequer after his 1868 election.

May became much closer to her father than either Willie or Beresford did, and remained so for the whole of his life. David Melville, with his commanding personality, was feared by both her brothers, and even though she adored him, by their mother too. But, May said, never by her. In old age, May wrote that her father was 'the wisest man I have ever known', but added that he had such a strong critical sense that he noticed faults even in those he loved. He never lost his temper, May said, but could not control a caustic comment 'when folly and stupidity were near'.

While rector of the parish of Great Witley, David Melville was made a canon of Worcester Cathedral, a position he was to keep for nearly fifty years, until shortly before his death at the age of ninety-two. It was largely through Canon Melville's influence that his patron and closest friend restored the beautiful cathedral. Melville, commenting from the pulpit on the rapid acquisition of vast private wealth from 'modern commerce and powers of modern invention', praised the Earl of Dudley's unselfish spirit in using much of his fortune to try to relieve 'wretchedness and destitution'. He told the congregation that the Earl had restored the cathedral to 'enlighten and relieve the darkness and distress of the people'. Standing high above the large congregation, Canon Melville's sonorous voice rang out: 'Everything about us – the seats we occupy, the marble floors we tread, the pulpit from whence I speak, the window that floods all this space with the tinted lights of the setting sun, the organ that floods it with solemn harmonies – all these and much more we owe to one who never thought he could help your worship here too lovingly and too well.'

But Dudley's charity did not end there: 'It is the most hopeful feature of the day that want and wretchedness have not now to be brought to the gate of wealth and luxury. They are sought out, often in the cradle of their misery.'

The new canon was soon drawing huge numbers to the cathedral to hear his stimulating addresses, and he also proved to be a humorous speaker and 'no mean raconteur' at social occasions. 'To hear him give the toast of "The Ladies", or to respond on their behalf, was a treat to be enjoyed and remembered,' a local newspaper reported after his death. He was, it continued, 'a churchman of broad sympathies' – exactly what his wife Emma's evangelical parents had been afraid of.

Emma Melville worshipped her husband, but his dominating character and increasing prominence did not help her to lose her natural diffidence and lack of self-confidence. Nevertheless, May wrote that she never lost her 'sparkling little Irish wit', and her sweet, loving character. Her kind help to the people of the parish and her 'pure' beauty made an impression on all who met her. Neither did she lose the piety of her youth; she remained deeply religious, and her faith helped her through later illnesses.

While her children were very young, Emma Melville's loving attention to their needs never appeared to May to be overshadowed by her highly sensitive disposition. She taught them music and found that May had inherited her lovely singing voice. I felt particularly excited to find that both May and her mother had good singing voices. I myself sang throughout my schooldays before studying at the Guildhall School of Music, and one of my daughters is fully launched on a singing career now, so I like to think that a genetic thread links our voices still today.

Even as a young girl, May's musical talents were recognized. In her teens she was welcomed into what was an elite intellectual and musical coterie in Worcester, where, among others, she made friends with the young Arthur Balfour, later to become Prime Minister. As well as singing, May played the piano and the violin, and discussed books with this group of distinguished people who were mostly much older than she was. One day she found a large envelope on her writing table at Witley Rectory; there was no indication of who it was from. Inside were the music and words of a song that seemed to have been composed specially for her. The song was called 'True Love is True For Ever'.

I discovered the crumbling sheet of handwritten music when I was going through some old tin trunks which had belonged to May, unearthed only recently in a family attic. Straight away I took the song round to a pianist friend who played it for me. It is typically sentimental in Victorian style, but the tune is very pretty and quite affecting. I sang as my friend played, and wondered if it had been May who had last played the music and sung the words. 'Trusting and tried, no chain can bind stronger than that sweet tie. True love is true for ever, true love can never die,' the song concludes. When May put the music away in the black trunk years later she wrote a note on the envelope, explaining that she had found it on her writing table. Then she added: 'I sang this a great deal – I never knew who it was from.'

So even in the 1860s, when she was very young, May already had a secret admirer.

May was about sixteen when she noticed her mother suffering from 'acute nervous breakdowns'. Whether these would have been what we now call depression, or were simply neurotic behaviour, is hard to say. Reading through so many old papers, I have not found a single reference to anyone being 'depressed' at this time, though May refers to it in her own son years later. 'Sad', 'gloomy' and 'melancholy' were the words most often used. It may also be no coincidence that May noticed these 'breakdowns' in her mother at around the time when she would have reached her menopause.

The breakdown of Emma Melville's health led to changes in life at Witley Rectory that affected Canon Melville too. His wife began to go abroad 'for her health', as did so many who could afford to at that

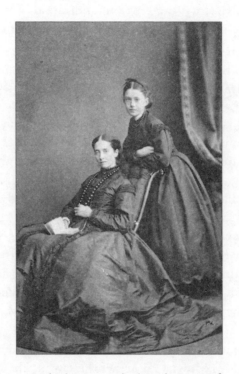

May, standing, aged sixteen and already part of cultural life in Worcseter, with her delicate little mother, Emma Melville.

time, leaving her husband alone for long periods. Their children were growing up. May observed that her father was often 'sad and gloomy'. Having resigned himself to the fact that his eldest son Willie, although 'splendid' in appearance, charming and witty, was much happier with an active rather than an academic life, his father was looking for an opening in the Colonies for him. His younger son Beresford was at school; despite the fact that his childhood injury meant he had been 'much with the doctors' and missed lessons during his early years, he had now won a scholarship to Marlborough. And May, David Melville's favourite child, would soon be of marriageable age. All his children would be gone soon, but it was May's company that he knew he would miss most.

Just when David Melville was beginning to despair of finding anything he thought suitable for Willie in the Colonies, he heard of a scheme being started by a man called Henley to take young men out to become early pioneers in the Argentine, which was then, in the 1860s, little known. Mr Henley had been already and claimed he had a contract with the Argentinian government to bring out young immigrants who would be granted a piece of land each, so they could settle there and help to colonize part of the country. He promised to keep them for two years first and teach them how to manage their land. For this he would charge the parents of each boy three hundred pounds – a substantial sum. Henley managed to gather together 150 hopeful boys; Willie was one of them. David and Emma Melville were glad to hear that the group were to be accompanied by a clergyman and a doctor. Poor May, however, was broken-hearted by the prospect of a long separation from her adored brother. 'It was a bitter day for me when we parted,' she wrote. But she joined in her parents' high hopes for Willie's new life, little dreaming of the hardship and struggle which lay in store for him.

The Melville family heard nothing from Willie for many months. When they finally did it was a story of disaster. After the long voyage out to South America he had arrived at Rosario, on the coast of Santa Fe province in the Argentine. From there, travelling by bullock cart, Mr Henley had taken his 'tired and bewildered group of boys into a wild and remote part of the prairie', far from civilization. They set up camp, and then Henley gathered the boys together. He confessed that the land he had promised them had not materialized and that he had already spent all their money. He placed his revolver on the ground in front of him and told them that since he had deceived them any one of them could shoot him. He must have known that none of these young, innocent boys would be able to do this, and the exhausted and dismayed group could do nothing but retire into their tents for the night. When they woke next morning, Henley, together with his 'clergyman' and 'doctor', who turned out to be frauds, had disappeared, taking with them most of the stores and any money there was.

Stranded in a foreign and fairly hostile environment, some of the boys set out at once, hoping to walk to the nearest town or village; they were never seen again. Willie stayed behind. Then smallpox broke out in the camp. May wrote that only Willie 'and a few others with grit and courage remained', nursing the sick and burying the dead. Finally Willie and the last few strong boys reached a town and continued their struggle for survival, working at any job they could find.

When David and Emma Melville heard at last that their son had survived they were relieved, but they continued to worry about him. For Willie, years of hard work and disappointment lay ahead before he made a successful life for himself out in the Argentine.

Canon Melville's 'intimate friendship' with the First Earl of Dudley never waned, and the two families were inextricably linked during all their years at Witley together. May wrote that Lord Dudley, and later his wife Georgina too, 'became a feature in our lives'. The Dudleys were rich on a scale that seems inconceivable today. Apart from their inherited wealth they were industrialists who earned enormous revenue from, among other things, coal mines. The trustees of the young Lord Ward had bought Witley Court from the impoverished Foley family in 1837, when William was still being tutored at Oxford by David Melville. At first the trustees let Witley Court to Queen Adelaide, widow of King William IV. Then, when William Ward came into his inheritance at the age of twenty-eight in 1846, he started remodelling the house, gardens and church on a gigantic, classical scale, and at staggering cost. Gradually a country house was transformed into a Palladian palace. But although he spent so much on creating a sumptuous and extravagant lifestyle for himself, William was thought of as a good man and a generous benefactor, as David Melville well knew. He received an earldom in 1860 in recognition of his services to the public, and became the First Earl of Dudley.

Perhaps the most exceptional and certainly the most unexpected building in Witley is the church of St Michael and All Angels. Attached by a passage to Witley Court itself, the church is where Canon Melville held his services, and where May was later to be married. It is an early-eighteenth-century Italianate basilica; never would you expect to see something like this in the depths of Worcestershire. The exterior is an incongruity in itself, but the interior, with its ornate gilded papier-mâché mouldings and beautiful painted ceiling, is even more of a surprise. Now thought of as England's finest baroque church, it has an extraordinary history. In 1747, it was a plain brick country church. The First Lord Foley had owned Witley Court, but died before his dream of rebuilding the church was realized. His widow and son, now the Second Lord Foley, were planning to carry out his wish when they heard that the Duke of Chandos, as a result of losing the huge fortune he had inherited from his father, was being forced to sell, piece by piece, his enormous palace, Canons, at Edgware. Canons had been described by Daniel Defoe as 'the most magnificent palace in England'. The sale of such a wealth of treasures was a bargain-hunter's dream.

Canons incorporated a splendid baroque chapel, where Handel had been the organist. As major parts of the chapel were also being auctioned off, Lady Foley and her son were struck by an enterprising idea: they would recreate the wonder of the Canons chapel at Witley. So this is why Witley church is flanked by ten tall Venetian-style painted-glass windows, contains the ornate organ on which Handel once played, and has a wondrous ceiling covered with Italian paintings and elaborate, gilded plasterwork. All this was dismantled at Edgware into numerous pieces, and brought by wagon to the depths of Worcestershire. To this day, a visit to the parish church of Witley is an awe-inspiring experience.

I went to Worcestershire in the course of my research for this book on a dazzling weekend at the beginning of June. The verges were speckled white and yellow with cow parsley and buttercups. It was one of those moments when even someone as addicted to travelling abroad as I am thinks that nowhere can be quite as beautiful as England in early summer. And Worcestershire retains an unusually peaceful, old-fashioned feel.

I had come to expect coincidences since I had become interested in my story, and one of them occurred when I heard a programme on Radio Four about Witley Court, just when I had discovered May's connection with it. On the programme a local historian, Ruth Butler, talked with passionate interest about the long-vanished, opulent life of Witley Court, of the ruin it became after a serious fire in 1937, and of its remarkable church. So I contacted Ruth to ask her if she knew whether May's home, the old rectory at Witley, still existed.

Ruth was the perfect guide, being completely bound up with the heyday of Witley Court; she even wore clothes to suit the late-Victorian period: a long, tight-waisted skirt, with a frilly, high-necked blouse. Ruth's riveting gossip about the house parties, banquets and glittering balls during the second Earl's time brought the vast ruin to life. Eagerly she described Edward VII's visits, the blushing chamber-maids he dallied with and the so-called Bastard's Wing, also known as the Cuckoo's Nest. She showed me the train tracks where a small train had brought tons of Dudley coal daily into the centre of the building to heat the gigantic rooms. Then we walked towards the church, which was as impressive as I had imagined. As we stepped inside, the bell in the church tower rang eleven o'clock. The sound of it within the church was rich, reverberating, deep and full, as it must have sounded to Canon Melville when he prepared to take his services there, and to May as she walked back down the aisle on her wedding day.

But I most wanted to see the old rectory, where May had played with her brother Willie, where they had done their lessons together under Canon Melville's strict eye, and where May had grown up into a talented young woman, admired by all who knew her. I felt I knew this house well, not only from reading May's recollections of it but from studying, over and over again, a collection of photographs which Amy had taken for her 'loving old uncle Willie', as he called himself, in the Argentine. Amy's pictures showed every bit of the rectory: its grounds, its trees, its nooks and crannies; everything she thought would remind Willie of his happy childhood at Witley with his sister May.

The house itself was still familiar and intact, structurally unchanged. From the outside only the ivy had gone. But where was the view over flowering gardens to the lake? Where were the lawns that stretched between wide herbaceous borders to the water's edge? Directly outside the handsome front of the building, the dark, dead flatness of a tall leylandii hedge blocked any view at all. Only from the third floor of the house could the lake be seen, as it was obscured by a large modern house set in an incredibly neat garden, with lawns that looked like an advertisement for grass seed. The lovely, extensive grounds of Witley Rectory had been divided into six plots, each with a house on it. Inside the old rectory, however, the well-proportioned rooms where the Melvilles had lived had not changed in shape. The fine polished oak staircase and wide landings were as they had always been. It was a comfortable house with a friendly atmosphere; it would have been good to live in. The shutters on the windows remained, and Canon Melville's study was still used as one; as we walked in I could almost see his long figure bent over the writing table.

In 1874, the year after May married, her new husband Captain Gaskell, a keen gardener as well as a soldier, had redesigned the gardens of the rectory, and planted many shrubs and beautiful trees. In 1905, when May's son, my grandfather Hal, went back to Witley on his honeymoon, he revisited the rectory where he had stayed so often during his childhood with his grandparents. The rector who had succeeded Canon Melville was not there, but Hal, who had inherited his father's interest in gardening, looked around. His reaction was violent, as he wrote to his mother:

> Oh, such dreadful things have happened at the rectory, they have chopped to the ground all the tall laurels round the pond, felled the big trees by the spring pond and the beautiful elms on the bank by the gate to the school, and chopped off and maimed every other fine tree they could lay hands on, and are scraping out the pond and planting d—d conifers in spots on the front. Luckily the beast [he refers to Canon Melville's successor] is not here or I should throw him to the ground and stamp on his stomach.

Sadly, although a beautiful copper beech tree remains today, d——d conifers are still in evidence in the divided grounds of Witley Rectory.

I drove on from Witley to Worcester in the late afternoon. In the clear, golden sunlight of early summer the sight that faced me was breathtaking: old houses clustered round the cathedral, which soared up above them against a flawless pale-blue sky. The dark river, which had flooded badly just a few months before, was glassy smooth and covered with swans. It was a timeless, idyllic scene. I walked across the green under towering old plane trees and through the doors of the cathedral.

By the Victorian font I met a young librarian whom I had talked to on the telephone when I arranged my visit. Like Ruth Butler, he looked as if he belonged to the nineteenth century rather than the twenty-first. With his fitted dark suit, wire-rimmed spectacles and neat, glossy hair parted in the middle, he would not have looked out of place in Canon Melville's time.

My great-great-grandfather's plain sandstone tomb is in the cathedral cloisters. At the centre of the large cross at the head of the tomb is the Melville family motto, '*Denique Coelum*', meaning 'Heaven at Last', a fitting epitaph for a theologian at the end of a long life. In one corner of the impressive nave, spiral stone steps lead up to the library, which runs the whole length of the building on one side, under huge ancient beams, and contains one of the best collections of medieval manuscripts in England. Here the librarian introduced me to Canon Iain Mackenzie, a medieval scholar. The canon, who was about to retire, was exceedingly erudite and had a dry wit; both characteristics, I realized, that had so often been attributed to Canon Melville.

Iain Mackenzie comes from Lochalsh in the north-west of Scotland; his regional accent is musical, with softly rolling Rs. He showed me King John's will, dictated by the king when he was dying of dysentery, caused, the canon assured me, by 'drinking fresh cider and eating pears'. Then I looked with amazement at King John's thumb bone, dug up from his tomb in the cathedral. I was dazzled by Aristotelian treatises, and finely illuminated manuscripts with colours made from pure gold, lapis, emeralds and rubies; it was riveting to see what an incredible wealth of knowledge existed in medieval monasteries. But nevertheless, the canon added with a wry smile, the dissolution of the monasteries was very necessary, because the monks had become so dissolute.

Jolting me back to the purpose of my visit, the librarian reappeared with some photographs of the ageing Canon Melville, taken at the cathedral in 1898, the year that Burne-Jones, who had become his friend as well as his daughter's, died. In the photographs the old canon's limbs look extraordinarily long and thin, his brow high, his eyes piercing within their deep sockets. Although eighty-six years old, he was still preaching regularly, with his well-known energy and passion.

'He had a certain look in his eye,' observed Canon Mackenzie as he examined the photographs. Canon Mackenzie also had, I felt, a certain look in his.

The sound of evensong began floating up through the rafters of the cathedral into the library. Dust-speckled shafts of evening sun stretched from the small windows along the shelves of books and manuscripts. Canon Mackenzie took us out by another door onto College Green, where David Melville had lived after leaving Witley Rectory until he died in 1904, at the age of ninety-two.

I also knew College Green at Worcester from Amy's photographs, which show the bowed figure of the old canon in an upholstered wheelchair outside his house in the year of his death. His hair and whiskers are long, fluffy and white under a black skullcap. He wears a dark cape over a long, pale, quilted dressing-gown. His legs stretch out far beyond the step of the wheelchair. He is reading. His devoted nurse Mary Collard holds an umbrella above him to shield him from the sun.

Now, at the start of the twenty-first century, children were playing in the last sunshine of the day on College Green. I shook hands and thanked Canon Mackenzie for giving me such an enlightening time. A car parked in front of mine had a printed notice on its side window: 'Priest on Call'. Frivolously I asked the canon, 'Couldn't you get me one of those for my car in London to keep the parking wardens away?'

He replied with a smile, 'I think you should have one saying

"Voodoo Priest on Call" – that would be more effective.'

Perhaps, I told myself, this afternoon had been the next best thing to meeting Canon Melville himself.

CHAPTER TWO

A WORCESTERSHIRE BRIDE

IN THE EARLY SPRING OF 1870, WHEN MAY MELVILLE WAS SEVENTEEN years old, she wrote to her father from Switzerland, where she was travelling with her 'Uncle D'. I have been unable to discover who this uncle was, but David Melville had eleven brothers and sisters, and his wife Emma only one brother called Valentine, so I presume Uncle D was a Melville.

'My own darling Papa,' wrote May, 'I am so happy that it is quite useless to think of going to sleep.' May described the long day that had just ended, and her first experience of a glacier. Rising at four in the morning, they had climbed up to a great rock, which stood at a spot where three glaciers met, surrounded by 'a magnificent circle of intensely white mountains which looked near enough to touch with one's fingers'. May reassured her father that she was protected from the glare by tinted spectacles and a veil. 'Oh Papa!' May enthused. 'It was like a new world to me, this wondrous sea of ice. We seemed such little mites on a great white river . . . the ice fall was just above us in great pinnacles, mountains of green ice tossed and twisted about, with bottomless crevasses.'

May's early enthusiasm for travel, beauty and new experiences was to continue for the rest of her life. Those three things are high on my

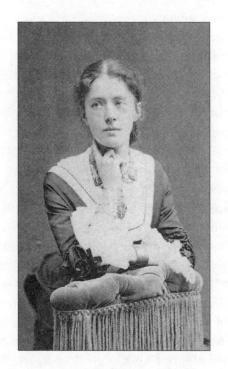

May at the time she met her future husband, captain Gaskell.

own list of the greatest pleasures in life. In later years May's constant travelling was often explained as being on doctor's orders, for her health, but even when she complained of tiredness and pain, the excitement she felt at the first sight of an impressive building, an exceptional work of art or a beautiful landscape was undiminished, and her interest in people she met helped distract her from the fatigue and discomfort of long journeys.

At the end of her long letter from Switzerland, the young May informed her father about the time of her arrival in London on the night mail from Paris. She said she was looking forward to a visit with her father to the 'Barracks'. As it turned out, there was someone of particular interest to May at what I now realize must have been the army barracks at Kensington. A lifetime later, in her seventies, when she was sorting out her papers, May pencilled a note on this letter, which she had presumably found among her father's things after he died. At the top of the first page she added: 'Written by me when I was seventeen before going to the "Barracks", where I met my future husband.'

I have several photographs of May taken at around this time. It is frustrating that the formally posed photographs of people during this era give so little idea of their true character. Because of the long exposure they hardly ever show a smile or the animation that creates a personality. Burne-Jones so often referred to May's laughter in his letters, yet I have no hint of what her smile was like. All I can see is that she had light-brown wavy hair, parted in the middle and drawn back in a thick twisted chignon behind. The short wisps of hair which escape at the front are very curly. Her eyes are widely set and were said to have been pale blue; in photographs they have a gentle, dreamy look. She has a nicely shaped face, with regular features. But it is her soft mouth, with its pretty cupid's bow, which is a perfect shape and size. When Burne-Jones did his last drawing of the forty-five-year-old May, shortly before he died in 1898, he characteristically idealized her looks, but her lips appear identical to those in photographs of her as a young girl. I can see why May Melville, combining a pretty face and elegant figure with intelligence and vitality, caused a stir when she visited the barracks at Kensington with her father in the spring of 1870.

May's husband-to-be was a soldier, Henry Brooks Gaskell. When

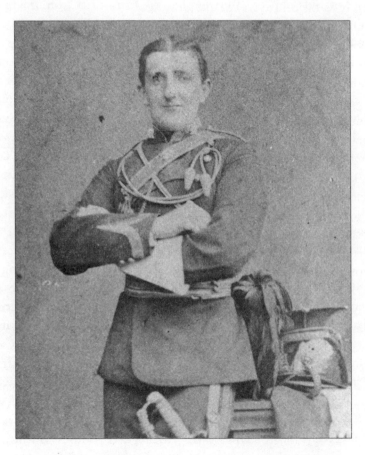

Captain Henry Brooks Gaskell in the uniform of the Ninth Queen's Royal Lancers, a smart cavalry regiment. He doesn't look very attractive, but I can see that he is a Gaskell, and the large nose is evident.

May met him he was twenty-four years old, a captain of the Ninth Queen's Royal Lancers, a smart cavalry regiment. I have an official Ninth Lancers photograph taken at the time May met him. He does not appear either handsome or sympathetic to me, but once again it is difficult to tell because of the stiffness of the pose. His hair is parted severely in the centre and greased down, his eyes are rather mournful, his nose and chin exceptionally large, and his lips thin. It is hard to imagine him sweeping the lovely, talented May off her feet. But his uniform, tasselled sword and plumed helmet are impressive, and he was, after all, from a family that had both money and land. Henry Brooks was the eldest son of Henry Lomax Gaskell, who owned Kiddington Hall in Oxfordshire, as well as two smaller estates. Henry Lomax had ten children and a warm-natured wife called Alice, who adored Henry Brooks, her firstborn child. Her husband, I was to find out, bullied both his wife and his children, and had a terrifying temper.

I searched through the old tin boxes unearthed for me in family attics, but could find no other letters to give me a clue as to why Canon Melville was visiting the barracks at Kensington, or about May's first meeting with her future husband. However, my search was not in vain. I came across a small envelope on which May had written 'H and I'. Inside was a leather folder containing two dance cards, one for a ball at Kiddington Hall and one for the nearby Woodstock ball. They were both dated November 1871, when May was eighteen. Coote and Tinney's Band played at the Kiddington ball. May's dance card was full; she danced quadrilles, gallops, lancers and waltzes with many partners. But it was Captain Gaskell who had the lion's share of her company. With him May danced the 'Snowdrop' waltz, a gallop called 'Fizz', the 'New' lancers, a quadrille with the exotic name 'Princesse de Trebizonde', and a final waltz, 'Dream of the Ball'. At the top of her card May had pencilled in her comment on the evening: 'Perfection'.

Henry Lomax Gaskell had inherited a large fortune from his father, the first Henry Gaskell, a solicitor in Wigan. This hard but extremely astute man was known all over Lancashire as 'the Devil of Wigan' because he squeezed every halfpenny he could, as well as farms and land, from his clients. He was also known for his caustic tongue and pungent wit. The Devil, who spoke with a broad Lancashire accent and who lived modestly himself, was determined that his son should become a landed gentleman, so he stipulated that a large part of the fortune he left should be spent on a country estate. It pleased the Devil greatly, shortly before he died, when Henry Lomax married an heiress, Alice Brooks.

Alice was the pretty daughter of Samuel Brooks, a well-known Manchester banker who was not only shrewd, but genial, humorous and generous. This could not be said of the stingy, severe Devil of Wigan, Henry Gaskell, who saved every penny he made. Samuel Brooks entertained on a grand scale and gave his friends and family lavish presents. As a wedding present he bought Alice and Henry Lomax a vast amount of silver and silver plate. But this was only a token; when the young couple moved into Kiddington Hall, he presented them with an astonishing housewarming present: he paid for the building of a large bachelor's wing, two laundries and a grand stone and marble conservatory which ran all down one side of the house. It may have been this touch of the nouveau riche which, decades later, made Burne-Jones, who much preferred the Gaskells' large Jacobean farmhouse, Beaumont Hall in Lancashire, tell May that he thought Kiddington 'pompous, ugly and common'.

Nevertheless, Kiddington Hall is an imposing house. Shortly before Henry Lomax Gaskell bought the house as a young married man, it had been restored by Sir Charles Barry, who designed the Houses of Parliament. It was Barry who added the large plate-glass windows which give the house such wonderful views and light. But it is the setting of Kiddington that is exceptional. The gentle tree-studded contours of the landscape and the romantic lake, with its island and waterfall at one end, can be seen through every window on two sides of the house. It was created from an early design by Capability Brown and was to be the inspiration for many of Amy's experimental photographs with her revolutionary Kodak panoramic camera in the early 1900s.

When May and Henry Brooks took over Kiddington after the death of Henry Lomax in 1889, May found a portrait of her husband's grandfather, 'Old Gaskell of Wigan', in other words the Devil, and hung it above the library fireplace, where it stayed for generations.

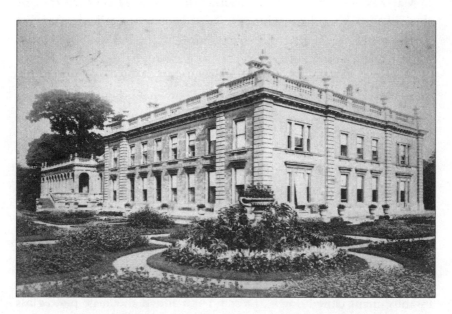

Kiddington Hall, the Gaskell family home near Woodstock, in Oxfordshire, at the time that May lived there.

She told her children that she had put it there 'as without his talents we should have had no house at all'. She urged them to study the picture: 'Look at his massive head, clever suspicious eyes, and jaw of iron will. It is not a face to forget.' My aunt Diana, who grew up at Kiddington with my father and uncle years later, still remembers the portrait; she says the Devil was dressed in black and had a nose like an eagle. 'I used to gaze with horror at his severe and stern face, and think what a terrifying father he must have been,' she adds.

May never knew her future mother-in-law Alice Gaskell, though she said she admired everything she heard about her. Alice was a most loving mother to all her children and ran Kiddington with great care, efficiency and taste, despite having little support from her husband. She remained devoted to Henry Lomax, even though he proved an extremely difficult man to live with. His temper was totally unpredictable; he was unreasonable, and often violent. 'No one ever knew when it would cloud everything, or the cause of it,' wrote May. Sometimes for days, almost weeks, he would not speak – a characteristic which I soon realized was inherited by his son Henry Brooks, by Henry's son Hal, who was my grandfather, and to a lesser extent by my father Tom, though he had no temper at all.

Henry Lomax could be exceedingly harsh; often he would shout at one or other of his six sons, telling them to leave the house and never return. Their reaction was to go and drink in the village inn, but when their father, who was the landlord, discovered this, he had the establishment closed down. This did not prevent at least two of his sons having serious drink problems later, so much so that one of them, James, was simply recorded as having 'gone to the bad'. May's children would sometimes refer to their 'wicked uncles', because in the Family Bible kept at Kiddington, with the names of several generations of the Gaskell family inscribed on the frontispiece, their grandfather had had his three most offending sons erased. The last anyone heard of these 'wicked uncles' was in my grandmother's time; she told her daughter Diana that when she was first married she felt sorry for the uncles, as they were very poor, and that she would go and visit them 'in the Brighton area'. But during their childhood at Kiddington it was on his eldest son that Henry Lomax, for no obvious reason, was particularly hard; perhaps it was because he was his heir, and clearly his wife Alice's favourite. This harshness caused Henry Brooks to turn against his father. 'No love was felt on either side,' May told her children, 'it was only for love of his mother that your father ever lived at home after he joined the Ninth Lancers.'

Having borne ten children, one of whom had died when he was ten, and with an impossible husband, it was no wonder that poor Alice's health and spirit suffered, and, sadly, she did not live to see her eldest and favourite son married. A year after he had danced happily with May Melville at the Kiddington ball, Henry Brooks lost the mother he loved. Despite the difficulties of her married life, Alice had never complained, and no one outside the family, May explained, would have known that anything was wrong. But her close family knew. At one point her brother had urged her to get a separation and had even drawn up papers for it, but although she kept them in her desk, they were never signed. Finally, when she knew she was dying, aged only fifty but looking far older, she told the family doctor, who had become a friend, that she was 'glad to go', as she could 'bear no more'. May told her children that Alice had died 'worn out', but her death certificate states that the cause of death was 'softening of the brain, epilepsy and paralysis', none of which I have found mentioned elsewhere. In my researches for this book I have learnt to doubt death certificates.

Henry Lomax was fiercely opposed to his eldest son's proposed marriage to May Melville. May was no heiress, and her father, though clearly distinguished and respected, was a parson. From a hand-written leather account book kept by Henry Lomax from the late 1850s through to the 1860s, it appears that he lived very comfortably, though the Gaskell family would not, at that time, have been considered among the truly rich. However, Henry Lomax sent his sons to Eton, and regularly bought more horses and carriages and new liveries for his servants, as well as decorative objects, pictures and furniture for the house. The account book shows that he ordered large quantities of the 'best champagne', many hogsheads of fine French wines and a staggering amount of old port, despite the fact that he was so disapproving of his sons' drinking and regularly gave contributions to the Kiddington Temperance Society.

Surprisingly, Henry Lomax gave expensive jewels to his bullied

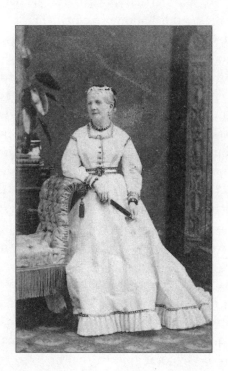

Henry Lomax Gaskell's sweet-natured wife Alice, who put up with his violent temper and bullying until she died 'worn out', aged fifty.

wife, Alice – or the repairs to jewellery are put down as for his wife. However, in a section entitled 'Presents', in which he names the recipients, there are often jewels bought for no named person. In July 1860 he bought 'A fine diamond festoon necklace with three diamond stars and gold chain to form also ornaments for the head, in morocco case.' This cost a staggering £1,075 – getting on for £50,000 by today's values. Perhaps he was apologizing to Alice for all she had to put up with, or could the necklace possibly have been a gift to another woman?

Through his father, Henry Lomax had also inherited two lesser estates: Beaumont Hall, a farm in Lancashire, and a Scottish estate, Cambus O' May, which eventually went to his second son John Francis. But he does not seem to have inherited the astute business sense of his father and father-in-law, so that what had started as the Devil of Wigan's large fortune gradually dwindled. I often wonder where all the jewels I have read about in wills and papers are today.

May would later tell her children that during their engagement Henry Brooks behaved with great patience and self-control in the face of his father's objection to their marriage. May did not enjoy her visits to Kiddington at that time. Henry Brooks's eldest sister Alice, who was only twenty years old, had courageously taken up the position of head of her father's household after the death of her mother and was in charge of the large family, but with a brooding, bad-tempered father this was an extremely difficult task, and the atmosphere in the house was tense. Finally, perhaps as a result of the charm and strength of May's character, and his daughter's obvious tact, Henry Lomax relented and the marriage was allowed to take place. But could his original objection have been a more discerning one? Perhaps he had thought about Henry and May's different backgrounds and talents; perhaps he had sensed that they might not find what they needed in each other. May's love of art, music and literature always came foremost in her life, while Henry Brooks apparently told 'barrack-room jokes', and above all loved shooting and fishing. Later on, however, he did show an imaginative streak in his creative gardening at Kiddington.

Henry Lomax gave May a beautiful diamond and opal bracelet as a wedding present, and she would later tell her children that soon after they were married her father-in-law became quite fond of her. She said he took an affectionate interest in her young children, and she always tried to remember this, 'as there is very little else that is pleasant to remember except his abundance of wavy white hair and the bluest eyes I ever saw'. May did admit to her children that after her father-in-law died, she and Captain Gaskell had sealed the family vault at Kiddington, 'as neither of us ever wished to lie there'.

On the last day of December 1873 May Melville, aged twenty, was to marry Captain Gaskell at her childhood home, Great Witley, in Worcestershire. The ceremony would take place in the unique church of St Michael and All Angels, where her father was rector. May was known and loved in the village of Witley, and in the surrounding district. Encouraged by her father to 'enter into the troubles and the joys, the pleasures and the cares of young and old, of rich and poor', May had started visiting the poor and sick at an early age. The *Worcester Journal* reported that everyone who knew her became endeared to this pretty girl, for her gentle manner and 'numerous acts of kindness'.

Such was the good feeling towards the Melville family that the village community wished to 'honour the young bride and give some expression to the high regard in which her father is deservedly held'. They decided to decorate the entire village for the wedding, and their efforts were praised for being 'elegant in design and tasteful in execution'. For his part, David Melville invited all the schoolchildren of Witley to a tea party at the rectory during the week before the wedding. There was a splendid feast of cakes and jellies, a conjuror, and presents for everyone, which were handed out around that 'newly popular institution – the Christmas tree'. On the wedding night itself David Melville was to provide dinner at the Hundred House Hotel, an elegant building which is still a hotel today, for the heads of all the families in the parish, and for the church choir. The dinner afterwards was pronounced as 'capital'.

On New Year's Eve, the day of the wedding, there was a thick fog in the morning, but this soon cleared. A dry, fine day followed which encouraged large groups of people from outside the village to walk in and attend the ceremony.* The wedding service was to be at noon. There were great preparations in the rectory. Emma's dress was of thick white satin, trimmed with Brussels lace. The Melvilles could never have afforded such a sumptuous dress, but the Countess of Dudley, wife of her father's closest friend, the Earl, gave it to May. There were six bridesmaids of May's own age, a bevy of young womanhood. Each of them, dressed in white muslin with cherry-coloured trimmings, carried a fan inscribed with the words 'Ring out the old, ring in the new', from Tennyson's song. These were a present from the bridegroom, as a memento of a very special New Year.

Under the awe-inspiring ceiling by the Italian painter Belucci, Captain Gaskell stood waiting for May in the church, accompanied by two other soldiers. He wore the dashing uniform of the Ninth Queen's Royal Lancers. Then the tall, imposing figure of David Melville could be seen in the doorway. On his arm, delicately pretty and small beside him, was his only daughter, May. They walked slowly up the aisle, between packed pews. The wedding ceremony was performed by May's godfather, the Bishop of Rochester, who, as the Reverend Thomas Claughton, had married his friend David Melville and Emma Hill in Ireland, twenty-five years before. The Earl of Dudley and his young son Lord Ednam watched from a front pew. May's beloved brother Willie had travelled all the way from the Argentine to be there for this important day.

Mendelssohn's 'Wedding March' peeled forth from Handel's organ, and the bells rang as bride and groom left the church across a carpet of flowers. Before going on to the rectory for the wedding breakfast, May visited the Countess of Dudley, who was not well, in her palatial bedroom at Witley Court, which adjoined the church. There is no mention of May's mother Emma, either at the wedding or the rectory.

---

* I wanted to find out what the weather was really like on several key dates in this story, so I paid an enjoyable visit to the Meteorological Office. Once I started looking at some of the early weather reports, written in spidery script with a quill pen, I became entranced by much more than the days I was looking for. As well as entries of rain, snow, sun, storms and so on, there were charming notes such as 'first butterfly', 'lilacs in bloom', 'pear budded', 'lunar halo' – which seemed to occur frequently – 'a ladybird seen', and numerous other intimate observations. On 6 October 1863, the entry for the Worcester area read simply 'earthquake'.

By this time Emma's health had already broken down, so I presume she, like the Countess, was too ill to attend the festivities. For May, the only daughter, who loved her 'gentle little mother', it must have been sad not to have her there.

At the rectory, Mr Mountford, a caterer from Worcester, served a lavish meal. Many toasts were made and the 'numerous and costly' presents were admired. The Earl of Dudley was generous in the extreme, but then his wealth was extreme. His towering Christmas tree at Witley Court is reputed to have sparkled with real jewels, which he would give away as presents. He gave May a turquoise and diamond necklace, with two diamond bracelets, as well as a triple-string necklace of large pearls. The Countess, who had given May her wedding dress, also gave her a silver dressing case, which was eventually left to my grandmother in May's will. She had more pearls from the Duke and Duchess of Hamilton, and a pearl locket from Captain Gaskell. The couple were given plenty of silver, and enough Dresden china to last a lifetime of breakages. Indeed, I remember eating off this china during my childhood visits to Kiddington Hall.

The extent to which May had won the hearts of the locals was evident when she left her home. A large crowd surrounded her when she came out of the rectory onto the drive, where a carriage was waiting to take the bride and groom to a train bound for London. Many tears were shed. The *Worcester Journal* reported that as the carriage creaked to a start, 'a shower of slippers' was thrown after it, which gives us a rather different image from the familiar old tin cans clattering at the back of a bridal car. That night May and Henry stayed as guests at Dudley House in Park Lane, before setting off next morning for a traditional three-month honeymoon 'on the Continent'.

When May wrote her various family reminiscences, for the benefit of her children, grandchildren and 'for those who come after', she never mentioned her own marriage. Nor did she comment on the character of her husband. Not much about Henry Brooks seems to have been passed down through the generations, though proof of his gardening skills can still be seen at Kiddington. In the later years of their marriage, May and Henry Brooks appear to have led very separate lives, which is not surprising considering their different interests. I would have had no clues about their relationship if, as a result of my quest, letters had not been unearthed in various family attics, and read for the first time in decades; I also made a crucial discovery among Lord Milner's papers at the Bodleian Library in Oxford. But I was told that a huge bonfire of papers had been lit impulsively after May's youngest daughter Daphne, who had been left all her mother's personal things, died in old age. Clearly, as is so often the case, much has been lost, but at the same time, to my constant excitement, much retrieved.

In a battered tin trunk labelled by May with the address of the last house she lived in, 28 Albion Street, London, I found a bundle of letters. They were from May to her husband and from him to her, spanning the fourth year of their marriage, 1877. There were also letters from May to her mother Emma, and two diaries of an adventurous journey she and Henry Brooks had made together in America. The letters, well over 120 years old, are very fragile and difficult to decipher, particularly those from Henry Brooks, written on the thinnest paper in a spidery hand. But as I held the brittle paper and touched the ink that had dried on those very pages so long ago, the young couple became real people to me. Yet again, as when I'd touched Burne-Jones's paintbrushes in the library, the past began to seem like the present.

May and Henry's first child, Amy, was born on 26 November 1874. At least that is what Amy's tombstone says. Her birth certificate is the only one there is no trace of, but a newspaper cutting states that she was born in London. May and Henry still had no home of their own when, not long after Amy's birth, May found that she was pregnant again. This time a son was born, at Kiddington. The 'curly headed boy', whom May often referred to with sadness in later years, died soon after the birth. May always maintained that if the 'stingy' Gaskells had not insisted on her having 'an ignorant country doctor' at her confinement, the child would have lived. 'It was a great grief he was lost,' May wrote to her daughter Daphne many years later, 'and it was only because I was not allowed to be in London, and a country doctor lost his head. How I pleaded for London, but the Gaskell family persuaded your father that it was unnecessary expense.'

Henry Brooks Gaskell had been in the Ninth Queen's Royal

Lancers for eight years when he married May Melville. In 1865 his father had paid a high price, £1,857 – roughly £85,000 by today's values – to establish his son as a soldier. The money included the purchase of Henry Brooks's commission, his lieutenancy, and the solicitors' substantial fees. The sum also covered the cost of sending two chargers, dogs, and regimental saddlery to Dundalk in Ireland, where the regiment was stationed. A sword had to be bought from Wilkinson, as well as a splendid uniform and the young officer's personal servants' liveries, which came from Hamburger and Rogers. Noted too were Henry Brooks's entrance and subscription fees to the Naval and Military Club, a large portmanteau and hat box, numerous shirts, and other sundries.

Major General Sir Hugh McCalmont, who joined the Ninth Lancers in the same year as Henry Brooks, wrote in his autobiography:

> Soldiering in Ireland was very enjoyable in those days in view of the excellent sport there was to be had, the good will that was displayed by the peasantry, and the hospitality that was met with in country houses ... it was common practice in the Ninth at that time for us to drink claret at breakfast in the mess. It would be difficult to find a more cheery gang than were the Ninth Queen's Royal Lancers.

Claret for breakfast! No wonder Henry Brooks and his fellow soldiers were happy.

Henry Brooks's last entry in the army list was in 1873, the year he married May. Although he continued to be called Captain Gaskell for the rest of his life, he was in fact a 'late captain'. His regiment was stationed in India from the following year, but it was to shoot game and not as a soldier that he decided to set off to 'Cashmere' at the beginning of January 1877, leaving May and two-year-old Amy behind. Reading the letters he sent to May during the nine months he was away, it seems that his time was spent on long marches in the Himalayas, shooting almost every day. The most likely reason for Henry's decision to leave his family and go abroad for so long was that he and May had no home of their own yet, and that he found life with his father at Kiddington intolerable.

Before he took over the Kiddington estate himself, Henry's favourite occupation was shooting – to such an extent that his nickname for May was 'Tiger'. He wrote from the ship off Tunis on the way to India:

Darling Tiger, last night I sat next to a Mrs Raymond, wife of an old merchant captain. They are both horrid cads, she pockets the oranges at dessert and nudges you in the ribs when she talks. There is a pretty unmarried girl called Miss Lee, her father eats with his knife – I must try and get the steward to give him a really sharp one as he deserves to cut his mouth. An old man with a young wife got on at Gib, she has yellow hair and an awful temper, neglects the poor old thing utterly and walks around with a clergyman. Her husband's teeth fell out while he slept on the deck. She picked them up, put them in her pocket, shook the old man, talked to him like a demon, and then bolted downstairs followed by the clergyman.

The ship reached India in April. Henry was happy to escape immediately from the intense heat, noise and dirt of Bombay, and he was soon camping in the mountains of Kashmir, shooting ibex. Surrounded by a landscape of staggering beauty, soothed by the cool air and gentle silence, he wrote to May:

One has plenty of time for reading and thinking. I often think of you my darling. I think this journey will do me good in more ways than one as I often think how unkind I sometimes was to you, and I am determined to try to make you much happier when I get back. I have also learnt to value your love more and if possible to love you more.

After only three years of marriage, something was clearly already wrong. May, however, was delighted with this letter, and wrote back:

Your loving words, my husband, were worth letting you go to receive, this absence will prove to each other how dearly we love. You may be pleased with me letting you go, and what you call my 'pluck', but these little tiny virtues are nothing when I think of your loving, self-denying thoughts of me, and your true heart. I always feel I could trust you far better than I could trust myself. You are so safe, Henry, and if an angel from heaven were to tell me you were unfaithful even in thought, I would not believe

it . . . I hope that we will say when growing <u>happily</u> old together that
India has been our greatest blessing, for it will teach us the other's worth.

But life at Kiddington alone with her morose father-in-law was too much for May. She too was soon on the move. She set off for Italy, taking with her Amy, the nurse, and her father. Before they left England, Canon Melville went to Kiddington and confronted his daughter's father-in-law, old Henry Lomax, about the need for May and his son Henry to have a house of their own. Mr Gaskell complained that it was selfish of Henry to have gone abroad for so long, abandoning him at Kiddington. Canon Melville firmly replied that it had been in the old man's power to arrange that his son and daughter-in-law should have a house of their own, and an increased allowance to pursue a country life in England. May wrote to her husband and reported their conversation, adding that her father had commented afterwards: 'Mr Gaskell wants to have it all take, and no give, with Henry.' As if to coax her husband back to England, despite his mean father, May pleaded:

Still, darling, I think we must feather a little nest for ourselves, even if the
feathers are of the commonest, do not you feel it would be much happier?
I do.

With her husband so far away, May settled in at the Grand Hotel Villa d'Este, still today a luxurious hotel, set in beautiful grounds on the shores of Lake Como. May took singing lessons, and started learning Italian. Canon Melville read and wrote, and went for long walks around the area. The nurse played with little Amy in the lovely gardens. Henry Brooks wrote that he hoped May was 'getting fat now you are away from the worry of that stingy old beast', referring to his father. May sent him a photograph of herself to reassure him. 'Look how fat I am. Are you pleased?' she wrote. In many of the letters Henry repeated his hope that May was getting fat – perhaps he preferred plump women, or perhaps May had lost weight after Amy was born.

Even if May was physically blooming, the romantic beauty of Lake Como caused her to long for her husband. Late one night she wrote to him:

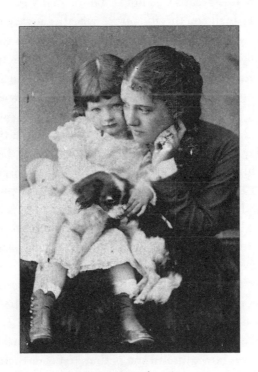

May with Amy in 1877, while her husband Henry was shooting game in India. She probably had this photograph taken to send him.

I never saw such a perfect show of stars, and they are all reflected in the lake at our feet like little moons. Listen now to what would be perfect – you should be sitting on the easy chair close by the open window and I would be on your lap, with your dear arms round me, telling me how you had wanted me, missed me, and how happy you were to be back. The nightingales would help to make it a dream of delight.

But May knew this dream was not to be for many more months: 'Do tell me whether I tell you this too often, whether it wearies you to have so many "pretty" speeches told you.' She begged him to 'remember it is the past I like best in your letters to me'. It sounds to me as if she already felt unsure of his love. May had worried in a previous letter that she was 'not good enough' for her husband. She was only twenty-four years old.

Amy shared May's large room at the hotel, while the nurse slept next door. May had filled her room with pictures of her Henry, and she wrote to him that Amy would run up and kiss a picture, saying, 'That's Amy's Papa.' One day, on a walk, Amy had pulled her hand from May's and rushed up to a heavily moustachioed stranger, calling 'Papa, Papa.' May told Henry that there had been no word from her father-in-law in England, or from any of the other Gaskells. She said they had not even acknowledged the photographs she had sent them. 'But no doubt it is the scramble of the London season,' she wrote. 'Everyone is going wild, I hear, about a new beauty, Mrs Langtry, with eyes that take the world by storm.'

I cannot feel too sorry for May. Writing again to her distant husband, she says how grateful she is that, to cover their time in Italy, he has increased the 'very generous' allowance he normally gave her, as otherwise it would have been 'a bit of a squeeze' for the 'frisky tours, and etceteras' she so enjoyed. 'And remember to bring me home some nice Indian things,' commanded May with a new air of confidence, 'such as shawls to make drapes. I do so like those embroidered in the same colour as the stuff.'

May stayed in Italy all through that summer with her father and other visiting friends; they enjoyed restful weeks in comfortable hotels, punctuated by intensive sightseeing tours of Verona, Padua, Venice, Bologna, Ravenna and Florence.

May loved the romance of Venice, but it made her miss her husband even more. She saw a balcony that reminded her of Romeo and Juliet, and she 'longed for my Romeo'. Eventually, because letters to India could take six weeks, her Romeo replied that he would like to meet her in Venice on his return in October. 'There is no hurry for our going to England. I am sure I don't want to see my beast of a parent, and I think it would be very jolly for both of us to go afterwards to America.'

Henry Brooks had heard that there was good shooting to be had in the Rocky Mountains, and instructed May to find out about 'expense etc'. Meanwhile, he continued to crisscross the valleys and hills of the Himalayas on long marches with his fellow officer friends and their coolies, shooting whatever game they came across, either on foot, or on horseback when some kindly maharaja would lend them some horses. The scenery was spectacular, the going sounded very rough indeed, but the exotic flowers and plants instilled in Henry Brooks an interest in botany which was to remain with him for the rest of his life. From August he began to talk eagerly of how it would not be long until he and May were together again.

At the beginning of September, after May, sounding upset, had written to him about a flirtatious Italian who had followed her around the hotel she was staying at, Henry Brooks was clearly rattled. He wrote from Harding's Hotel in Simla:

> *You are a naughty little woman to let that man flirt with you but I am*
> *sure it was his fault. I knew that you would find it hard to resist flirtation,*
> *though I also knew that you would resist to the best of your power; you*
> *don't think I should have left you alone if I had not trusted you, though I*
> *think you are the only person in the world that I do trust. I don't think*
> *you could ever abuse my trust, God keep me from thinking so, as I believe*
> *it would ruin me body and soul . . . you are the only thing I care to get*
> *back for, you have the whole of my love, I never think of my relations, and*
> *I could not flirt here if I tried, although there are plenty of women ready*
> *to play that game.*

Henry Brooks sailed from Bombay on 14 September 1877 on the P&O liner *Venetia*, via Aden and Suez. On 11 October, May was bobbing about in a gondola beside the quay at Venice, with little Amy at her side, waiting for her husband's arrival. First 'a monster Italian vessel' loomed on the horizon, then a merchant ship from Liverpool, then a boat from Egypt. May felt nervous and impatient. At long last, very slowly, the sleek steamship *Venetia* moved silently across the still green water towards the waiting crowds.

'We rowed close to her,' May wrote to her mother Emma in Witley, 'and there I saw my darling standing watching. For half an hour we were side by side, looking at each other, then she stopped and we were together.'

Henry, she said, found Amy 'very, very pretty'. She added excitedly that they were to stay two more weeks in Venice before wintering in Rome for two or three months. 'Then we must think seriously about our future plans. Henry alas is no more inclined to settle, quite the reverse.'

Their stay in England after the winter did not last long. By mid-August 1878, when May must have been about two months pregnant with my grandfather, they boarded the SS *Bothnia*, bound for New York, with a group of Henry's shooting friends. Three-and-a-half-year-old Amy stayed in England, at her grandparents' with her nurse. May was the only woman in the party. 'Ship quite as horrid and smelly as I feared, cabin worse, spirits poor,' May noted in her diary. The next day, 12 August, the derided ship, owned by Burns and McIver of Liverpool, set sail. Seasickness immediately afflicted many of the passengers, for which a remedy of 'one teaspoonful of lime-water in a wine glass of water every half hour' did little good. 'A rough sea does not encourage the pen of a ready writer,' wrote May, who gave up her diary until their arrival in New York, 'after days of such utter misery and prostration that the memory is odious'.

Although New York was 'hot, hot, hot', the luxury of a large warm bath with plenty of soap and water was bliss, and May's spirits revived. She took a tram up Broadway to Union Square, and was particularly impressed by 'the wonderful advertisements', and by 'the elevated railway over the street', which she saw when they went to get money from Wall Street. In Del Monico's restaurant May quite forgot her seasickness. Here, she and her party of men tucked into oysters, soft-shelled crabs and scallops, accompanied by buckwheat cakes and fried sweet potatoes, a meal which they all pronounced 'A1'.

Many women callers came to see May at her hotel and she was 'touched' by the outgoing nature of Americans, so different from the reserve of the English. The ladies of New York seem to have envied May as the only woman among so many young men. In her diary she wrote that she was surprised by their 'outspoken preference for the male sex, and the absolute necessity for crowds of men to give them a good time'. That evening at a dinner, May sat next to 'a clever American', Mr Gerard. He told her, May recorded, 'that it was a curious fact how the American race was gradually approaching the Indian type, that the cheek bones were getting high, the nervous temperament more excitable and that the doctors allowed five more pulsations of the heart to the minute in Americans than in Europeans'. A curious observation indeed.

Everything changed for May and her party when they left sophisticated and comfortable New York life behind, and set out for what now sounds like a quite gruelling tour of America. The more I read about Victorian travellers, the more hardy and adventurous they seem in comparison with modern tourists. With her pregnancy advancing, May bumped across desolate plains, hills and mountains by stage-coach, experiencing the contrasts of burning heat and intense cold. There were many delays for fear of Indian attacks and highwaymen, who, they had been warned, were 'most dangerous'. It was a good thing that little Amy was not with them on such a rigorous journey. At the start, after crossing the remote and featureless prairie for days, May wrote in her diary:

This life is debasing, our chief amusement is watching to see which of us grows dirtiest quickest. I feel quarrelsome, time is slow, dirt vile, and self hot.

On another day, however, her entry was:

Morning glorious, stage punctual, horses good. Spirits were like champagne, a dashing cowboy cantered beside us for two or three miles and then cantered away into the morning light across the prairie.

The young May was perhaps becoming as conscious of 'the male sex' as the American women she had met in New York were, for at another point she observed:

> *There was a very handsome specimen of a young ranchman, living utterly alone. The sunset was glorious, and a crescent moon rose over the loveliest pink hills.*

The ultimate goal of the expedition was to shoot game in the Rocky Mountains. Here they found elk, antelope, deer, buffalo and bears. They camped in spectacular positions from where they could watch the sky turn from 'blue to gold, purple, and pink' as the sun went down over the jagged mountains. May wrote in her diary:

> *The evenings are rather nice, our men become more communicative in the firelight, but there is a grave reticence about them when they return successful, which is very baffling. The better their luck, the more sad they become, it is a strange fact.*

The exception was Lord Granville, who just seemed to be continually depressed; he was obsessed with killing a bear, which he never did.

Although May wrote pages of ecstatic descriptions in her diary about the wild and spectacularly beautiful landscape they travelled through, the sunsets and the early dawns with their changing colours and light, and the feeling of adventure, there were times when she missed her home comforts:

> *Began to think camp life not all it might be. Fried elk four days running is wearisome, the sun burns, the tents grow dirty, washing clothes is not amusing, the horses keep getting lost.*

Towards the end of their time it began to snow, and the nights were cold and frosty. Although she never mentions her pregnancy, May did not feel well; she had bad toothache and her face was painful and swollen. Even so, there were days in this wilderness when she sang and drew and felt 'an intense sense of happiness' with her Henry. Nevertheless, when writing to her mother, she was again thinking

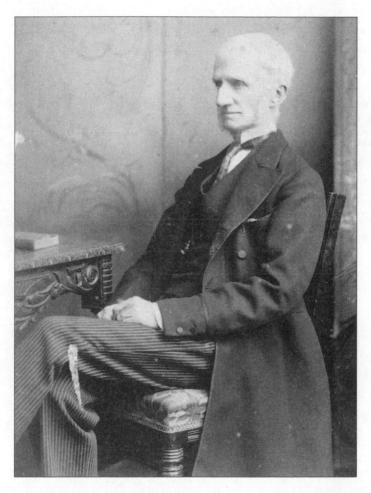

The temperamental Henry Lomax Gaskell. The nose he inherited from his father, the Devil of Wigan, is evident here, and has been found in each following generation of Gaskell men, and in May's younger daughter, Daphne.

about settling down with her husband in a house of their own. 'Henry is such a darling,' she told Emma Melville, 'only he likes roving far better than I do.'

After they returned to England at the start of 1879, there was to be no more roving for a time. May was now six months pregnant, and she was at last reunited with Amy. Henry, May and Amy went to live in a rented house, 6 Chapel Street, off Park Lane. It was here, on the cold wet morning of 15 April, that Henry Melville Gaskell, my grand-father, was born. That afternoon there was a gleam of sunshine and the weather brightened. Amy, who was now four and a half years old, with her thick dark hair cut in a bob, was brought in to see her new brother by her nurse, Miss Cooper. Lively, and very pretty, Amy chattered constantly. The new baby was tiny and delicate, but his nose was on a different scale from the rest of his little face, already showing that he was unmistakably a Gaskell. This eldest Gaskell son, May decided firmly, though once again christened Henry, should always be known as Hal.

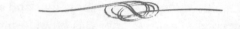

CHAPTER THREE

WIFE AND MOTHER

OLD HENRY LOMAX GASKELL REMAINED GRIMLY AT KIDDINGTON. Henry and May, who had moved into another rented house in London, in Hyde Park Place, would sometimes take their children to visit Grandfather Gaskell, but the country life the family enjoyed most was with May's parents in Worcestershire. The Melvilles gave them the warmest welcome, and, despite Emma Melville's uncertain health, would often look after their grandchildren for long periods while May and Henry travelled abroad. It was from the rectory at Witley, in the early autumn of 1885, that Amy, aged nearly eleven, wrote to May to complain about her little brother Hal, who was now six and a half. Amy clearly felt she had a responsible position when May was away:

> *My dear little Mother . . . I do not know what to think of Hal, he behaves disgarsfuly at the table at breckfast. Wast of all when he has an egg he genrely deposets it in his lape. His misic is awful, his lessons are awful, alltogether he is going to the bad. Not a word of French has Hal said yet . . . Your loving little Amy.*

But none of this bothered Hal, for it was in the garden, the woods and the fields of Worcestershire, like his Uncle Willie before him, that

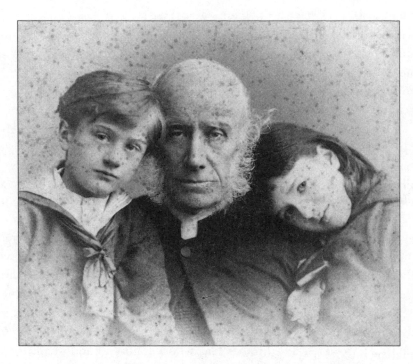

I love this picture of Hal and Amy with their grandfather, the striking canon David Melville.

young Hal developed a passion for the countryside, which was to become his greatest love.

Hal was not like other little boys; a sensitive, shy child, he showed signs of being a loner from an early age. With his small frame, large beak-like nose, humorous blue eyes and quirky imagination, he looked and behaved differently from his peers. He was artistically creative, with a funny, original mind. He was greatly attached to his family, which by 1887 included a younger sister, Daphne. He loved being with his sisters, and, when she was there, with his pretty, tender mother. He loved home life. However, at that time the sons of well-to-do families were sent away to school, while their sisters remained at home with governesses. So, in the freezing January of 1888, May had to take her only son, an increasingly emotional little boy, to his first school, Stonehouse, far away in Kent. It was hard for both of them.

May waited for Hal's first letter home with apprehension. She already realized what a highly developed sense of drama her little boy had, but when that first letter arrived, passionate and wildly spelt, it provoked intense maternal anguish.

> *My dear mother, this is perficly ofal . . . I cried al the time from when you went away and al the night . . . i jumped up and cried and sed oh mother oh mother I am dunfor . . . my word is <u>troo</u> and if you <u>dont</u> I shall take mademoisels knif and thrut it into my body . . . I will wether you no or not . . . this is for the last time that I shall . . . I dont want to dy but I serpose <u>I</u> <u>cant help it</u>. dear mother dear mother but I must . . . Goodby mother.*

Hal had written the last five words in a shaky, fading hand. The lettering became smaller and smaller until it dwindled to nothing, giving the impression that he was dying as he wrote. He accompanied the letter with a drawing of 'mademoisels knif' which showed blood running down the sharp blade, and another drawing labelled 'me afterwards', in which Hal depicted himself falling over, with blood spurting from his chest as he cried out, 'dunfor'.

As soon as she could, May made the journey to Stonehouse School to comfort her son, but her visit only provoked a fresh burst of misery. Hal now told her that the other boys were bullying him. Almost as soon as May left, he wrote:

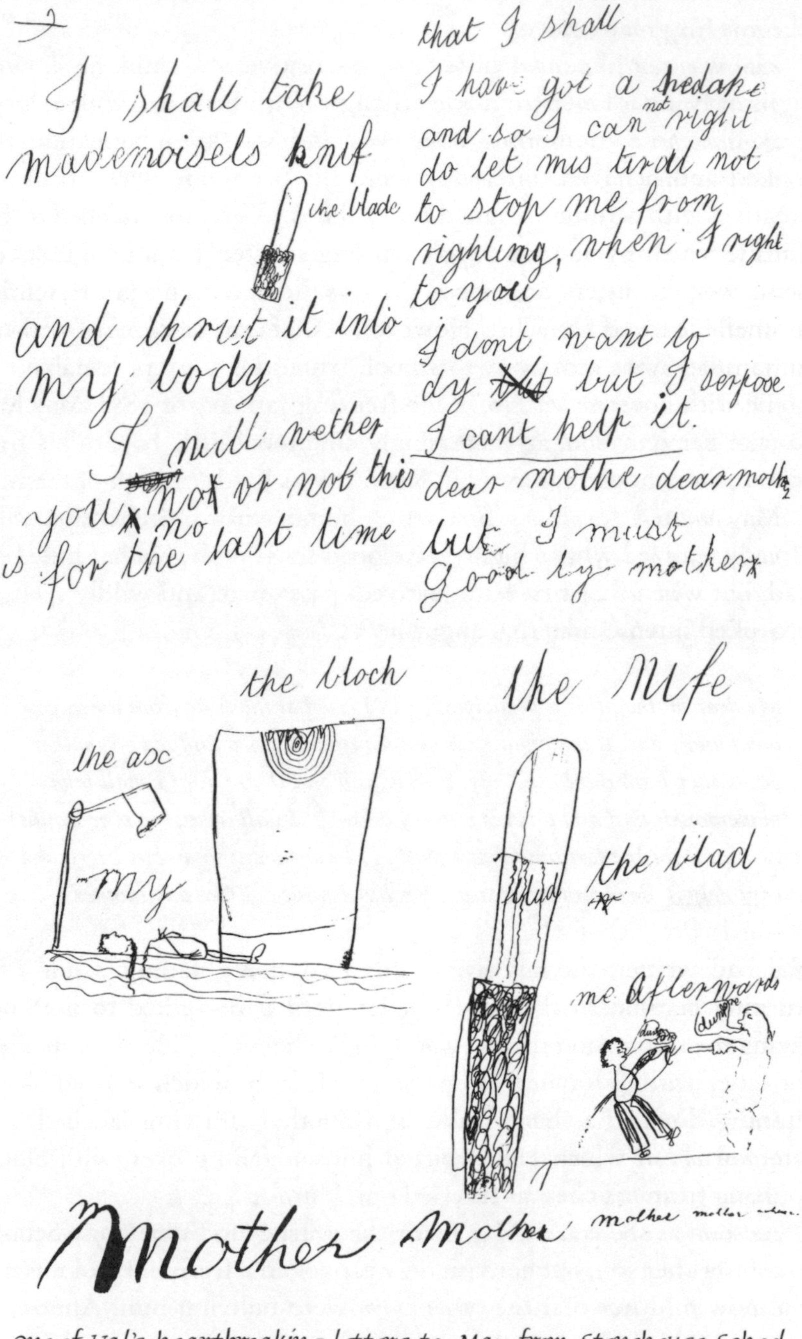

I shall take
mademoisels knif

that I shall
I have got a hedake
and so I can not right
do let mis tirdl not
to stop me from
righting, when I right
to you

the blade

and thrut it into
my body

j dont want to
dy but I serpose
I cant help it.

I will nether
you not or not this
is for the last time

dear mothe dearmoth
but I must
Good by mother

the bloch   the lfe

the asc

my

the blad

me Afterwards

Mother Mother mother mother

One of Hal's heartbreaking letters to May from Stonehouse School.

*Oh mother oh mother, I want to go to another school please . . . I have
been crying since I saw you . . . the boys are geting worce and worce and
everything is geting awful . . . realy mother it is awful . . . I shall die for
greaf if you don't be quick . . . what I say is tru realy it is . . . all my leter
is tru mother tru . . . I prey oh oh oh mother have piti on me I am crying
do do let me . . . goodby my dearest mother.*

This letter was followed during subsequent weeks by others in the
same vein, frequently ending with 'oh mother' written countless times
in smaller and smaller writing until it diminished to nothing, as if his
unhappiness was making him actually disappear.

The headmaster, Mr Stone, wrote to a friend of his who knew the
Gaskell family, about this most emotional new boy:

*Hal Gaskell has a highly imaginative soul, and consequently he aggravates
his sorrows by reflection. I don't think there is any bullying, even of the
mental kind, which to such a boy would be the worst. The constant
writing home in which he indulges may, I dare say, be a salutary relief to
his feelings, but his statements must be taken with a full grain of poetic
salt.*

At the beginning of the following term Hal's letters were as
miserable as ever. May wrote to Mr Stone and suggested keeping Hal
at home for another year. His reply came quickly, a seemingly harsh
but perhaps perceptive letter. Yet what appears to us today as an
implied threat that Hal might become a homosexual if he doesn't
learn to stand up to the bullies might have been taken by May as a
warning that Hal might not become as stiff-upper-lip and masculine
as men were then expected to be:

*Hal is a very difficult case to deal with, but I think your best plan is to
leave him here to work himself clear of all his troubles. I talked to him
seriously last night, and he promised he would do better. I believe the
malevolence which he attributes to the other boys is imaginary. You must
not take what he says as pure truth, he invents and exaggerates, and if this
habit is allowed to be successful will be most mischievous. I think you may
know the sort of man he is likely to turn out if he is humoured. I am sure*

there is nothing like brutal bullying, but if he is so unmanly he must bring on himself a good deal of silly chaffs, which won't hurt him. Do not encourage him in the idea that he is 'unlike' other boys – there are many sensitive boys who fight their terrors and apprehensions and live them down. I am certain that many of his grievances are wholly imaginary, and that they would disappear in a moment if only he would face them.

A month later May received a more optimistic letter from a junior teacher, Mr James, who had been kind to Hal and sympathetic to May. From the start he had made a real effort to reassure May about her fragile little son, writing to her as often as he could. Now, he said, he wanted to relieve her recent anxiety; Hal seemed to have settled down at last, and was getting on well with the other boys:

He is quick enough at his work and lacks no power in any direction except that of self control. He also has a way of drawing upon his imagination very liberally.

At the same time, Hal wrote to his mother in much neater hand-writing, which somehow gives the impression that he was far less desperate.

I am getting on alright . . . I am now trying to get a prise at the end of the term to please you and father . . . Mr Stone sed to me Hal is the person I admire he used to get bad marks but now the table is turned. I have tried and I can get on very well and now I wonder why I did not try before. I was very silly and now the examinations are coming I am going to work my hardest. I am going to chear you up mother. I am going to try to do well.

A letter covered with drawings of sailing ships and steam trains followed:

my dear mother . . . the boys say that I am one of the best jumpers in the school and I have jumped a jump that the top of the school canot do. Please get me a book of all sorts of things about engines with pictures of them to draw because I have settled that I am going to be an engineer. That is why I wanted to go down to the station so often.

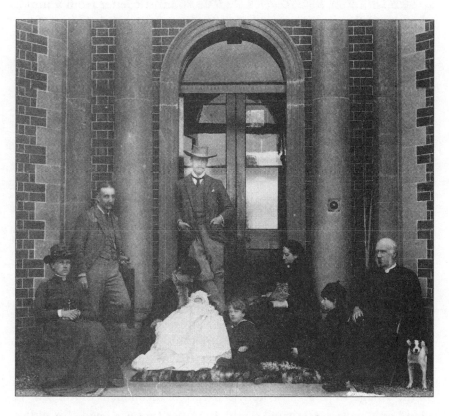

Family group at Witley Rectory, 1887. Right to left: Canon Melville, Amy, grandmother Emma, Hal, Berry in the doorway, May with baby Daphne, Henry Brooks Gaskell, Berry's wife Sydney.

Presumably he meant Paddington Station, not far from Hyde Park Place, where May and Henry lived in London at that time.

Hal was nearly ten years old now and May thought he really did seem happier at school, although he was still prone to strong emotions that he found difficult to control. A few months later, his grandfather, Henry Lomax Gaskell, became ill at Kiddington. Hal wrote to May:

> *I don't like being hear very much this term because I am always thinking of grandfather. It is rather beastly, I do not know what to do but I have to restrain myself . . . mother, this is a very short term, perhaps I shall come back before grandfather dies. But still everyone must die sometime must not they mother. It is nearly time for him to die, he has had a long dreary life perhaps it is better for him to die. I hope he will have a nice death, but still it is better not to tell every boy, I will keep it in me as much as ——— I can.*

Hal did not see his grandfather again.

> *My dear mother I am so sorry the grandfather is dead. I felt it very much that I would not see his face anymore but I suppose you must cheer up after a while Miss Tyrrell [his matron] does not know what to do about those trousers. Goodby your loveing Hal.*

Henry Lomax Gaskell died of cirrhosis of the liver. The quantities of 'best champagne', 'fine French wines' and 'old port' with which he had filled the cellars of Kiddington Hall must finally have taken their toll, and it may well have been that his past contributions to the Temperance Society and fury with his sons when they went drinking in the village were because he was aware of alcoholism in himself. It could only have exacerbated the bad temper that had made his wife's life so unbearable. And could his eldest son Henry have consoled himself with drink as a result of a bad relationship with his father, and so become a more difficult man himself?

Only one of Henry Lomax's sons was at his bedside when he died, and it was not his heir. May wrote to Amy, who was fifteen and studying in France:

The funeral was simple and impressive and the sun shone down. I was
sorry for them all and the poor little grandfather who was leaving the
world forever. I did feel for him as we lowered him into the grave.

It would seem that May's feelings for her father-in-law and those of
his grandchildren were warmer than those of his son. But there were
problems to deal with. May explained to Amy:

Father is very, very busy, and has to face no end of difficulties and worries.
We now have all the work and looking round as to what our lives are
going to be, and what our income! First of all you must face a
disappointment for we shall be poor for two or three years, but we hope by
the time you come out we shall be able to be all happy and comfortable
together.

May finished her letter by telling Amy that she could buy a boa instead
of a collar if she liked, but that it must not be an expensive one:

We cannot spend much money until next July, as we have none to spend.

The poverty May pleads after her father-in-law's death must have
been partly because Henry Lomax's will – ten foolscap pages of tiny,
dense handwriting – was immensely complicated, and any inheritance
was not immediately available. Henry Brooks was one of the
executors and although as the eldest son he was to inherit Kiddington,
it appears that the house had to be let out for about three years because
of the time it would take to settle the complex affairs of the estate and
liberate some cash. Henry Lomax's substantial estates and investments
were apportioned in different ways between eight of his children, four
sons and four daughters. Of the other two, one son, Walter Edgar, had
died when he was ten years old and another, James, had 'gone to the
bad' and been disinherited; I can find no record of what happened to
him or when he died. Another son, Samuel William, was clearly a
problem too; his father stipulated that he would inherit an income only
if he was 'not at my death outlawed or an uncertificated bankrupt'.
The names of both James and Samuel William had been crossed out
in the large Family Bible.

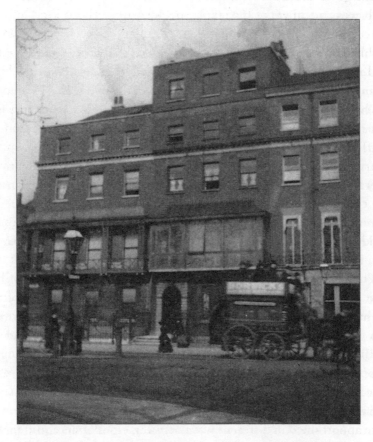

The tall central house is Number 3, Marble Arch, May and Henry Brooks Gaskell's house, which they moved into in 1890.

Henry Lomax left his Scottish estate, Cambus O'May, to his second son, John Francis, who appears to have been his favourite. In the will he refers to him as 'my dear son', but there is no such endearment for Henry Brooks. However, the will specifies that all Henry Lomax's 'wines, spirituous liquors, ales, ports and other consumable stores' should go to his eldest son. Although the old man may have been harsh with members of his family, he was not without kindness and appreciation to others who had helped him in his last years. On his deathbed, in October 1889, he added a codicil to his will, witnessed by his doctor and a male nurse. He left a generous legacy to his long-serving butler George Brown, 'in acknowledgement of the attentive way he has nursed me', and sums of money to all his other servants, both in his houses and on his estates. To the head gardener and the bailiff at Kiddington he made an additional, odd bequest: a suit of mourning for each of them, presumably to be worn at their employer's funeral.

Despite her warnings to Amy about a period of poverty, it does not sound as if May and Henry Brooks suffered too much. They moved from Hyde Park Place, on Bayswater Road overlooking the park, to a more substantial house, 3 Marble Arch, looking straight down Park Lane and across Hyde Park. With Kiddington temporarily rented out, husband and wife travelled abroad together for much of the year with groups of friends. When they were in England, May was more socially gregarious than Henry Brooks. She had become confident at house parties in grand country houses, even though she was often alone. 'Henry chose not to come because of his being shy,' she told her mother more than once.

Although she was not an aristocrat, May's intelligence and beauty were noticed and her social life had begun to enlarge two years before the death of her father-in-law, after a particularly distinguished house party she and her husband had been invited to in November 1887. But Henry Brooks had made his excuses and May, although she was now thirty-four years old, was slightly nervous when she went alone to stay at Escrick Park, a stately home in Yorkshire belonging to Lord and Lady Wenlock, set in a 450-acre deer park. Prince 'Eddy' of Wales was to be one of the guests. Among others was Lord Charles

Beresford, an admiral and well-known 'wag', who was tattooed all down his back. He was reputed to have once telegraphed the Prince of Wales in answer to a last-minute invitation to dine: 'Very sorry can't come. Lie follows by post.' To May, it was an illustrious group.

During the weekend, May had written to her mother:

I am very much amused here, and don't feel out of it as I expected. The Prince is very 'unprincey' and is quiet but rather full of jokes, and inclined to bearfight and is rather silly, but he is pleasant, and not a stiff element. Lord and Lady Charles Beresford are very funny in different ways. She is a type I don't often come across and her small audacities and coquetteries and guiles and wiles are so queer. Lord Charles has a flirtatious eye and a most ready wit. Then we have Lady de Gray, with her radiant eyes that light up the room with beauty and glorious health and strength. Lady Pembroke is vastly interesting but her husband is more – he is delightful. He is beautiful, and clever and thoughtful, and talks on all sorts of things with a simplicity that only great minds have. Lord Elcho has the reputation of being a great deal to most women, but I cannot see his charm. Then we have Captain Greville, equerry to HRH, and Lord Alwyne Compton, and a Swede with no name I can repeat.

The Wenlocks, the Pembrokes, the Elchos and Arthur Balfour, whom May had known in her Worcester days, were among the principal members of a circle of beautiful, cultured people in the highest echelons of society who were at that time forming more and more of a 'gang', as they had begun to be called. They recognized in May qualities they most admired: intelligence with sensitivity, personal beauty, a passion for literature, art and music, and a strong, independent spirit unusual in wives of the day. For her part, May must have been attracted by their belief that women should not have to do everything with or for their husbands, and that within their circle they were able to speak out and to assert their individuality. To be involved with this group of friends was a chance to be emancipated in a way that had previously been thought impossible in male-dominated Victorian society.

This aristocratic circle, known as 'the gang', had been drawn together by their interest in avant-garde art, literature and music.

They loved each other's company and patronized the most distinguished artists, writers and musicians of the day, the painter Edward Burne-Jones being arguably their favourite. In the late 1880s it is said that Lord Charles Beresford, who was himself part of the circle, commented that since they all spent so much time discussing their souls, he thought that 'the Souls' would be a better name for the group. The name stuck. In 1889 and 1890, at two dinners given by Lord Curzon, later to become Viceroy of India, the key members of the circle gathered together and were officially recognized. Although, being such a clique, they could seem irritating to outsiders, they were a lively addition to an often stiflingly conventional society. The Souls have been described as anti-philistine, disapproving of what they considered the many aimless pursuits of their social contemporaries, such as hunting and shooting – just what May's husband Henry enjoyed.

Now that May had become known within this influential cultural circle, she started to be invited to more literary and musical events. She was still singing herself, and in her letters she mentions more than once 'singing to the soldiers' in the Tower of London. One afternoon she was asked to visit a bedridden old lady called Mrs Hodge, who liked to gather around her 'all sorts and conditions of charming men and women of talent' to listen or take part in music and readings. That day there were ten guests, including another female singer, a well-known reciter, and a painter called Charles Barber, who had painted Queen Victoria with her dogs, and the Prince of Wales's dog, Fozzy. Barber was also a gifted musician. But the person May was most excited to meet was the famous painter George Frederick Watts. She told her mother:

> He was very quiet, with an extra refined head, and gentle courtesy of manner, a little frightening by his retiring gentleness. Gradually we began to talk, and spent most of the time so, except when music was going on. He gave me a most kind invitation to go and see him, which I shall certainly do.

That same evening, at a dinner party, May's appetite for culture was stimulated once more. She was glad to see a previous acquaintance,

Thomas Woolner, the sculptor and poet, 'a rough, noisy, powerful and tender hearted man'. But it was the poet Robert Browning, an old man by then, whom she had never met before, who took her into dinner; 'a meal he most thoroughly enjoyed', May told her mother.

> *His talk was ceaseless and interesting, but before we had been five minutes together I had annoyed him by saying that as a rule I thought geniuses managed their lives badly, or something to that effect, whereupon he took it as a personal insult and poured out floods of eloquence! He gave me his own anecdotes of Carlyle, Goethe and Tennyson, but what I liked best was his talk about Shelley. All this he said very close to my face, and emphasised it with his finger, sometimes within an inch of my nose. I suppose it is necessary that these men of talent are hugely conceited. To hear Woolner talk you gather that Woolner is the greatest man of the day. Listen to Browning and he is certainly the one man above all criticism. After my singing he came up and said thank you and went on to tell me how thoroughly he had studied music – au fond – adding 'and I can write fugues quite well'.*

Although May's life was full and distracting, she was never without a certain anxiety. In one letter to Amy, she referred to feeling soothed by sucking 'cocaine lozenges'. Cocaine was at that time a new drug, used as a local anaesthetic, a nerve tonic, a gargle, and in throat lozenges. It was thought to be perfectly harmless, although I would have thought it was stimulating, rather than soothing. May's main worry was about her odd little son Hal. Although he had become more settled at school, he was still prone to outbursts of emotion if things went wrong – which they did, in a dramatic way, one bleak winter term.

> *My dear mother, we are having fearful misfortunes – last night one of our school fellows one of the nicest and best died of brain disease – things are getting worse as days go on and I hope that nothing else will happen – his name was H Freshfield. Last Wednesday he was playing cricket with us and caught a lot of catches poor boy for his last time – it is fearful. But I am greatly afraid there will be one more – Mr James who is seriously ill in this house. But poor H Freshfield died without any of his relations. Oh I*

long long that this will soon be over. It is too much for me but I must be as brave as I can to be as good and as liked so much as these two.

Mr James was the young master who had been sympathetic to May, and kind to Hal. In Hal's next letter the worst had happened.

Last night at half past ten Mr James died he was only about thirty. I am fearfully sorry and wretched about it. I could not help crying when I heard of it. He has been the best master we have ever had, and the nicest, and he died so young of inflammation of the lungs. The masters were all very done up in trying to keep Mr James alive but it was of no use. His poor father has been too late to see him die. I shall not get over it for a long time. Will you please send me my foxes head. Goodby your loving Hal.

Towards the end of each term, Hal would become very excited about his return home for the holidays. He sent his mother a drawing of a house called 'the house of quick time'. In the smoke wafting from the chimney are the words: 'Time passes quickly, fly, fly, fly.' Hal adds: 'Time passes like a bang and I come home.' In anticipation, he would ask May about his little sister Daphne, about Mademoiselle, the French governess, about the toy engines and boats he loved, and some-times about his father. A concern for his mother, who was so often away, began to be apparent. Possibly he sensed that something was not right between his parents: 'Oh mother oh mother are you getting on alright?' was now a frequent cry in his letters. Did it ever occur to May that if she had a more settled lifestyle it might make a difference to her sensitive son? From our perspective it seems obvious that May's absences would make Hal more insecure, yet regular travelling abroad was the pattern of life for so many well-to-do Victorian families, and they believed that being sent away to school would turn their sons into stronger, more independent boys.

May's extended travels meant that home for Hal and little Daphne during the holidays was often in Worcestershire with their Melville grandparents. This could have given them much-needed security, as it did for me when I stayed with my adoring grandmother during many school holidays, because my mother lived abroad with my diplomat stepfather. Amy, now aged seventeen, was studying art in Paris, but she also visited her grandparents regularly on College Green beside Worcester Cathedral, where the Melvilles had lived since they left the rectory at Witley.

In late October 1891, May and Henry Brooks set out for Egypt, leaving Hal and Daphne, now aged twelve and four, in the care of their grandparents once more.

The Gaskells were to sail down the Nile with their close friends Lord and Lady Waterford and a small group of friends. The Waterfords lived in County Waterford in Ireland, at Curraghmore, a large estate that the family had owned since 1170. Today, the house still contains an ancient Eastern crystal ball, believed by many throughout the generations to cure infected cattle. May, who had arranged to travel from Egypt to meet Amy in Italy in the spring, would be away for nearly seven months, missing Christmas and Easter with her two youngest children. Daphne was to spend the whole time with the Melvilles in Worcester, while Hal would stay there during his school holidays. May knew they would be looked after well by the devoted grandparents and their trusted servants. There was also a new governess, Caroline Balsiheck from Germany, who was known as Fraulein. She had replaced the 'Mademoisel', as Hal called her, whose knife he had threatened to kill himself with when he first went to Stonehouse School.

May's letters to her father while she was in Egypt show how devoted she was to him, and how concerned about his well-being as he grew older. The distinguished canon was seventy-nine now, but he was still working as hard as ever, and preaching to rapt congregations in the cathedral at Worcester. May wrote to him on 11 December 1891, not long after the start of the three-month cruise on the Nile, as their 'dahabeah', one of the long houseboats used on the river at that time, sailed slowly downstream towards Luxor. She realized, she told the old canon, that letters sent by the mail boat which was due to catch them up that evening should just reach England by Christmas Day.

I wish my own darling we could be together, but I shall think of you so much, so much. Are you taking care? Are you buttoning up the cape when

*you run through those drafty cloisters? And are you keeping your skull cap
on in the Cathedral?*

May wanted him to look after himself well, in the hope that he might
be able to join her in the spring in Italy with Amy.

*Perhaps you could meet us in Venice and we could drift through those
northern lakes and towns once more together . . . In these long sunny
hours I picture you so often. I see your darling gray head reading the Pall
Mall Magazine by the lamp in the library when the afternoon service is
over, and being brought your cup of tea, and Daphne's imperative little
squeak to which you are always attentive. I see you all and kiss you, and
trust to heaven I may see you, just so, next Christmas . . . This is a love
letter, not an Egyptian letter. Ever your loving May.*

May's mother Emma wrote to her regularly with reports of
Daphne, who was now showing herself to be as odd a little character
as her brother Hal. Unfortunately, she also had just as big a nose,
which dominated her small and delicate face. Decades later,
Daphne was to tell her daughter how for most of her life she had
prayed every night that when she woke in the morning her nose
would be smaller. Emma, an adoring grandmother, wrote on one
occasion:

*She was rolling her hoop in the garden when I asked her if she had any-
thing to say to you, 'Oh yes, tell her I always begin to think of her when I
am rolling my hoop – I don't know why – and I send her the only kiss I
have – a huge kiss, and I'll come and give it to you.' It was a dozen kisses
at least.*

In her letters, May told her father of magical experiences as their
party sailed peacefully down the 'noiseless river'. She described the
monumental sights of ancient Egypt along the way, the exhilarating
rides on camels far into the desert to have picnics, the guards of honour
who watched over them, consisting of 'the wildest of Arab tribes', who
in those surroundings 'look far more dignified than we do'. Near
Aswan, a tribe called the Bicharines particularly impressed May:

They are the finest looking lot, hair plaited and frizzled, their bodies wrapped in white cotton but generally naked to the waist. Though perfect savages they are nevertheless beautiful, high bred, and graceful.

At Aswan, too, they met the English army officers stationed there:

a capital lot, as plucky and good as could be, they have made their houses charming and are as keen as mustard about their gardens. For eight months of the year they never see a European lady, so they treated us very well.

In February, they were retracing their way back up the river. May told her father:

The Nile is quite a wonderful sight now. It is a highway for pleasure and health-seekers. Yesterday seven steamers passed us, and two sailing boats like ours. We sometimes wave to friends as they pass.

May was amused by one of their party, Canon MacColl, who was clearly known to Canon Melville.

The little canon is a great success, so adaptive and agreeable. He has taken a violent fancy to sporting, and stalks vultures and hawks with a revolver he brought out, while we sit laughing. He is frightfully dangerous with this weapon, but undaunted, getting up at six in the morning to get a chance.

So the peace of the silent river must quite often have been shattered.

The canon also felt passionately about Irish Home Rule, frequently discussing it with Lord Waterford late into the night. William Gladstone had introduced his first Irish Home Rule Bill when he was Liberal prime minister once more in 1886, but it had been defeated.* At the beginning of 1892, at home in England, feelings were

---

* In 1893, after Gladstone's re-election as prime minister for the fourth and last time in August 1892, his second attempt to introduce the Bill was passed by the House of Commons but again rejected by the Lords, leading to his resignation in 1894.

increasingly strong both for and against Home Rule for Ireland, but far away in Egypt, May was clearly beginning to tire of listening to arguments on the Irish Question:

I tell the Canon and Lord W that even if they begin with Egyptian antiquities, or the reform of the House of Lords, we are sure to end on Irish Home Rule. Last night I went to sleep on deck as they were drifting towards Ireland again, and at eleven o'clock we went to bed, leaving them in full swing, agreeing to agree and disagree with admirable temper.

At home in Worcestershire, the Melville family were waiting nervously for an exciting moment: May's brother Willie was expected from the Argentine on his first visit home since he had made the long journey for May's wedding almost twenty years before, when he was still working at one job after another in order to survive out there. He was now a successful man; about fifteen years before, he had heard that the Drabble family (a 'black sheep' ancestor of the writers Margaret Drabble and her sister A. S. Byatt) owned huge tracts of land in Buenos Aires province. It is not known if he had an introduction to the family, but he hired a native tracker to take him across the country to where their land was, oversaw the building of their estancia, and then continued to manage the vast estate.

May longed to be with her parents to greet the brother she had always loved so much. At last, the Nile mail boat brought a letter from Emma Melville.

Darling child, Willie is actually here and I wish you were also to make us all perfectly happy. My dear he is magnificent! I met him in the hall. My first impression was 'What a splendid man!' My next was 'What a sweet soft voice!', the third 'What a delightful kindly face' and fourth 'What a strong pair of arms', as he hugged me to his great heart and sobbed 'Mother!' Then we found Father and Daphne in the library. You should have seen Father's face. I could only see Willie's back, his noble back, and Father's delight as he exclaimed — 'Well, you are a fine fellow.' He is so well made that his movements are light and easy, and his feet are beautiful, long and narrow. I told him Amy would want him for a model. His colour and whole appearance bespeaks health and strength and what is wholesome and happy. He left his Spanish beard in town but kept the moustache, which covers that same cupid bowed mouth I used to admire. His hands are large and shew hard work. I am proud of them. His hazel eyes, with their twinkle of fun, are not changed at all. Soft and tender, his manners are perfect – his talk slightly tinged with Spanish. There is the old fun and sparkle in his talk mixed with the shrewdness men get who have knocked about as he has. He forgets no one and nothing it seems. There is a perfect excitement over him wherever he goes – some knowing and some guessing who he is. He is a son to praise God for. Father can't gush as you know, but I can see he is proud as a peach of him, from head to foot.

Although Willie Melville was to stay in England for some time, his arrival had made them all, including Daphne, who was just five now, more anxious to have May back again. 'Ah, dear little mother, I wish she was here,' said Daphne to her grandmother. 'I would hug and kiss her, oh I wish she and father would come home.'

Willie himself was eager to see his only sister and intimate childhood companion again. He said to his mother, 'I am rather anxious about the dear girl. Glad indeed I shall be to see her back again, but it is better I think in one way seeing the family by portions, rather than all together.'

So Willie went off to stay with his younger brother Beresford, who was fighting for a seat as an MP in Derbyshire. Beresford had recently married a rich and forceful widow, with the unlikely Christian name of Sydney, whom May later found difficult.

Willie himself was still unmarried at this stage. Emma told May:

What a mercy he is not married, he is all our own. We cannot part with him again. We must close our eyes – and oh how he loves you. He said he 'blubs' over your letters and hugs Daphne for you – he bid me tell you that they were firm friends already. I looked out of the drawing room window on Tuesday morning and saw them squatting under the birch tree making tooth powder out of the dust, and thought how natural it was to see them together. I heard Daphne tell him 'My heart is in mother's, she knows it is.'

By March, May felt that her Egyptian journey had been long enough. She was avid for news of England and scoured the newspapers that reached them on the boat. She read a 'wonderful speech' that the Prince of Wales had delivered in the House of Lords, which Lord Waterford remarked was so good that Canon Melville could have written it. May wrote to her father and told him this:

> *Lord Waterford says no friend he has except you would be capable of it. What a contrast the subjects I am writing about, and the life I am living are. Now it is an absolutely placid hour, in the middle of a hot still day. The only sound is the creak of the schadoofs* [these were wooden mechanisms on the banks of the Nile which brought up water], *the slight ripple of the current and the lazy chatter of the sailors. Lord Waterford and I are writing in the saloon and the rest of the party are being broiled on deck. I think we have been away long enough in Egypt, but it is a wonderful winter to look back on, and we none of us feel as if it was real. I suppose gradually I shall begin to know a whole winter has gone and that all we have seen exists. Meanwhile it is a floating haze of no definite limits, and might equally be a dream or a reality.*

The dreamlike haze ended when the party reached Cairo again, and moved on to Alexandria to board Lord Waterford's yacht, *Mera*. Here the silence of the Nile seemed far away. A striking sight greeted them. Egypt was a British protectorate at that time and the whole of the British fleet was in the harbour, as well as Egyptian and Italian warships, dressed overall with flags. This was in anticipation of the Firman, an edict in the form of a document from the Ottoman sultan in Constantinople, which was being brought that day to proclaim that the sultan recognized the new Khedive, or viceroy of Egypt, a twelve-year-old boy called Abas Hilmi. May wrote:

> *As the Turkish yacht hove into sight the whole fleet saluted. The yacht anchored close to us so we saw the gold stomached pachas take the Firman across to the mainland.*

Later in the day, Lord Waterford's younger brother, the flirtatious Admiral Lord Charles Beresford, whom May had first met at Lord

Wenlock's house party, invited them to lunch on his ship, the *Undaunted*. Before they sat down to eat there was a service. As once before on her journey through the wilds of America, May found herself in all-male company. She wrote to her mother:

> *You would have laughed to see me sitting in the midst of the officers gravely facing five hundred crew. I was the only woman, and my voice sounded so funny with the great mass of male sound in the hymns. The ship was wonderful, like an extraordinary floating fort.*

May now parted from her husband and set sail on the Waterford yacht for Italy. There, to her great excitement, she was to be reunited with Amy and travel with her for a few weeks before they both returned to England. May had not mentioned Henry Brooks in any of her letters from Egypt, but she now wrote to her mother of their parting in Alexandria:

> *Nothing could be dearer and kinder in this world than he has been to me on our 'honeymoon', indeed, altogether for the whole five months. It was a perfect time.*

When I read these words I was puzzled. Was May just reassuring her frail mother that all was well with her marriage? I knew that by the end of that year, 1892, May would already have formed a close friendship with Edward Burne-Jones. I knew also that she met the painter in the spring, very shortly after her return from Egypt and Italy. From his letters to her it was clear that she had confided in him almost at once, telling him about some secret unhappiness in her life, and that he had offered her comfort and a promise of total discretion. What could have gone wrong, I wondered? Or was May to find when she saw her husband again that he was not so dear and kind as she told her mother he had been in Egypt?

May's return to England in the early spring of 1892 marked, in many ways, the beginning of a different stage of her life. Her daughter Amy, having finished her studies in Europe, was to be 'brought out' in London society. Kiddington need no longer be rented out and the family was starting a life of their own there. In the early summer they were also to take over Beaumont Hall, near Lancaster, a large Jacobean farmhouse belonging to the Gaskell family since it had been acquired by the Devil of Wigan, which had been rented out for years. May wanted to move builders in as soon as possible to their North Country retreat; she had a real flair for doing up houses.

Once installed at Kiddington, Henry, having spent so much of his life shooting things, found a more creative occupation. Inspired no doubt by Capability Brown's sculptured setting and the beautiful long lake, he began to replant the garden and grounds. He started with various rare trees, and then, on a lawn which sloped gently down to the lake, he created a rose garden, still known today as the Rosary. It was designed to an Elizabethan model, and amongst the roses he planted 'rare Elizabethan white strawberries'. A cedar tree planted by Henry Brooks also survives at Kiddington – my uncle, when he was an old man, remembered nostalgically 'the smell of cedar needles in the grass'. In the silence of Kiddington's surroundings, broken only by the sound of birds, which seemed to echo off the surface of the lake, Henry Brooks found a satisfaction in his gardening that was to stay with him for the rest of his life, a closeness to nature which perhaps from then on became more important to him than his wife. As his father had done before him and his son was to do after him, he seemed to withdraw into himself. He spoke little. It was almost as if trees became more important to him than people.

But for May, people were supremely important, and it was at their house in London, 3 Marble Arch, that she most liked to be. In London her social life flourished, and she began to give the cultural and political dinner parties that she became well known for, and which included many of her friends among the Souls. She was, people considered, the perfect hostess, with a capacity to enjoy her own parties, the secret of making her guests enjoy them too. They would write her appreciative notes of thanks, even poems. One guest, who did not sign his name, wrote after a dinner in August 1892:

> *She bloomed – as bloom the fragrant flowers*
> *Of may-bush after April showers –*
> *She sang – as pipes its liquid lay*

Sweet Philomel on may-bush spray –
So flower and song – with friendship rife –
make May-days of the days of life.

May was also in demand as a stimulating and attractive dinner companion. But it appears she did not entirely abandon her wifely duties. One close friend, 'dear Godfrey Webb', was a clerk in the House of Lords; a much-loved 'raconteur and wit', he had become known as the 'doyen' and 'court jester' of the Souls. Webb wrote to May in verse when she cancelled a 'diner a deux':

Oh Lady of the Marble Arch
I gather to my sorrow
That you refuse, or do not choose,
To dine with me tomorrow –

Your Henry is the instrument
With which you thus betray me,
Though surely he could dine content
With pretty daughter Amy –

Yet I'll believe, not meanly stoop
Your charming note to garble,
Though Arch your smile I'll not revile,
Or say your heart is Marble.

When May's 'pretty daughter Amy' came back to England in the spring of 1892, she was almost eighteen years old. She was to 'come out' that summer, and the constant balls of the season would soon begin. For generations, Amy has been a mysterious legend in our family, probably because all anyone seemed to have been told was that she had died young, 'of a broken heart', and had been beautiful. Without the photograph albums in which she features so prominently, I think she would have been completely forgotten. But Amy's passion for photography, and for posing herself in romantic self-portraits, meant that most of us grew up with an image in our minds of this doomed relative and her world, even if we had not quite gathered her name or who she was.

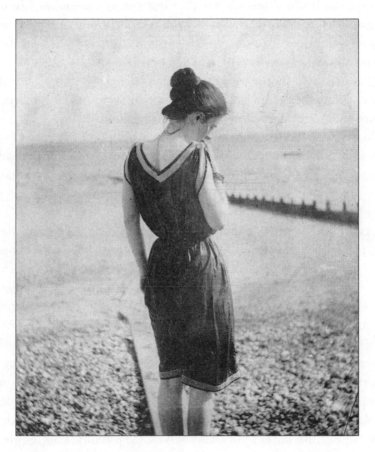

Amy, in her bathing costume on the beach at Bognor Regis, showing that her figure was lovely even without the help of corsets.

Looking at photographs of Amy, I cannot see her as exactly beautiful, but with her abundant dark hair arranged in a swooping bun, her creamy skin, her straight nose, prettily shaped mouth and strong chin, she is certainly striking. She has her mother's elegance of carriage, and from one photograph where she is wearing a bathing costume, you can see she had a lovely figure: slim but gently curvaceous. In other pictures the tight corset makes her waist unbelievably small, even for that era. In close-up pictures her large eyes, shown in one family portrait as dark blue, are particularly striking.

'She attracted by the softness of her lovely eyes,' wrote May about her lost daughter years later, 'but those eyes were piercing sharp, and penetrated to the core of the nature that responded.'

May gave Amy the best bedroom at Kiddington. It was a corner room with high, wide windows reaching almost from floor to ceiling. These windows, which faced both south and west, framed spectacular views of the lake and park. With their large expanses of sheet glass they filled the room with light and sunshine.

As I found out more about Amy, it became clear to me that she had great charisma and allure. In her mother's words, she was 'a wonderful mystic creature of wayward charm'. As Amy grew from a carefree girl into a contemplative young woman, a somewhat perplexing, moody character began to emerge. Amy had always been her mother's favourite child, but now, as she was about to come out in London society, May's feelings for her eldest daughter seem to me to have had, at times, the passion of a love affair. It must have been perplexing and perhaps painful for May to watch her perfect little girl grow into a complex, bewitching, but sometimes melancholy young woman.

May was now thirty-nine years old; she had probably reached a stage in her life familiar to many wives, even today. Family life was changing and she was getting older. She started to complain of weakness and unspecified ill health. Her first and 'best-loved' child was almost grown up, with looks and appeal which threatened to surpass her own, her husband was increasingly shut away from her in his own world. At home, May was beginning to discover the cruelty of silence.

May was hungry for words and conversation. She turned increasingly to her friends among the Souls, particularly to Frances Horner, who has been called 'the High Priestess of the Souls'. Frances was married to Sir John Horner, a quiet, erudite, yet humorous man who owned an old family estate, Mells Park, in Somerset. May and Frances were already close friends, but they were soon to have much more in common. For many years, since long before her marriage, Frances had been worshipped and adored by the painter Edward Burne-Jones. It was Frances who took May to meet the painter in the garden studio of his house in Fulham, on the outskirts of London, during that spring of 1892.

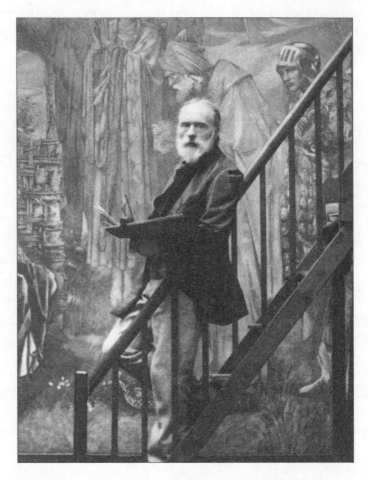

Burne-Jones in his studio in 1890, two years before he met May.

CHAPTER FOUR

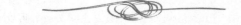

THE ARTIST'S MUSE

THE PRE-RAPHAELITE PAINTER EDWARD BURNE-JONES WAS AT THE height of his fame when May Gaskell met him, at the start of the 1890s. He was nearly fifty-nine years old. She was just thirty-nine. Burne-Jones, both in his painting and in his life, had always searched for perfection and beauty, most often in female form. Later he was to explain to May:

> *I mean by a picture a beautiful romantic dream of something that never was, never will be, in a light better than any light that ever shone, in a land no one can define or remember – only desire – and the forms divinely beautiful.*

The divine forms in his paintings were inspired, recognizably, by women Burne-Jones knew; and he also told May that he liked to 'live' in his paintings. So for him, real life and fantasy intermingled, and became inseparable.

Burne-Jones's first ideal of beauty was someone he never knew: his mother. Tragically, she died within a few days of his birth. His father's grief was intense and long lasting; during the first years after his young wife's premature death, he was unable to show love to the child he believed had caused her to die. So the lonely little boy grew up with a sense of guilt, and the impression that his mother had been a perfect woman. He felt he would have loved this ideal woman with all his heart. Perhaps because he was never able to give her this love, he spent his life searching for women who could match his mother's perfection. His lifelong artistic quest for pure and absolute beauty was part of this, and the perfect women he found became subjects in his paintings, where he further idealized their looks.

This need to love far more than to be loved had led Burne-Jones, throughout his life, to fall for many 'perfect' women, both models and social acquaintances. Sometimes it was simply admiration, at other times he became hopelessly infatuated. Despite these recurring passions, his wife Georgie remained steadfast throughout a long marriage. Only once did he stray almost too far. Burne-Jones's ideal was spiritual, celestial love, but he was, after all, a man. A few years into his marriage, Burne-Jones allowed a friendship with a young and, as it turned out, tempestuous Greek sculptress, Maria Zambaco, who was also his model, to become a full-blooded affair. Ultimately and inevitably it ended badly. Although his marriage survived, it was never quite the same again. Much more controlled, but deep and long lasting, was his friendship with Frances Horner, daughter of his rich patron and old friend, William Graham. He had known Frances since she was a teenager, and used her frequently as a model. He fell in love with her early on, and was never to lose his affection for her.

But the last romantic obsession of Edward Burne-Jones's life was to be Frances's friend, May Gaskell. Once again, he thought he had found the perfect woman. Only a few months after he met May he wrote to her, 'I love you beyond all reckoning, beyond all measure – you are quite perfect – body and soul you are perfect, perfect.'

May had been introduced to Edward Burne-Jones at a dinner party, but as he was to tell her later, 'I used to think, well, not that you disliked me, but that you didn't much like.'

It was the spring of 1892 when May's friend Frances first took her to meet Burne-Jones properly at the Grange, 'in the wilds of Fulham', where he and his wife Georgie lived. In the mid 1860s, when the couple had moved there, the house had been surrounded by fields, but

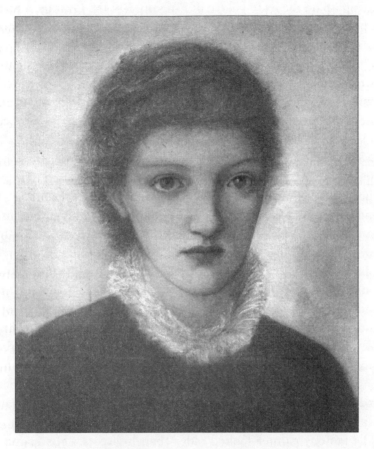

Frances Graham, painted by Burne Jones in 1879. She married Sir
John Horner in 1883 and met May in the late 1880s through their
friends amongst the Souls circle.

by the time of May's first visit, the fields had become streets of terraced houses, with a station of the Metropolitan District Railway, West Kensington, nearby, and omnibuses passing the door. London was creeping up on the leafy village of Fulham. But the Grange, a historic old house behind high walls, with its large, flower-filled garden, remained an oasis.

The artist and writer Graham Robertson described a visit to the 'old red-brick house behind an ivy-covered wall'. He remarked on the quietness, and that it was 'pretty and secret and romantic – like the house of the Sleeping Beauty'. Apart from a pale drawing room whose windows looked out on to the garden, the rooms were dark. The house was sparsely furnished with uncomfortable but decorative contemporary furniture, some painted by Burne-Jones himself. The walls of the hall were hung with green paper, designed by the painter's best friend, William Morris; most of the wallpapers and fabrics in the house came from Morris's company, the Firm. On the walls hung many of Burne-Jones's own paintings, as well as those of other Pre-Raphaelite artists, which enriched the darkness with their glowing colour. There was also the famous portrait of Burne-Jones by his old friend Frederick Watts. All who went to the Grange talked of the beautiful garden, with its wide flower borders, its little orchard of apple trees, and its peach, plum and apricot trees trained against a sunny wall. This is where Frances and May must have walked on that spring day in 1892, past a row of lime trees, across the lawn shaded by a fine old mulberry tree, to meet Edward Burne-Jones in his garden studio.

The famous painter looked older than his years. His frame was slight, his straight hair white and thinning on a very round head. Under an exceptionally wide brow and prominent cheekbones his pale face tapered to a snowy white moustache and pointed beard. His large, grey-blue eyes, described as 'dreamy', had a serious, penetrating look that could suddenly light up and become mischievously smiling. Graham Robertson found this characteristic 'startling', as if, he said, Burne-Jones was 'half priest, half jester'. Frances Horner wrote in her memoirs that he loved laughing and that this made everyone around him laugh too. From his letters, Burne-Jones seemed very aware of his appearance, and often told May later that he was ugly, or 'a funny little thing that glares'. One day he wrote:

Do you remember that nasty old cheval glass in my studio, that I have for
reversing the aspect of my pictures, and seeing where they are most amiss?
I just caught sight of me in it, by accident, I did – and it is virtually
impossible you could ever look on such a thing without repulsion.

But he need not have worried about his looks; his widely acknowledged talent, charm, 'golden voice', wit, wisdom, understanding and
gentleness were the qualities that captivated women.

During the year before he met May, Burne-Jones had often been
unwell, with the result that he became depressed, and uninspired in
his work. He had reached universal fame during the last few years,
but he may perhaps have sensed that the craze for the romantic
medievalism of his pictures might not remain in fashion for ever. All
his life he had had a tendency to melancholy, but painting always
lifted his spirits: 'If I can only work – it has saved me always – saved
me through the most miserable times.'

His other recipe for happiness was to be able to fall in love, and,
almost as importantly, to offer comfort to women. Although he was
still writing affectionate letters to Frances Horner at the time he met
May, she was happily married and living in the country with her
family, and he clearly wanted something more.

This he found in May, in whom he sensed a sadness calling for his
compassion, and who appeared to yearn for comfort and understanding as much as he felt he did himself. In an early letter to her he wrote:

you won't hide anything from me will you – I am to share all your
unhappiness, and enfold you and comfort you with tender love – I will
keep myself well in the background, but I will go to you or bring you here
as often as ever you like – and I'll write gently and softly to you every day
and afterwards in my heart you shall find refuge from all bitterness and
grief . . . whatever comes of it or happens I dedicate my days to you. I can't
help it, pity and love together have been too much for me . . . all is easy
with you – to talk, to write, to be in harmony, to love – all too easy – poor
little me.

May was clearly anxious that the strength of Burne-Jones's feelings for her should not become publicly known, for in another letter he wrote:

You shall be obeyed in what you ask, and in everything – but indeed that is what I too want most of all – for our friendship to be a profound secret – the least manner or rumour of questioning jars and vulgarises whoever it is who asks – I want this to be a most holy compact – I have come to you without a thought for myself – all you give I shall take reverently and very very gratefully; I dare say it will never be more than I have to day – it shall be enough – I pray to God it will never be less, don't make it less if you can help – now and then if you can give me an hour like yesterday it shall be a gleam of heaven to me. None shall hear the faintest whisper of this friendship which is a real heavenly friendship for you, to help you and sustain you and make you want to live. You shall bless the day when you opened your heart to me – it was a week ago today – if one said it was three months I could better believe it. I will try very hard to put nothing in my letters that shall ever recall the little secret I told you . . .

So it appears that when they were first alone together, May and Burne-Jones had each confided secrets to the other. What can have been the secret which made May so sad, I wondered, that had even made her want to die, so that Burne-Jones reassured her that his friendship would make her 'want to live'? I sensed that it must have something to do with her marriage – but what exactly I had not yet found out. I also wondered what Burne-Jones could have confided to her – could it already have been a confession of love, or did he let her know that over the years he had become disillusioned by his own marriage? It could have been something to do with his ill-fated affair with Maria Zambaco, to whom there are obvious references in his subsequent letters, though never by name:

You won't think again of what I said will you – except to feel quite certain that I am the surest of friends upon whom you can fling yourself for help . . . But keep my little secret – bury these things deep in your heart – it is a mystery now but one day you will understand. And one day when there is an hour without interruption I will tell you a long story that shall

make dark faces clear to you – I don't a bit want to tell it because even to
go over ancient sorrows is a little to renew them – but something in the
tale may be of use to you – and, as I should say in the pulpit, of spiritual
application.

Burne-Jones was a compulsive communicator. No one has ever quite understood how he was able to write so many letters each day at the same time as working hard on his painting. Before long, added to his usual constant correspondence with other friends, he was secretively writing up to five letters a day to May: 'people may think I write about once a fortnight or three weeks – we won't let them know the truth'.

A boy took his letters at intervals during the day to catch several of the seven daily posts. Burne-Jones wrote at his easel, he wrote in bed, he wrote wherever he could throughout each day and into the night; anything to be continually talking to May. But this outpouring of written words did not seem to interfere with the concentration and inspiration he needed to work; his personal life, his passions, his fantasies and his dreams were an essential part of his paintings. May, with her gentle looks, her sensitivity, and an artistic judgement which he also respected, became a necessary muse to his creativity.

Burne-Jones would pin pieces of paper onto his easel in order to write anything that came into his mind while he painted. As a result his letters seem indeed to be a stream of consciousness, with little punctuation and many dashes, almost like a long e-mail message might look today. For her part, it is easy to see why May, who herself loved writing and conversation, but whose husband was becoming increasingly silent and withdrawn, found this new friendship both comforting and inspiring. The letters also made her laugh. Burne-Jones had an endearing, sometimes almost childish wit. With his painterly eye and acute mind he observed life and people in a unique way, and was particularly hard on himself:

I feel just twenty and to look at me is to look at the survival of the stone
age – hair like moss – hairs not hair – skin like old book bindings – eyes
fading out, nose a lesson to the art student what to avoid – mouth at least
with the decency to hide itself in hairs – are you laughing?

Two years after he had started writing to May, Burne-Jones told her that during that time he had sent her over seven hundred letters:

I am always, all day long, wanting to talk myself out to you – for with you only I think aloud – and that is easy and happy – it has been a wonderful fortune for me to have known you – in a moment when I am with you all fatigue and wear of life and all sadness disappears, by nothing less than magic – and I am ten years old again . . . do you like me to write so much, or is it overmuch – pretend you like it for it makes my chief happiness – verily it does – goodbye – oh it is hard to leave and yet am I not always and every moment your E.

The intimate correspondence between Victorian men and women outside their marriages can be surprising when read today. The word 'love' is used liberally, romantic private moments are referred to nostalgically, there is a tender, personal concern. Yet more often than not, the correspondents were not what we would now describe as lovers in the physical sense. Perhaps these intense friendships were tolerated because divorce was rare, and numerous couples were trapped in dead marriages. In any case, within a household at that time so many letters came and went daily that even such a constant correspondence may not have aroused suspicion. Although the Victorians were more formal than we are in social conversation, they were far less inhibited about revealing their innermost feelings and emotions when they wrote letters. Few of us now, for fear of ridicule, dare expose our sentiments, even privately, in the way that our ancestors did. The Victorians and Edwardians expressed affection for their friends in a way that only lovers, and perhaps not many of them, would choose to do now.

From the very beginning of their correspondence, Burne-Jones told May that he would not jeopardize their friendship by keeping her letters. In fact he had been caught out in this way many years earlier, when his wife had found a letter from Maria Zambaco in his pocket. When one of May's letters came, he told her he would read it 'again, and yet again', carry it on him for perhaps a day, and then burn it 'up in a blue flame'. He urged her to do the same with his letters, so that 'there can be before us a life of mutual help and strength, to make us bless the day we met'. But although years later May agonized about not having obeyed him, she clearly could not bring herself to burn his letters. In a note found with the letters after her death, May admitted that 'some' had been destroyed, and when I was looking through them I noticed that with a few she had cut out part of a page, which was tantalizing.

One day, visiting him in his studio, May noticed a letter from another of his female friends, most probably Frances Horner, lying open on a table, and it made her wonder if he might be as careless with one of hers. Burne-Jones wrote to her that night:

Have no fear about your letters. I hide them on me and have only one to guard   I left the letter out for you to read on purpose, feeling you had a right to see it if you liked – I thought it beautiful of you to refuse – still it was your right – and when you wouldn't look at it I compared you in my heart to others and said 'she is perfect – there is none like her' – there is none like you.

Burne-Jones's letters to May were full of yearning, particularly at times when May had been away from London:

And I have waited for the hall clock to strike long enough – and today is a great day, for you are coming – so long since you came – you have forgotten how long – forgotten almost that you ever came – forgotten I should think the Saturday afternoon when you first came and I gave you some good advice by the window – and yet that is only two months ago – time is a funny thing I must say – sometimes years go by and nothing happens at all, and sometimes a lifetime is packed into a month – and Lord what a change in me – oh love of my innermost heart and life, what good is my love to you? You must tell me once a month at least that I make some little difference in your life – for darling I am pouring all my soul at your feet.

But he would also tell May about his day, and about visitors to his studio, including models who came to sit for him. Sometimes they were not English:

This morning I drew from a Pole – the Pole wouldn't sit still . . . a strange looking creature – you could never guess what is in her mind, and whether evil or good – hermetically sealed. I am sorry for them often, it must be hateful to come and sit for money – but I make it easy – nothing I love so much in the way of work as drawing out the hidden experiences . . .

After a group of Frenchmen visited him, he complained that they 'parleyvooed at poor me for three hours', and spoilt his day, as when they finally left it was too dark to continue working. Nevertheless, he assured May, he had treated them politely:

. . . we parted with many deep bows and assurances that Hastings and Waterloo were forgotten and hidden in a remote past.

Sometimes Burne-Jones appears overwhelmed by the strength of his emotion regarding May:

I have just come back from the theatre and I have seen you – and God knows I am happy and content – you looked well – better than you have looked yet – and beautiful – you are not to laugh – you looked so beautiful – wasn't I stupefied and dumb – I couldn't speak – I had looked and waited all evening and yet when I saw you speech fled from me – I can't remember what you said or what I said – was it very stupid of me – what took hold of me so I couldn't speak, I who can gabble to you by the hour together . . . Now my heart is set on this friendship, and my eyes are there and will never be removed – let's make it quite beautiful. I will worship you with my whole soul to the end – goodnight.

May still sang at social occasions quite often. Burne-Jones was enchanted when he heard her lovely voice: 'The music was sweet – sing to me whenever there is a chance for I shall love it.' He would also listen intently when she played her Steinway grand piano at dinner parties. One day he told her that he had heard his daughter Margaret playing a favourite air on the harpsichord:

. . . and suddenly as clear as if the walls of the room had opened I saw you – it was clear as a vision – I saw you at the piano there – I heard you sing

*— I saw your mother and father — and then in a moment I saw all your
life — and as I thought of you I fell into a passion of tears that I think no
one saw — pain excites me and sometimes I have had a strange exaltation
at a time of pain — it was that I suppose — but oh me, how you hold my
life in your hand — it is seldom enough I cry — but I saw you in the room
at the piano singing, a quite young girl — and for a few moments I did
verily feel the agony of heartbreak.*

May must have known from Frances about the famous painter's
habit, over many years, of falling passionately in love. But his attentive
worship clearly made her feel special in a way that her husband did
not. Even if she knew that he had proclaimed his love to many others,
and indeed, at the beginning of their friendship, probably continued to
do so to Frances, Burne-Jones's admiration was something May needed.
She loved his wit, his observant eye, his warmth, his intimacy, and his
lack of pomposity; all things she felt were missing in her home life.

As it had been notorious within artistic and cultural circles, May
must have heard something of Burne-Jones's earlier affair with Maria
Zambaco. As his model, Maria's dramatic Greek looks had inspired
Burne-Jones to produce some of the best paintings and drawings he
had ever done. The affair resulted in inevitable pain and misery, and,
with Maria's volatile temperament, in a public drama. There was
rumour of a suicide pact, and then she did indeed attempt suicide.
The affair shook Burne-Jones deeply, and permanently changed his
relationship with his wife Georgie, although she was to stand by him
devotedly, even if at times somewhat sternly, to the end. In a well-
known portrait Burne-Jones did of his wife, Georgie looks decidedly
long-suffering.

Burne-Jones knew that his impulse to seek out friendships with
'perfect' women would be with him always. He needed them to be
part of his dreams and fantasies, and to feel, as he looked at his paintings, that he was living with them. But he was determined not to
repeat the disaster of the Maria Zambaco affair. In his letters to May,
he referred often to his 'celestial love'. Yet physical longing lurked
beneath the romantic surface. Later he was to tell May, 'you see I am
a monk with a craving for a life with a woman — and am doomed at
the outset'.

Burne-Jones confessed to his assistant, Thomas Rooke, that he had a 'fear of lust', yet he did not disguise the more earthy side of his nature in his letters to May, even if it was in jest: 'But I should like to eat you; yes I really mean eat – set teeth in and chew up as I can't see how I shall ever have you all to myself in any other way.'

When writing to May late at night in bed, Burne-Jones's passion became most extreme:

> *You see I think you perfect – nay but I do worship and reverence you and live on my knees to you, and my eyes on the ground. I do love you with all my whole soul and life.*

At one point he began almost every letter with an abject declaration of love:

> *Day by day my love grows about you – what a friend it will be soon – hard work to make it a friend – so soon it could become a wall of fire – it shall not be fire – it shall be nothing but shelter and delight to you . . . and I shall never hurt you only I must love you for ever now – I have found my faith – I cannot leave you – do with me what you will – I have watched you and know you in these long months that are like years – and I know you through and through and give myself to you.*

Burne-Jones himself realized his outpourings were 'more than you quite bargained for'. But at that time his physical longings seemed to become harder and harder to contain:

> *. . . fly to me in all sorrow and I will unfold you and caress you and spoil you and pet you and say little comforting words . . . I gave you a heavy time this afternoon sweet lady – yet before I sin I am sure of forgiveness – so I go on in my wickedness . . . directly you had gone the strained nerves relaxed and I fell into a deep long sleep – and you will let nothing and no one in the world ever push me from you? Goodnight – it's just as if you are near me, as if gentle arms soothed and held me.*

May appears, not surprisingly, to have been slightly overwhelmed by all this passion: 'Two or three times yesterday you looked pained and troubled at me – did my hands hurt you? Or were you sorry for me?' However, in another letter he refers to May's hand as 'that little kind hand, that can cling and hold so tightly'. It sometimes sounds as if they had moments of what in my schooldays we called heavy petting, but, as Lord David Cecil pointed out in his long essay about Burne-Jones, opinions were divided about just how far the painter went with the important women in his life, and intense sentimental friendship between married men and women, thought to be within the bounds of propriety, was an accepted custom of the period.

If May was taken aback by her new friend's ardent proclamations, it did not stop her replying to his letters. They appear to have been almost as constant as his. But they did not make Burne-Jones sure of her affection:

> *I seldom have courage to open a letter from you at once – I try to prepare my mind for some disappointment or sorrow – at first I thought they might say 'goodbye' and was frightened – I don't fear 'goodbye' now – but still I hold off from opening – time travels fast in these histories, and the rivets are driven home in me now, it is too late – give nothing you will ever have to take away from me.*

Burne-Jones was aware that when he was unwell, tired or weak, his letters became more frenzied. At the end of a long outpouring to May, he wrote:

> *When I am stronger I will control my words – I know I pain you by my letters and yet they are as tame as I can make them – of course they pain you but you are so patient and sweet – and the nicer you are the worse I get – but give me time – I can learn to master myself. I must learn to do it that's all.*

And to show her he was trying to control himself, he would write about lighter things, such as his dislike of dogs, which in his drawings he always portrayed as grotesque, snarling creatures:

> *I don't want animals in my life – and especially not a dog – I might have loved an elephant before I met you – or a lion – and am always weak about cats as you know, but a dog never.*

Nevertheless, Burne-Jones continued to tell May repeatedly that all he wanted was to comfort her, and to be able to love her, but that he expected nothing in return except the pleasure of her company, whenever she would grant him it. But no relationship can be as simple as this. In one of what he called his 'night letters', when he was at his least emotionally controlled, he showed the depth of his neediness: 'I catch myself now constantly hunting in your face for some little sign by which I can tell what love you give me.'

Two nights later, he wrote to her again from his bed:

> *Another night letter for you, beloved, but why do you like them? . . . Do you really like to be with me? When you say you are glad to see me it is still hard to believe . . . when I hushed you you were beginning to say it was a shame for me to give such love and get so little back – and so it would be if you had ever given me more, but I knew the conditions beforehand and chose my road . . . ah love can't be won, nor got by asking, not if Apollo asked, whose golden mouthed prayers Daphne fled from – nor got by pity, that is the poorest of all roads, nor by desire – and a woman keeps it from the best man under the sun and gives it to one less worthy – and a man does the same – if asking would get it for me I might try.*

In another night letter, he seemed more confident that May had come to feel real affection for him:

> *There – I have seen you, and I'm content – no burning fever like last night . . . sometimes I must go mad with my passionate love and be unhappy – such a starved life I live – at any rate tonight is peace – how good you are to me – oh love you are good to me – in the day when our souls tremble at the judgment you will get mercy for the mercy you have shown me . . . darling I shall do nothing that has not you for inspiration to the end of my sane days – and you are the soul of my life – and now good night – come to me in a dream – you didn't come last night, I wanted you so grievously – come tonight.*

As their friendship developed, Burne-Jones told May more about his past life, and it was not long before he mentioned his mother, who had died only six days after he was born:

Sunday was September 3rd – I always keep it with what piety I can – that was the day my Mammy died – on the sixth day after I was born . . . It used to be the saddest of days at home, whilst my father remembered things, a day of tears, and the show of tears, and I used to hate it when I was tiny . . .

In another letter, talking about women, he again refers to his mother:

I should like to be kind to all women and I don't think I ever hurt one yet – no, never willingly. I don't think it is ever out of mind what hurt I did when I was born, and I was quite old as a child, ten or twelve, when my father still took me once a week to my mother's grave, and used to sit crying – and when we walked in the streets he would stop at places and would tell me that hereabouts my mother was tired and could walk no more, or that at another place something amused her – the grave was in a churchyard on a hill called Holloway Head, and I thought it was the same name in the Lord's Prayer, and duly prayed night and morning 'Holloway Head be thy name'. I hope it made him laugh . . . it is never long out of my mind, and I am always ready to cry with it – so I'm good to women . . .

In the same letter, Burne-Jones confides in May about someone who must have been Maria Zambaco. The ill-fated affair had raged passionately for about a year and then painfully on and off for many years afterwards. He still felt guilty about it:

. . . the one who hurt me was not wicked a bit – it was a hard life to lead and she broke down – that's all – she minded so much and so much feared to hurt that it drove her to cheat – she thought I couldn't like her if I knew she was passionate so she hid it always – but I should have liked it all the more you see, for it is the one thing that is beautiful to me, and pardons all – but there it was – for the first years it must have been an unbearable life to her – it was to me – who can be a wicked hell of passion if I let go – and I never forget hearing of her crying all night or walking about in rain outside the house when I was ill, for hours and hours.

Burne-Jones was comfortable with his feminine side, and perhaps that is why he felt such an affinity with women. He wrote to May:

You are sweet, you are such a woman, and so true in all where truth matters most that you shine far beyond men – men bore me often, and I resent their airs and their silly pomp – and their ambitions sicken me or make me laugh.

Although Burne-Jones preferred women to men, the designer and writer William Morris had been his closest friend of all since they were together at Oxford University. His few other male friends, among them Ruskin, Rossetti and Swinburne, had exceptional minds and talents. He explained to May that he would 'bow down to heroes', but that it was women he admired most. He said bluntly: 'Most men are nothing to me – I can scarce remember their faces from one day to another.' In a later letter, again talking of men in a derogatory way, he urges May, with perhaps a little jealousy, 'you'll never let the nasty things come near you, will you, – will you?'

Now that May came so often to visit Burne-Jones, especially at times when he felt too ill to leave the house, he seemed to want her to make friends with his wife Georgie too.

It makes me so happy that Georgie welcomes you – some day come to see her for her own sake – she is the wittiest company, and very pious – I say pious because all things are serious to her – only she is bitter upon folly – she is not a Christian any more and yet she hates to be approached except on bended knees.

As that ironic dig suggests, he could be critical of his wife too:

I asked Georgie about her guests on Friday – that's her birthday – and she told me – oh heaven, such an incongruous lot – how strange she is – just the very people who can't get on together – if she writes and asks you to come please don't – I should be miserable or at least thoroughly uncomfortable – I shall have a hateful evening but it doesn't matter – I can bear anything now. If once she could guess – could once know what I should like and what I should hate – dear it does me good to pour out to

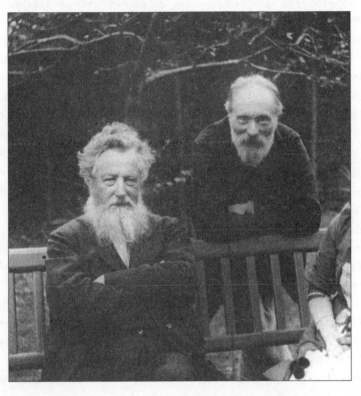

Lifelong friends: William Morris, still wild and wonderful looking as he aged, with Burne-Jones in the early 1890s. I like the humorous look in both their eyes.

*you – and I feel kinder after it – I look sometimes over such a waste of
years – so sad a retrospect – I could cry tonight.*

Burne-Jones had been prone to melancholy for years, perhaps ever
since childhood when, starved of his mother's love, he had felt guilty
of her death. His depressions came in phases, and affected both his
health and his work. He had been through a bad period before meeting May. But the excitement of a new passion, almost an addiction
with him, seemed to inspire him to work again, '. . . and my work is
getting better and better, isn't it?' Burne-Jones wanted May to involve
herself in his work and would often send off a letter in mid-painting,
impatiently demanding her immediate attention:

*. . . but come and look and see what I have done – does the white look too
cold? – I want it silvery white and not golden white, but I can't tell yet
and want your advice. Oh, do come and look – I wouldn't wait a minute
if you wanted me to come and look at anything.*

Light and warmth soothed Burne-Jones. He hated the damp black
days of winter and was often ill. May hated the cold too, but she, as
many well-heeled Victorian women would do for 'their health', used
to escape to sunnier parts of Europe during the grimmest months,
while Burne-Jones stayed hard at work in his studio. He continued to
write to May at the hotels she stayed in, such as the lovely Villa d'Este
on Lake Como, which she knew well from the early years of her
marriage. What a contrast May's life there must have been to the
grime and fog of London, which further depressed Burne-Jones:

*These are dark days – the mornings begin with an immoveable cloud that
never lifts . . . Dark, dark, dripping day – raw, desolate skies – and I can't
go out – and yet to stay in means ghostly nights and bogies – for the first
time last night my memories could not rally me – so heavy was the gloom
and feverish my blood – yet I clung to them – and almost prayed them to
help me.*

In the early March of 1893, after two months away, May was back
from her winter wanderings, but the days were still dark and held no

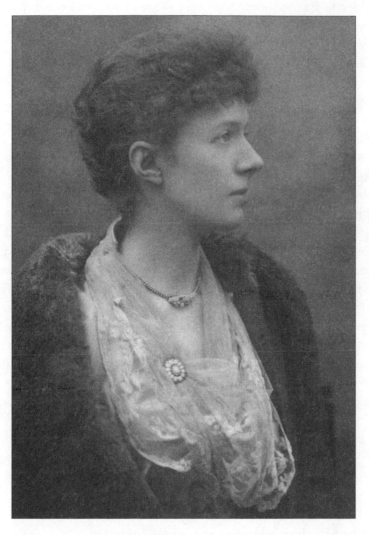

This photograph of May was taken in 1893, when she was forty years old. It may well be the one which she sent to Burne-Jones after he had begged her to have one taken for him. The image shows she looked young for her age, and that Burne-Jones's drawings of her were not as idealized as I had imagined.

promise of warmth. However, her return made everything seem brighter to Burne-Jones. Now that she was in London again he was desperate to see her as much as possible:

I hold all the week free for the chances you give me – for though my love is celestial my silly eyes hunger to look at you, and so I keep the week clear for little chances.

But before long, May had to leave England again. She heard that her mother Emma, who despite her fragile health had so attentively looked after her grandchildren in Worcestershire the year before while May and Henry Brooks were in Egypt, was dying in Rome. It was never specified what Emma Melville's long-standing illness was. May had once described it as a 'nervous illness', which may well have meant some form of depression. Whatever it was, she had gone to Rome in the hope that the beneficial effects of a warmer climate and complete rest would help; but to no avail. When the Melville family received news of her deteriorating condition, May, her father, her brother Willie, who had not yet returned to the Argentine, her younger brother Beresford, and Amy set out for Italy at once. They stayed by Emma's bedside for three weeks. Burne-Jones wrote sympathetic letters to May at the Hotel Royal Mazzin, hoping that her mother would recover. He made sure she knew that he didn't forget her:

I talk to you constantly – I am always telling you things while I work – I do bits of work to please you – if I read anything lovely I want to tell it to you – you are never removed from my side – that's how I live.

I found one letter written from Rome by May to her youngest daughter Daphne, who adored her grandmother:

Grannie is very weak, and she drinks out of a cup with a long spout like a baby. But she is so gentle and sweet and smiles and says thank you when she is able. When Amy came in yesterday with a pink cotton shirt on and her hands full of lilac Grannie laughed and said 'How pretty!' I go out every morning and buy some violets, or lilacs, or big blue anemones for Amy to wear.

But little Emma Melville grew weaker each day, until her heart quietly gave up. She was buried in Rome's Protestant cemetery, and lies there still under the palms and cypresses, along with Shelley's heart, the mortal remains of Keats, and many other distinguished foreigners. A large colony of stray cats have made the cemetery their home.

On the same day as the burial in Rome, the big bell of Worcester Cathedral was tolled at intervals throughout the morning, and in the evening Canon Knox Little, a distinguished colleague of Canon Melville, spoke to the congregation about the much-loved wife of their 'most venerable' canon and sub dean. He remembered her 'great personal beauty and charm'. 'We cannot shut our eyes or close our hearts,' he continued, 'to this very loving, very gentle, womanly life which has been removed from us.'

In the summer of 1893, it was more than a year since Burne-Jones had first met May. Their friendship had deepened, and it appears that it was mutual. The painter wrote:

> *What a beautiful letter you sent me – how beautifully you write of me and my devotion – oh does it really do that for you – really? Yes, for you never lie – it must be so, how difficult to believe it and yet I do – and it is the happiness of my life from now . . . I have watched your laughter and your grief and both are splendid and true – and I know I have found rest and security in this most perfect, blessed and beautiful friendship – ah that isn't the word for it – but what other is there – give me another – yet the highest you could give me would hardly be enough – something eternal I have found that deepens and makes splendid all my days.*

Edward and Georgie Burne-Jones owned a small, whitewashed house in Rottingdean, near Brighton, which they had bought in 1880, when the fields around the Grange in Fulham were fast being turned into streets by speculative builders and they thought they would need somewhere to escape for fresh air and quiet. Georgie went to Sussex more often than her husband, who usually stayed in London working, but occasionally he wrote to May from Rottingdean. He said he thought it 'a sweet place'; he enjoyed the 'clean air', drawing the black pigs in a large sty nearby, and the visits by his daughter Margaret's children. He also liked to visit the 'wonderful' village shop:

It is kept by a man called Tuppence. Nothing in the shop is worth half a farthing – it sells balls of string, and potatoes, and sand boots and galoshes, and geraniums in pots, and occasionally a cucumber, and Cassel's popular reader, and newspapers, and it has a circulating library of as many as eighteen volumes which sit on the shelf from year to year and never circulate, and if you go into the shop there is nobody to serve you with anything, no not if you stamp and knock for an hour. If you make a great noise Mr Tuppence comes out looking cross and says he hasn't got it before you ask for anything, and one of the insoluble riddles of the earth is why Mr Tuppence has a shop at all, but the riddle is so contemptible no one comes to answer it.

In October 1893, Burne-Jones's spirits soared to newly ecstatic heights:

It is such a life for me now – it is such a life – I am so happy – I can't imagine how anybody could be happier and I walked back in a golden sunset – was there a sunset really? I don't know – I can't remember – all the world was melted gold I think.

This time it was a secret plan to meet May the next day for an outing, possibly partly fantasy, that had made him so elated:

If it's fine tomorrow let it be Richmond – nay why not if it's wet – it wouldn't rain all the time – and it would be so far away and safe – better than Hampstead, and the British Museum we'll do in winter time. Oh let it be Richmond – the drive even in rain will be nice – so in the morning telegram and say 'Yes, Richmond, Paddington' and I will wait for you at the door opposite Praed Street Metropolitan entrance where the hideous hotel is at quarter past three – and off we'll go galloping in clouds of dust or splashing through puddles of mud – and we'll ramble there and talk, and dine at a window and tell tales – and one of us two will be grateful to God and stretch out a hand to the past and forgive it – a heavy past. I am happy now – I look up from my writing and into the fading sunset and

*have thought for twenty minutes or more – yes it's true as truth that I am
more happy this night than ever I have been since I was born.*

Once, the sudden arrival in London of Henry Brooks from
Kiddington must have spoiled a similar plan. Burne-Jones was
anxious for May's reputation:

*This coming up to town is most unlucky and inopportune, but it may be
good discipline – we might have given way to the comfort of each other's
society and been so constantly together that people would chatter – for I
can't resist you – you can do anything you like with me I warn you . . .
people may talk about me as much as they like and always have done –
now and then things come round to me, and are always lies – But I don't
want you to be in their vulgar lies – and the best lies in the world are
vulgar when they chatter about sacred secret things – slowly, bit by bit, it
will seem we are close friends – and people will get used to it – I don't
think people ever do say things about you – I never hear the faintest
murmur – but nobody tells me things, they know I am not at all the life of
gossip.*

Burne-Jones had always had several close women friends, and as he
was a famous man, this of course gave people fuel for gossip, but as his
passion for May intensified there were two women whose feelings he
had to consider above all. He had been devoted to Frances Horner for
many years and would remain so until his death, but her marriage had
long ago somewhat changed their relationship. Nevertheless their
friendship remained strong, and it was Frances who had brought May
into his world. After Burne-Jones received a letter from Frances about
an evening they were all three to spend together, he wrote to May:

*How I should hate to hurt and yet I must be true – but I would sooner
she would see by time – with all its gentleness than by one violent moment
– I know if I am driven I shall have to say – I mustn't be driven if it can
be helped. I cannot humbug about it – it is all too serious with me – it is
clear by now that it was no sudden passion of pity and sympathy – that
you see by now – it is my deepest me that is involved, and nothing could
come of deception, which I could never manage. I have no fear of the*

evening, you help so, are so bright and full of infinite tact – we will make
her happy – if she asks the question I dread I must try and evade it unless
you bid me tell the truth. It's a pretty letter, warm and loving and we will
be careful not to hurt – but she knows I am sure – it can't be helped – it
isn't you that has done it, nor had the least share in it – it was furthest
from your thoughts – my mind was estranged and free before I ever told
you – else I should never have been moved by you – I have never been
untrue – never – never – nor once lied about love – nor will I ever.

Burne-Jones may have tried to persuade himself that his new friendship with May would cause no upset. But surely Frances, who had
been adored by him for so many years, and who would have noticed
how much he had taken to the friend she had introduced to him, must
have felt more than slightly put out, however involved she was with
her own family life. It was evident that Burne-Jones now had less time
to give her. He told May:

> *There came a very short – and very disappointed sounding letter from*
> *Frances – vexed that she had asked what I refused – I am sorry to hurt,*
> *but I think she will make these plans no more – yes I do wish my letter*
> *had not hurt her, with all my heart – I can't bear to give that kind of pain.*

Most of all, of course, he did not want to hurt his wife, though he
must have often deceived himself about that. Georgie had clearly been
hurt at times during their marriage, yet she always remained calm.
Their relationship changed after the early years, but she believed,
correctly as it turned out, that she and her 'Ned' still had enough love
for each other to last until the end. Their lives became more separate,
but she stood by Burne-Jones devotedly. An intelligent, strong
woman, Georgie had the measure of her husband; she understood his
character and knew his weaknesses, but she also knew how much he
depended on her. Like many women married to a man they consider
an artistic genius, she let him have his way.

One of the many things Burne-Jones needed Georgie for was to
manage his affairs. He hated thinking about money, as he told May:

*I can't manage a bit and get into dreadful messes, that is where Georgie
has been so good – at the worst time she's never let me know and keeps all
the ugly rubbish out of sight – years ago I handed all over to her, and I
never sign a cheque even – or see money, except pocket money she gives
me when I go into town – I can't think how I live – perhaps my pictures
are really very bad and that's why they sell.*

Georgie certainly appears to have been a supremely loyal and long-
suffering wife, but she was also resilient, and had many admiring
friends of her own. Perhaps the closest of all these was her husband's
lifelong friend, William Morris, whose socialist views she also shared.
It was at the time of the Maria Zambaco affair, when Morris's own
marriage also had its problems, that he had become a close friend and
confidant of Georgie.

The friendship between Burne-Jones and Morris had blossomed
when they shared a copy of Malory's *Morte d'Arthur*, which they had
found together in a bookshop in Oxford, while at university. This
book, and the mystical world of the Arthurian legends, inspired both
men's work profoundly from then onwards, and they became closest
friends. But in 1883 Morris, who had been involved in politics for
some years, formed the Socialist League, a new Marxism-based movement. Burne-Jones felt strongly that it would be destructive for such a
brilliantly talented artist to become too involved with politics, and
feared that it would cause a rift between the two of them, which
proved, sadly, to be the case. Some estranged years followed when
Morris no longer visited the Grange.

However, by the time May met Burne-Jones, his friendship with
Morris had happily been rekindled and the two men were colleagues
once more. Now Morris was back every Sunday as he had been before
to enjoy a large breakfast at the Grange. Then, after the meal, the two
old friends worked and continued talking in the studio together.
Their joint work was an edition of the complete Canterbury Tales by
Chaucer, a huge project to be published by William Morris's
Kelmscott Press. Burne-Jones was responsible for the illustrations and
Morris the decorative borders. Burne-Jones told May:

All the time Morris is designing his borders here on Sunday morning one

*hears his teeth almost gnashing – at least gnattering and grinding together
– and so it was always I remember – and when I (your poor friend) work
I hold my breath, and when the stroke or the touch is over I have to sigh
heavily so that anyone hearing would think I was unhappy – and yet both
I suppose are done to steady the hand – but isn't it strange.*

The recovered friendship between the two men had its ups and
downs, its irritations and differences of opinion. But it was an inde-
structible partnership. Burne-Jones deeply admired his great bear of a
friend even if he didn't share his political views, and much preferred
seeing him at the Grange rather than at Kelmscott House, where
Morris lived with his wife Janey on the Upper Mall at Hammersmith:

*Of course I wish Morris was different in some ways – wish he had pretty
manners and grace in his welcome – or even the simulation of it – but it
couldn't be – he has to be what he is – and no one is like him or has been
for hundreds of years – some Viking of old was like him – probably never
again will such a being be. I come away from his house sadder always –
all year through I see him here – and he seems more at home – is less
constrained here, and more at ease – when I am there which is once in
two years at most I come away gloomy and depressed – the house feels full
of ghosts to me – a Wuthering Heights feeling about it all.*

But one day, Burne-Jones took May and Amy to visit Morris at his
house for tea. Afterwards May must have commented on his grubbi-
ness, for in a letter the following day Burne-Jones sprang to his
friend's defence:

*You said he wasn't clean – he is really underneath – but always pencils
and ink and the day's messes in work stick to him, and like to get on to him,
and if ever anything has to be spilled to make up the necessary average of
spilling, it spills on him. But he boils himself in tubs daily, and is very clean
really – but he needs more explaining than anyone who ever lived except
Swift – who was dirty inside – the nasty thing – and this one is cleaner inside
than is at all necessary . . . He liked the ladies who called on him the other
afternoon very much – that is tremendous – that is a conquest – he was
pleased you noticed his teacup and said he liked you to laugh at it.*

Presumably this was a reference to the size of teacup Morris needed to contain the large amount of tea he drank. It must have been clear to May by then that of the few men Burne-Jones did admire, Morris was the one he really loved.

Burne-Jones, who had a special affinity with children, became increasingly interested and charmed by May's three children, Amy, Hal and Daphne. He was soon writing illustrated letters to all of them, particularly to six-year-old Daphne, using a parody of her spelling:

> *darlink dafny, I foregot to say I do want a cat but I think I want a fat hevy tabby chap like Tommus* [the Gaskells' cat] *... I want a hevy fellow with a face like a poik py ...*

During his school holidays, Hal, who enjoyed drawing more and more, was given lessons at the Grange both by the Master himself and by his assistant Thomas Rooke. Daphne was as much of a character as her brother and had great charm, which she clearly exercised on Burne-Jones: 'Sweet little ray of real light is Daphne and her baby affection soothes me a great deal.'

But it was Amy, just grown up, who seemed to intrigue him most. At eighteen, Amy already showed signs of being an emotionally complex character, and possessed an air of vulnerability and flawless romantic looks that Burne-Jones loved. He wanted to paint her as a present for May, perhaps feeling it would create even more of a bond between them.

> *Presently we'll fix a time for a sketch of Amy – and you will bring her and stay with her all the time, to make it not dull for her, and watch it and see that I make it a little like.*

It was also a challenge for him as a painter, as he pointed out to May:

> *I don't easily get portraiture – the perpetual hunt to find in a face what I like, and leave out what mislikes me, is a bad school for portraiture but there is such sweetness in her face that I should like to draw her – and you should say every half hour if I am getting it better or worse.*

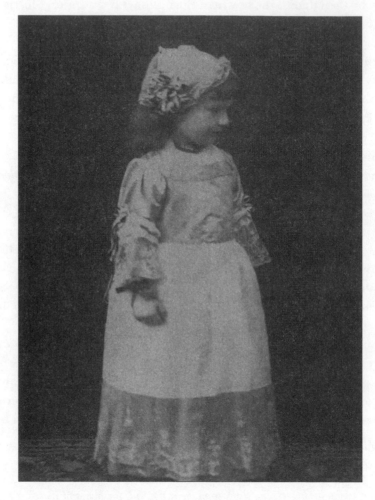

May's youngest daughter Daphne at the time Burne Jones first met her, when she was six years old.

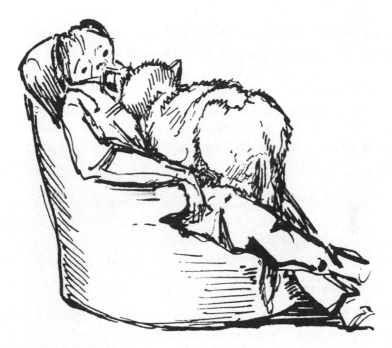

A drawing in one of Burne-Jones's letters to little Daphne: himself as he liked to be. He loved cats, and always drew them as warm and comforting creatures, unlike his many images of snarling dogs.

May knew the garden studio of the Grange well; it was where Burne-Jones received most of his visitors. But it was his upstairs private studio, where he painted Amy, which she came to know best. So began, first by sketches with May in attendance, later by long painting sessions with Amy by herself, the creation of an exceptionally beautiful picture. Even at the time, Burne-Jones told May that those who saw it liked it better than any other portraits he had done. It took the painter over a year and a half to complete, during which time he came to know Amy well, and to feel affection and concern for her.

Later on, when May was away on one of her more prolonged travels and Burne-Jones was perhaps feeling bereft, he wrote to remind her of the studio where she had brought Amy to have her portrait painted:

*Do you remember the studio – the upstairs one? Have you forgotten it –
to me it is full of memories of you – not one was made bitter for me – if I
feel any bitterness in there it was my silly doing – and do you remember
when you first came and said it was untidy – you said it was worse than
untidy – you made me live with Mrs Williamson for days and days.*

Mrs Williamson was Burne-Jones's studio cleaner; he drew countless
unflattering caricatures of her, fat and plain, bustling around in her
long black dress. He hated her destroying the peace as well as the
disorder of the studio. Burne-Jones continued nostalgically to a far-off
May:

*You sat here, and you sat there, and here you were most unhappy, and
there you laughed and forgot trouble in your sweet way. And there is
Amy's corner, and out of that corner she looked with far piercing eyes. As
for the garden studio – far be it from me to go and look at it yet. One
room full of memories is enough.*

Burne-Jones loved colour; in his paintings there are glorious shades,
deep or glowing, richly warm or ethereally cool. Yet in his portrait of
Amy, a young girl who preferred to dress all in white, and who at that
time spent most of her life being whirled round the dance floor
surrounded by a riot of colour at glittering social occasions, Burne-
Jones inexplicably chose to use no colour at all. The picture was just
black: black dress, black background; only her ivory skin glowed out
of the darkness.

I have found no clue why Burne-Jones chose to paint Amy in this
way. Seeing the picture is like looking at a marble statue on a tomb
within a shadowy church. It is as if the sitter was a young widow. Why
did he choose to dress this ravishing young girl in funereal garb at the
very start of her promising adult life? Burne-Jones was a spiritual
man. Did he feel compelled to paint Amy like this? Was it melodramatic of me to wonder if he could have had a premonition of her
fate?

dear Amy

Yes come in an old
frock — that can't hurt by being
wet — though if it rains I
suppose we shan't go —
but I shall have to
finish the sleeves for
your black frock one
day.

One of the many notes Burne-Jones wrote to Amy during the time when she came regularly to the Grange to sit for her portrait.

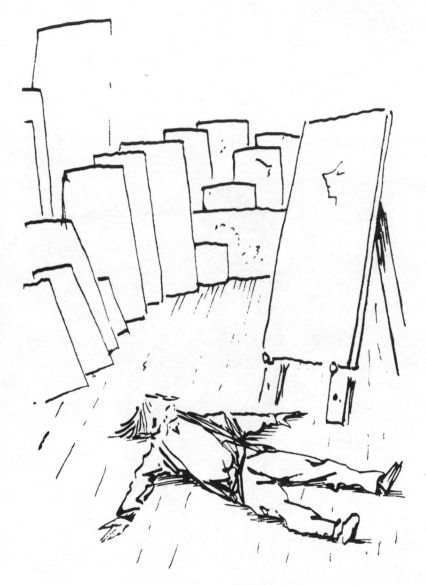

From another of Burne-Jones's letters to Amy, showing her face on his
easel and himself prostrate on the studio floor. He often drew himself
looking exhausted or pathetic.

CHAPTER FIVE

THE DARK PORTRAIT

DURING THE SUMMER OF 1893, MAY WAS AT THE GASKELLS' NORTH-
country house, Beaumont Hall, in Lancashire. The large Jacobean
farmhouse was near Lancaster, where it survives to this day, though
now almost swallowed up by the expanding city. The estate had
originally been one of the many rural properties acquired by Henry
Brooks's grandfather, the Devil of Wigan. May had recently decorated
and furnished it in the style of the Arts and Crafts Movement, which
had been founded by William Morris and his contemporaries. There
were one or two pieces of furniture painted by Burne-Jones himself.

The Gaskell children loved going up to Beaumont, and their father
enjoyed the shooting. But for May the more enclosed family life they
led there appears to have been difficult; she mentions in letters that it
was 'a strain'. Burne-Jones was aware of this when he wrote to her
soon after she arrived there that summer:

*I know it is a painful visit to you – how could it be otherwise – and I see
you all day long so unselfish, so helpful, giving and giving and taking
nothing.*

May's response was to invite Burne-Jones up to Beaumont. As he could often be, Burne-Jones was clearly irritated by Georgie on the morning he received her invitation. Enthusiastically, he replied at once:

> It is change I want, yes and need – not change of air only – but at Beaumont it will be change – such sweet change for me.

But before he left London, Burne-Jones heard terrible news. His watercolour painting of 'Love Among the Ruins', which he had painted years before, soon after the end of his affair with Maria Zambaco, had been irreparably damaged while being prepared for photographic reproduction in Paris. As May later explained in a notebook, the photographer, not knowing the work was a watercolour, had covered the surface with egg white to make it glisten. Burne-Jones's son Phil, who was in Paris at the time, brought the painting back to London. Devastated, Burne-Jones wrote to May:

> I have come home and seen the ruin – Love in the Ruins with a vengeance – all gone – as if the devil had hated it and had his way – and now be soft and nice to me – as if you were ever anything else – I am so sore I can't bear to talk of it – And I have made up my mind – I am going to you on Tuesday – to be comforted – I turn to you naturally – <u>please</u> we won't talk once of it . . . something good for me will come of seeing you – either courage, or new life, or comfort – something that in misery only a woman and only one woman can give.

Perhaps feeling that he was making too much of a fuss, Burne-Jones ended the letter with:

> But how mean of me – what glorious things have gone, by the side of which mine is such a wretched thing – but it was mine – very me of me, and I must be sorry for a bit – I will tell you the train – I don't care if it isn't comfortable – I want to go to you and would rather reach you through prickles and fire than through Pullman sofas.

And so Burne-Jones, in a dejected state, arrived for his first visit to Beaumont, and was comforted by May. The following spring, when she was staying there once more, and when Burne-Jones had already started work on an oil version of 'Love Among the Ruins', he wrote to May recalling the turbulent emotions of his visit the year before:

> How I remember those days – every moment of them – there was an unhappy walk, in a narrow green lane and I leaned over a gate and was very unhappy – a year had been cut away from my life – and my picture had been destroyed – it sat heavy on my heart, that last picture – how kind you were to me – and how truthful – and wouldn't cheat me even to please me . . . Since the day that I came from Beaumont I have not rested from work one day – and that is many months ago – There was a room – the school room, when I grew so very unhappy – and I felt I couldn't stay another night, and that it was more unhappiness than I could bear – and I even thought it unkind of you not to let me go . . . but the seat in the gar-den was a peaceful time – only twice I suffered too much and once was in the school room and once in the long lane, but now that time has dealt mercifully with me – it is all dear to remember – the grief has turned to delight and I think often of the green lane as of happier times.

In the early summer of 1893, Amy Gaskell had begun coming to Burne-Jones's private studio upstairs to sit for her portrait, wearing the black dress he had requested. After the first session with her mother, she came alone. Frequent reports of how it was going were sent to May:

> . . . oh this morning's work was nice. As the picture gets towards an end I will ask you to look at it, and tell me where it seems to you not like, but today's work was only learning something of her face and mapping the proportion in.

Another time he explained that he had 'cut off a bit of her inexplic-able little nose and she says it's better'. He clearly became fond of Amy in a fatherly way, and was aware of her changing moods: 'Amy was very sweet today, talked gaily and was happy.'

Soon Burne-Jones added Amy to his list of correspondents, sending her humorous notes and little sketches. By the summer of 1894, he had almost finished her portrait and did not see her so often. Amy's social life was full:

> *Darling Amy. Want a letter from you – know you hate writing – but want to know if you are merry and dancing away, and something about you. Wish you liked writing, I do – but you hate it – copy this out and send it to me and I shall know then that you are wishing me well – 'Dear Sir – I am sorry to hear that you are not well – but at your time of life you cannot expect to be frisking about, you must bear with your maladies and talk about them as little as you can – they are never interesting and frequently fatiguing – a young friend may perhaps be permitted a freedom which an old one is reluctant to take, and I hope that you will not be angry if I tell you that you are too much in the habit of saying you are unwell – be as unwell as you like, or must – but for heaven's sake be silent about it. My love and best wishes to you all. Yours truly, Amy Gaskell.'*
>
> *I shall be at the Stratford Ball tonight, <u>in spirit</u> – so be careful.*

Burne-Jones ended the letter with a little sketch of himself as a pathetic-looking spirit, floating forlornly above the ball in ghost-like robes.

After the summer, Amy was back in the studio for the last sittings. May was now allowed to come and see the portrait. It pleased her very much, and she could not wait to take it home to Marble Arch, although it was to be exhibited for a short time at the New Gallery first. But disaster struck. May received a desperate note:

> *Oh poor abject little me – I think I have quite spoilt the portrait of Amy – I don't think it will ever look nice again, and I wished you had carried it off the other night now – all day it has been slipping and slipping from my hands, and I tried so hard and had my heart so set to please you. If I hadn't cared so much perhaps I could have done better – the picture is spoilt – perhaps irredeemably – my heart so heavy with failure and disappointment – don't ask to see it – we'll talk when you come, but be kind, and don't ask to see the poor ruin – let me try to recover it first.*

Burne-Jones never recorded how he had spoilt the painting, but his efforts to save it were successful, as we know from the enchanting picture that survives today.

Soon after Burne-Jones had given the portrait to May in late 1894, and after she had allowed it to be shown at the New Gallery, she hung it at her London house, 3 Marble Arch. The Cumberland Hotel now stands where the house used to be; my father used to take me to lunch there as often as possible, because he said he could just remember going to the house to visit his grandparents when he was very young, and so felt a sort of bond with the hotel. The family photograph albums show that, in typically Victorian style, the interior walls of the house were covered from top to bottom with paintings and drawings, and the rooms filled with elaborate furniture. I can recognize some pieces that are still in my brother's house and others that belong to a cousin. The sofas and several cushions were covered in William Morris fabric, there was a William Morris screen in the drawing room, and both May and Amy's bedrooms were hung with William Morris wallpaper.

I can identify, hung on the walls, many of the drawings Burne-Jones gave to May. Some of these I have managed to see since, but there are others nobody seems to know the fate of. There were several platinotype reproductions by Burne-Jones's close friend the photographer Fred Hollyer, which perhaps he himself gave to May. On her bedroom mantelpiece are many photographs in frames, and above her dressing table, lit by candles, a reproduction of Frederick Watts's portrait of Burne-Jones, the original of which May knew well from her visits to the Grange. Over her bed is another beautiful photogravure reproduction, of a painting from Burne-Jones's Briar Rose series: the story of the Sleeping Beauty, which shows the king and his courtiers asleep. Next door, on Amy's bedroom wall, is the most exquisite painting in that series: the Sleeping Beauty herself lying in a rose bower, waiting for her prince's awakening kiss. On the other walls, however, are a surprising number of religious pictures, perhaps indicative of Amy's search for God, which May mentioned after her death.

But more identifiable than anything else, on the wall above the piano in the drawing room of the house at Marble Arch, is the recently finished portrait of Amy. 'My picture,' Amy wrote proprietorially

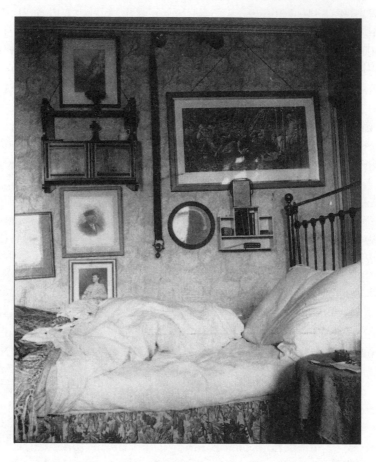

Amy's photograph of May's bedroom at Marble Arch, with William Morris wallpaper and a photogravure reproduction of one of Burne Jones's Briar Rose series to the right. The unmade bed looks as if May has just left it.

under the photograph of it in her album. Burne-Jones warned May
that he felt it would not be discreet to put too many of his gifts to her
on display in her London house, and a few years later the portrait of
Amy appears in photographs of the elegant dining room at
Kiddington Hall. After May's husband died, the favourite painting
must have gone with her to rented houses in London. In the early
1930s my aunt Diana, May's only surviving grandchild, used to visit
her grandmother at 28 Albion Street, the house where May lived for
the last seventeen years of her life. Diana vividly remembers sitting
having tea under the picture of the beautiful aunt she had never met.
'Granny didn't talk much about Amy by then,' Diana told me, 'but
because of that picture I always felt her presence.'

My heart was thudding with excitement as I drove down to Andrew
Lloyd Webber's house for my promised first viewing of the legendary
painting. I had been told of his wonderful collection of Victorian
paintings, bought over many years. But what makes the collection
exceptional is that it isn't as if you are at an exhibition or in an art
gallery; instead, you enter a Pre-Raphaelite world. The pictures hang
on the walls of a very private house, in whose rooms the theatrically
Victorian décor seems chosen entirely to suit them. They are subtly
and perfectly lit. Walking from room to room amongst such a feast of
beautiful women gives an impression that is almost orgiastic.

I passed through the luscious room devoted to Rossetti, full of
women who would nowadays be suspected of having their lips
enlarged with collagen injections. Then I came into an inner hall
devoted to Andrew's extraordinary Burne-Jones paintings. At first all
I was aware of was colour; great sweeps of colour with all the rich,
warm and varying tones that I had associated with the painter. As in
the previous room, I again found myself surrounded by women, but
these were purer and more virginal looking than Rossetti's sensual
beauties. Then suddenly I was conscious, without really seeing it, of
another presence, something no less beautiful but a complete contrast
to all around it.

In front of me, at the bottom of the stairs, was the picture. It was
even darker than I had imagined from the reproductions I had seen,
almost inky black. Here at last was my great-aunt Amy, a ravishing

nineteen-year-old girl, at the time when she had just come out in
London society, a girl who appeared to have every advantage you
could think of. 'My daughter Amy, just out and lovely,' was how May
described Amy at this time in her family reminiscences years later.
Now I was able to see for myself that smooth translucent skin, glowing with youth and promise, the glossy dark hair, and the gentle
features, which seemed to invite tenderness and love. The mysterious
charisma of Amy seemed to me evident even in this youthful portrait.

During the summer season of 1894 Amy danced at ball after ball and
gathered quite a retinue of beaux, mostly the kind of young men who
spent much of their time shooting and hunting. They were the sort of
people Burne-Jones had no time for. He complained to May about one
such fellow:

> And the more I think of it the more dreadful that man grows – Amy's
> friend – oh poor Amy . . . do you remember his face? And the back of his
> head? Did you notice the back of his head? This is what happens in the
> hunting field. But in the next life it will be his turn to be hunted. Can
> that aplomb and assured manner of being made perfectly, inside and out,
> which marked every accent of his, be acquired? Or is one born to such a
> manner. He had the way of a man accustomed to conquest. And if they
> laugh up in heaven as I hope they do sometimes, what fun they must have
> over him. And Amy bore your teasing prettily.

It is obvious that May was sometimes exasperated with the changing moods and foibles of the eldest daughter she adored. At these
moments Burne-Jones took on himself the role of her adviser:

> The time will come, a few years hence, when Amy will make up to you
> and be a mighty comfort, stay and strength in your life – and when it
> comes about remember I prophesied it . . . so cuddle her up and talk to her
> as if she were a grown woman and ask her advice – and never say things
> for her good – indeed you are the last to do that. But be soft and sweet to
> her – I know you are, but I mean perpetual patience. Forgiveness wins at
> the last – she is clever, that I'm sure of – quick – swift in mind – she will
> repay all.

When I was reading through May's letters from Burne-Jones, I noticed that she had pencilled in remarks such as 'wonderful, loving letter' or 'wild, unhappy letter' on some of them many years later. One she had simply marked 'sacred', probably because it brought back particularly poignant memories of both the daughter and the friend she had lost:

Amy was a pet last night – we were quite alone for she asked for that – and we talked without ceasing all dinner time and all evening through, and at about half past ten I had a fly to take her warmly back. I had the talk with her I had wanted so long, and had no opportunity for – and it came very easily – and I understood her perfectly in all her words. I did not go reckless into this talk, and I measured the words of love I used about you – and all she said in reply was loving and graceful about you – she said she continually saw just when and where she could help you and she longed with all her heart to do it, and always as certainly a fit of stubborn silence came upon her as if to mock her and she couldn't move or speak though she longed to and I said 'Don't try to speak, go to her and nestle up against her and bury your cheek in her neck and say nothing.'

Whether she was at Beaumont, Marble Arch, Kiddington Hall or abroad, Amy, having inherited an artistic eye from her mother, spent much of her time practising photography. She had the latest model of Kodak camera – a very large, rectangular box made of leather-covered wood: 'My Kodak,' she would call it. It was Amy, of course, who had taken most of the photographs I had loved to look at in my father's house. Often she used herself as a model, always looking away from the camera, but carefully posed, in a way that shows how sure of her own attractions she was. The self-portraits were achieved by squeezing a rubber bulb at the end of a long cable attached to the camera, in order to activate the shutter at the right moment. At other times she would set up a romantic scene, such as herself on the lake at Kiddington, and direct someone else to take the picture with her camera.

Amy recorded life at each of her homes photographically, and froze in time the interiors of each one. When I study them with a magnifying glass I can almost feel I am in those rooms. Through the lens of her Kodak, Amy captured her family, gatherings of friends, and the servants, whom she often used as models for posed portrait photography, for instance Ralph, the Gaskells' London butler. Burne-Jones took a special liking to Ralph, whom he saw whenever he called at Marble Arch; in one letter he suggested to May that Ralph might like to come and see his studio. From time to time Ralph accompanied the Gaskell family up to Beaumont, where Amy also pictured him with Pratt, the genial-looking round-faced butler from Lancaster, who had a ruddy complexion. In contrast Ralph appears olive skinned and good looking, with straight, shiny dark hair, fine thoughtful eyes and a distinguished aquiline nose.

In Amy's first photograph album you can see little Daphne's kindly young nurse Boyne, with her smiling eyes, and her older governess, the rather swarthy Miss Neurotsos, who was Greek. A group photograph of the Beaumont servants, taken in 1894, shows Rose Iles, young and blonde in a pretty white dress; the housemaid was to become May's personal maid, and stay with her until her death in 1940. 'Granny never went anywhere without Mrs Iles,' my aunt Diana told me. But the most intriguing photograph of all, and the one I have studied most, is the eerie and prophetic one Amy took of herself: 'dead'.

When I was nineteen years old, roughly the same age as Amy then was, my godmother, who was also a close relation, sent me a copy of a touching letter from Burne-Jones to Amy. It gives an early hint of her melancholy temperament:

> *Dear little Amy, what is to be done? How are bonny maidens to be made happy – I don't know. If I knew the troubles of your mind I might be able to advise – perhaps even then I couldn't say anything to help thee – I would give a great deal to have you happy and at peace.*
>
> *It would not be fair, at this end of life to tell you what I have grown to think about the quest after happiness – it would sound like poor dry cheerless words. The happiness I have sought for and pursued I have missed – if I ever reached any I lost it soon, that which comes to me comes by surprise, in a quarter where I least looked . . . Dear, I have often thought it a pity that the word 'happiness' should ever have been made and put in a dictionary to beguile us . . . And some say it will be hereafter, and some*

that it will be presently – if we don't snatch – and some say courage is
better even than happiness and to be Lord of oneself, and some find peace
in endurance and are too proud to lament – and some there be who find
contentment in the pot-house – the 'Live and Let Live' which is our
nearest tavern I observe to be always thronged. And often I have a mind to
go there and see what delight it would bring.

At the end of the letter Burne-Jones urges Amy to come and stay at
the Grange with him and Georgie and their son Phil:

I don't like to press you – for it is such a quiet house and few things
happen here – work every day – but if ever I could help you, my dear,
with all my heart I would . . . Georgie is a brick about troubles and
sorrows and as wise as the Delphic Sybil. And I am very fond of you and
would take mighty care of you.

Soon after this, Burne-Jones wrote to May:

I am so glad you think kindly of that plan for Amy to come here by and by
. . . Georgie loves damsels and is the best company in the world for them –
you will write to her won't you. I want her to feel you have some friend-
ship for her, and would trust Amy to her – she shall not have a dull time
either – Phil and I will take her to amusements and the days shall not
depress her. And somehow, somewhere I will get a little of her confidence.

These letters made me suspect that Amy might have had, even at that
young age, a tendency to depression which could well explain later
events in her life. Was there a problem with one of her beaux? Or was
she increasingly troubled by the tension at home between her mother
and father, perhaps even disturbed by her mother's close friendship
with Burne-Jones?

In January 1894, the prime minister William Gladstone offered
Burne-Jones a baronetcy. Between then and 1898, Burne-Jones, who
considered the old man a close friend, would often mention him in his
letters to May, and tell her about his visits to Hawarden Castle, the
Gladstones' historic home in Wales. He remarked that it was a 'real

marvel' that 'a house that has seen in its time and known all that is most famous and important in this world should remain so untouched by glitter and so simple and innocent'.

Burne-Jones described his walks and talks with the distinguished politician, who was three times prime minister. After one such visit he told May:

> We were out two hours . . . and we talked a good deal about Latin things, and Greek things, and about Scott, a nice talk – I loved being with him and was never tired of looking at his face – only once he frowned and drew his fierce eyebrows together and shook himself and put his stick down firmly – and this was when he had to mention George the Fourth.

After another Hawarden visit, Burne-Jones complained that people always assumed he talked politics with Gladstone:

> What stuff it is to suppose one talks for show on such occasions – we talked very simply – very cosily – we never once mentioned politics for as usual gentlemen are kept aloof from all nauseous and hateful topics . . . nothing worth repeating was said by either of us . . . I rather hate brilliant talk but that I have said a thousand times – we talked about things we loved, gently, in an autumn afternoon, in the autumn and afternoon of life – and no one could have taken away anything to remember, nothing less for show, or more cosy and more heartily meant could have been said by two ancients.

Ultimately, the two ancients were to die within a month of each other.

Georgie was fiercely against Burne-Jones accepting a baronetcy. Echoing the painter Frederick Watts, who had refused one on the grounds that such honours were for politicians, not artists, she thought it was not appropriate for her husband. Morris, with his socialist ideals, would never have considered it. Burne-Jones himself was torn. He said: 'I half like it and half don't care tuppence.' But his son Phil urged him to accept the honour, and then chose the motto *Sequor et attingam* – I will follow and attain.

Nevertheless, it is unlikely that Burne-Jones accepted the baronetcy just for Phil. As the son of an unsuccessful Birmingham frame-maker, he himself had hyphenated his name so that he was not plain Mr Jones: he was undeniably a bit of a snob. Even if he sometimes complained of the frivolity of high society, he enjoyed being taken up by well-born ladies, as long as they were beautiful and cultivated.

May was not a class snob, but she was certainly impressed by fame and achievement, neither of which she had found in her husband. Her regular dinner parties at Marble Arch included glamorous friends among the Souls, such as the Horners, the Wyndhams and the Elchos, as well as eminent writers, artists and politicians, including Algernon Swinburne, Henry James, Arthur Balfour and Herbert Asquith. Burne-Jones was now often among the guests. One evening in 1894 May had, as usual, provided a lavish meal: there were six courses, starting with a delicate clear soup, followed by salmon, a chaudfroid of quails, saddle of lamb, chicken with beans, bacon and peas, a macédoine of fruit and vanilla ice. I know this because Burne-Jones, who had clearly been one of the guests, sent May a humorously illustrated menu on which the peas are presented in a black silk top hat, and the vanilla ice is an imperious female guest with an ice-cold

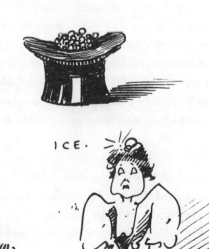

PEAS.

ICE.

expression on her face. At the bottom of the page a young man in a dinner tail suit gazes across at a young woman holding a fan; the couple are attached to each other by a thin thread, from which hang two hearts, flaming from above and dripping with blood from below.

Late that night, after everyone had gone home, May wrote a letter to Burne-Jones, which she sent by the first post next morning. An answer came swiftly:

> *I knew you would write to me last night – felt certain of it – you looked so beautiful, though you looked frail and ill – I watched you from the sofa and you looked like all the Queens of the world – and black velvet suits you finely – so did the silver buckle across your breast – and the white things all looked right – I turned now and then and thought you perfect in beauty.*

He then praised Amy, who, he thought, had 'great sweetness in her face'. But it was May he had watched most throughout the evening. Perhaps Amy was watching them both, and wondering. In his letter, Burne-Jones continued:

> *How nice of you to say that you looked across the table and thought 'It's mine' – yes, it is yours – only yours – not a bit left for anybody else – you looked across to me with eyes full of tender solicitude, to see how I was faring and the first moment you could you took me to your side, and let me stay. It's never easy to dine when you are by – the old instinct to look at no one else, hear no one else is in me – all else are shadows – I want to say 'Hush, she is speaking – I must listen to her' – and to behave politely is a bit of an effort.*

Burne-Jones's concern about May looking frail and ill is echoed by May's son Hal, who hated it when his mother was ill, which she more and more frequently appeared to be. Hal was now in his early teens, at school at Eton. He still retained the fanciful, odd nature he had had as a little boy. During one of May's mysterious collapses a worried letter from Hal arrived:

> *My darling mother, I did not know you were so ill, you never told me so.*

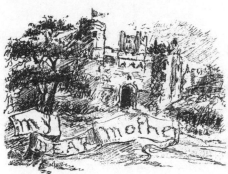

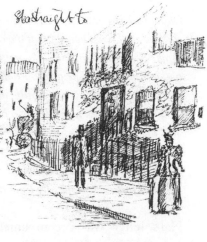

Sto straight to

my DEAR mother

On Friday I shall be with you
dear mother. I shall come down
by the 8.20 which arrives
at about 10.30 in London and

then I shall drive   And I shall come in .

like

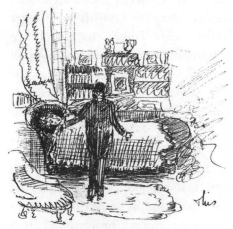

this

Good by dear mother
for 4 days

I hope you got my letter

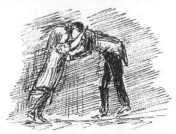

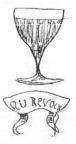

QU REVOIR

One of Hal's illustrated letters from Eton (note Windsor castle at
the top), planning to come home to Marble Arch and visit May on
her sickbed. At the bottom of the page, wearing his Etonian tailsuit,
he greets his little sister Daphne.

Oh mother you must rest rest and rest and try not to overdo yourself in everything, I have noticed that over and over again, and all for other people. Dear mother, I will do anything to make you better and everyone will amuse you and help you. I will do my utmost, and then slowly you will get better until you are quite well and we will all live happily ever after. You are like the flower who began in perfect health and beauty, and then the boy who is sickness suddenly plucks you and you fade in his grasp, but the little girl (your friends and family) takes you gently up, and with great care gets you back to your former health in water from the spring. This is a funny, perhaps silly little story that came into my mind.

Hal's letter was accompanied by some charming pen-and-ink drawings of himself, in his Etonian tail coat, coming home to Marble Arch, greeting May with open arms as she lay prone on a chaise longue, with only her face and curly hair showing above a checked coverlet. Lastly, Hal shows himself bending to kiss his little sister Daphne. Soon he wrote to his mother again: 'I hope that people are calling to see you, and Amy is gadding about, and father hiding all day, and I hope that you are able to get out now.' I wonder if this remark about his father was merely a reference to Henry Brooks's antisocial character, or was Hal aware of a more troubling situation at home?

A year or so later, May wrote to Hal at Eton after she had shown Burne-Jones some of his drawings. Hal replied: 'I am so glad BJ thought the sketches were better, and that I might be able to do something after all.' Hal was now intent on becoming a professional artist and was at his most articulate when he spoke of art:

Art seems to roll out like a piece of parchment, and with every roll of the day you see new things, and things you have not noticed before suddenly unfold themselves, and you wonder that you have not seen them before, at least so it seems to me.

The school holidays were what Hal lived for; as he grew older he could go out alone into the country, at Kiddington or Beaumont, and sketch as much as he wanted to:

*Every day that I go out sketching I feel more and more able to see into
and understand nature and consequently more able to put it down . . .
What I love is to go out with all my materials and get away from people,
dust, roads and ugly houses. Then I sit down where the birds sing, flies and
bees buzz and lambs and sheep are grazing, and I paint away until the sun
goes and the shadows get longer, but I don't notice these things 'til I wake
up and find it nearly dinner time.*

However, Hal didn't mind the dust, soot and noise of London
when he could visit Burne-Jones in his studio, and with luck even
have a drawing lesson from the great man himself. As Burne-Jones
listened to some of Hal's fantastical stories, he may have been
reminded of the imaginative child he himself had been. At the studio
Hal also met Thomas Rooke, who had been Burne-Jones's
studio assistant for more than twenty years. After the painter's death,
when Hal had left school, he was to study with Rooke in Paris, and
already at the Grange he had begun to learn much from him. But one
day Rooke appears to have been diverted from his usual devotion to
his work, and perhaps to his employer. Burne-Jones sent two
half-comic, half-serious letters to Hal about his assistant. It would seem
that Rooke was, most uncharacteristically, 'falling under the influence of
charming and fashionable ladies'. Presumably these ladies may have
been those who came so regularly to visit Burne-Jones, in whom Rooke
had never previously shown any interest. 'Rooke is in peril,' declared his
master, 'being an artist he is of course susceptible – I don't blame – but I
am anxious about him.' Referring to the 'charming and fashionable
ladies', Burne-Jones told Hal that Rooke now had a 'burning desire to
come to their assistance, to guide and help them', and that he himself had
been unable to distract him by talk of a more serious nature.

Before Hal could reply, another letter arrived:

*Dear Hal, it is just as I feared. Now do let this signal example be a
warning to you in time – here is Rooke advanced in years, of a naturally
sedate and placid disposition – with domestic responsibilities around him –
and just when I felt perfectly sure of him, and was accustomed to quote
him as a fine example of a single minded artistic life – here is Rooke,
crumbling under one's very eyes – we are never safe.*

But I beseech you, if now or presently, ladies were to go to you, and with almost tearful eyes, ask your help in designing book plates, fashionable shoes – fancy dress costumes, or ask your advice about the coiling of their hair, or the colours of their fans, or how far antimacassars are permitted amongst the cultivated – or whether black, blue or white becomes them most – to one and all and on all occasions say you can't, and won't, and don't know – and that you are going abroad, or about to enter the ministry – but at the very outset stop it.

There will be no more Rooke such as we know him – pious, simple, busy, a miracle of duty – there will be instead a frenzied, nervous, irritable Rooke – with a tendency to palpitations of the heart, a distraught manner, and a vague wandering eye – nor do I believe for a moment that this throne in the heart of the lady – whoever she may be – is in the least secure. Promise me that you will ponder over these things. Yours affectionately, BJ.

I wonder how seriously the young Hal took these very funny letters. Burne-Jones became more and more involved with all three of May's children, and even visited them when May was away. During one such absence, he reported to her:

And I went at the day's end and had a spelling lesson from Daphne – this time I got on better, and I wasn't so much scolded. She was a darling – and I pryed into her face to find traces of you, sometimes I do, sometimes I don't, her ways remind me of you keenly – and she showed me a letter she had from you – mainly in one syllable words, such a sweet letter, it was such a pretty letter – I saw Amy too – and bless her – I love to be loved by your children.

During one visit to Marble Arch, Burne-Jones asked Daphne what she would like him to draw for her. The little girl giggled, and came up very close so that he had to bend down for her to whisper in his ear that what she really wanted was 'Bottoms'. The next day a drawing arrived for Daphne. It was of a flower, but the five petals could be recognized as heart-shaped bottoms. With the drawing was a note to May: 'The name Daphne wanted me to illustrate – I have thought of it in many ways – as this – do you think this will do?'

When her mother was away, Burne-Jones wrote to Daphne even more than usual, and sent her many charming little drawings. While May was in Italy one spring, Burne-Jones wrote constantly to Daphne, almost always in fake childish spelling, as was his habit with her. It was as if he knew they could give comfort to each other when they felt abandoned by May:

My dere dafny – isn't it just so dredful without that Mama? Whats the good of getting up of a morning or washing or cooming ones hare – I shall not have my hare cut til your Mama comes back . . . I suppose she is at Jennover now – I remember Jennover when I was young, it is a staitly city on the sea.

Sometimes the tone of his letters might have made even the spirited little Daphne anxious:

I cannot think where your dear Mama is – she sed she was going to Itterly and perhaps Sisserley, but I have looked at all the maps of those countries and I cannot find her mentioned anywhere – surely if she was there look-ing so pretty they would be sure to put her on the map . . . I think she likes traverling and wont come back – I also think she has forgot all about us.

And as if to make poor Daphne worry all the more, he wrote:

Your Mama is probably now in the vicinity of Etna which is a burning mountain discharging volumes of fire over the nayberring country which terryfise the inhabitants.

Luckily, Daphne received more reassuring letters from her loving mother as well:

Your little letters made me laugh and cry – laugh because of the dear funny spelling and cry because I wanted you so dreadfully badly. I look at the little BJ drawing 'Daphne' I brought with me – I talk to you in my heart, and now I am doing it on paper. I kiss your eyes, I kiss your mouth, I lay my cheek against your cheek, I hold you as tight as tight – and finally you creep into bed beside me where I am writing and we have a

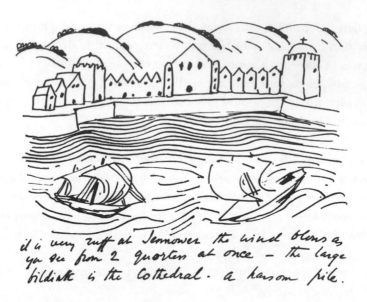

it is very ruff at Jennower the wind blows as you see from 2 quorters at once — the large bildiuk is the Cothedral. a hansom pile.

While May was in Italy Burne-Jones sent little Daphne this drawing of Genoa, using her childish spelling as usual.

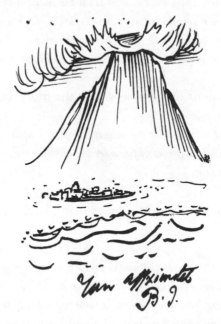

Your affectionate B. J.

Burne-Jones's image of Mount Etna sent to Daphne while May was there; one would think it might have made the little girl worry that her mother might be engulfed in flames.

*big chat all about everything. Write to dear BJ and ask him if he would
like you to come and see him one day soon at teatime. Write to him quite
by yourself. Never mind the spelling.*

Burne-Jones's interest in May's family was not limited to her
children; he also formed a real bond of friendship with her father,
Canon Melville. He called the old man 'my very specially dear friend
and contemporary', although the canon was twenty-one years older
than himself. Their friendship had blossomed after he went to
Worcester with May in the spring of 1893, to meet her father at his
house on College Green, next to the cathedral. The two men found
they had much to talk about, and Burne-Jones did what must rank as
one of his most lifelike pencil portraits, capturing perfectly the
distinguished features and expression of the old man. He later wrote
to May:

*Worcester was altogether sweet and I love it and my memory lingers about
it constantly – the little drawing room (though by the by I gave you trouble
there) full of ancient souvenirs – the little room you had lived in when
you were a girl – the piano – how it broke my heart to see. And in the
Malvern Hills to the west – my heart was so tender those days and my
hours content – I loved to see you with that dear father ministering to him
and lightening everything with your sweet brilliant passings to and fro –
the glidings in and out of doors that I love to watch.*

Even Georgie could not resist the charms of the learned old clergyman. In the summer of 1894, the year after Emma Melville had died
and at a time when May was away, it was Georgie who suggested they
should lend their house in Rottingdean to Canon Melville for a holiday, where he would be 'properly cared for and attended to' by their
caretakers, Mr and Mrs Mounter. She wrote to him:

*I hope you have some of the sunsets for which we value R'dean, when the
pink reflection in the East from the sun in the West turns the little church
into mother o' pearl. Also I should like you to know that the full moon is
larger than in London.*

When the canon arrived and found that Burne-Jones had had his own bedroom made up for him, he wrote gratefully to him in London, where he was working hard. A reply came swiftly, much regretting that he could not come down to be with his friend at Rottingdean even for a day:

> *But I think of you climbing the downs, and hope the weather will be warm and dry for you. So glad I am the little funny place amuses you with its white washed walls and scant furniture – indeed it is my idea of furnishing a little house – and I find it restful to go to.*

From their first meeting in Worcester, the two men wrote to each other about books, history, spirituality, education and other 'momentous matters', as Burne-Jones put it. But their communications were not all that serious. In one long letter written to Canon Melville in January 1895, Burne-Jones told the old man that he had decided not to go to the first night of *King Arthur*, a play at the Lyceum written by J. Comyns Carr, who managed the theatre. Burne-Jones had been persuaded in 'a weak moment' to make the designs for the production. Although Henry Irving was to play King Arthur and Ellen Terry was to be Guinevere, with music composed by Sir Arthur Sullivan, Burne-Jones told Canon Melville he had not really welcomed the commission because, he said, 'the Morte d'Arthur is a sacred land to me – I never wanted it to be dug up for public amusement'. Having been to some rehearsals, he realized too that it was a production he much disliked. So that first night he had stayed at home, as he explained to Canon Melville:

> *No, my dear, I didn't come before the scene between Irving and Ellen Terry and make a bow – I wasn't there – newspapers said I was but they always lie – I was at home, playing at dominoes – which is a game I like – and find that its mock anxieties, depressions and exultations chase out of my mind graver things . . . dominoes is very like life – a little skill helps if you can last out – but mostly luck has it . . . You have been ill, poor dear friend – and I wanted to send you thick woollen stuff to wear – underthings of fiery heat – but your daughter said no – that you were self willed and would have nothing of the kind . . . I only live because of hot*

things against me – every winter I have to add a new one, because I dare
not leave off in the summer anything I have worn – so I grow fatter and
fatter. You could tell my age as you can tell the age of a tree by its circles –
and as I am past the time when appearances matter, I mind little.

Burne-Jones's love of warmth, and of cats, which appear often in his drawings, is shown in one of the most engaging illustrations on a letter he wrote to Daphne; he portrays himself sitting in an armchair looking very content, almost completely covered by an enormous furry cat. He titled the drawing: 'How I like to be.'

Unhappiness and illness seemed to go hand in hand for May. By 1895, despite the comfort that her friendship with Burne-Jones gave her, her illnesses had become more frequent. Seeking strength and cures, and probably an escape from her marital situation, she went away more often. There were seaside hotels in Brighton and Kent, but for longer periods of recuperation she went to spa hotels in Switzerland. Sometimes Amy would go with her, and other friends would occasionally join her for a short spell. In May's letters I have found no clue as to exactly what her illness was, though I know she later developed arthritis and rheumatism, and often mentioned weakness and tiredness. In one letter to a friend she wrote:

I am a little better, but am still very weary, and heavy-hearted at times.
The doctor here says it will take many months to be stronger, and my
London man writes to me weekly with all sorts of directions. I am not to
be worried or tired for months!

In a letter to Daphne from one of her spa hotels, May described a dream she had. Although lilies of the valley were the flowers Burne-Jones associated with her, May also loved large scented lilies, and had some in her hotel bedroom.

I woke in the night to smell lilies and then dreamt I had lilies all round
me – I was quite dead – but I thought – how delicious – this is more than
I expected, one can smell quite well when one is dead.

As Daphne was very young, alone with her governess and separated from her mother, possibly worried about her, for weeks or months on end, this particular dream seems rather an inappropriate one for May to have told her. But then the idea of death is probably more frightening to us than it was to the Victorians.

One reason that May had such strange and vivid dreams could have been that she took chloral, a mixture of chlorine and alcohol, to help her sleep. Burne-Jones worried about this:

I was told you looked pale – I know that, and when shall you look strong again I wonder – Last night we talked at table about inventions in medicine and I told how Gabriel [Rossetti] had died half paralysed in brain because chloral had been given him for sleep – and everyone said it was perfectly safe – and now they find it kills, and maddens before it kills – and I thought of you – and down I would go on my knees to pray that you do not take that stuff anymore – will you promise me not to take it anymore – but you don't listen to me, or do anything I ask – do you?

Around this time, Burne-Jones seemed to be full of anxiety for May:

I wonder you don't dislike me these days and want not to see me – but it isn't your way and I think you are divinely made. And the kindest heart God could fashion was set beating the day you were born – No I have never known anyone like you – and if tears would only come I would sit on the ground and cry, so I think of you and all you are, and your ways and looks, and the pain you suffer. I will write every day, and chatter all the rubbish I can think of, and be very gentle to you for months to come – life is very hard for you, and your feet are bleeding with the thorns and stones – to see you suffer doth break my heart to bits.

But even if May needed time to try and cope with her own problems, Burne-Jones could not always disguise or contain his own longings and need for May's company and comfort:

... it isn't life without you – it is waiting and pausing and all glorious life in abeyance – if I were waiting on a platform for your train and had to wait six hours pacing up and down I should be happy – so I am happy

now, waiting for you – but with a restlessness, longing for the signal – I
feel as if I have had no life before this – nothing worth thinking of . . .
Meantime I miss your voice most dreadfully – the hundred things I want
to say – and ask you – I want to ask you about everything – want your
advice, your help, your sympathy over so much that fills the days and that
I cannot put into letters. Your letters have seemed far away from me . . . if
– if – if only – a mad hunger has possessed me all morning until I could
have cried with it – I could be so divinely happy today, could rise to any
height of splendid life today – if.

So far I had only been able to guess at the cause of May's unhappiness, which, from Burne-Jones's letters, was clearly becoming worse towards the late 1890s. It was surely connected with her marriage; I remembered how Henry Brooks had hinted, in only the fourth year of their marriage, as he had set off for months away in India, that he felt he had not always been kind to her. Then one day I was told that the Bodleian Library in Oxford held some letters from May Gaskell to Sir Alfred, later Lord Milner, the British statesman and colonial administrator. I knew him only as one of May's many acquaintances. Burne-Jones had commented, after meeting Milner at one of May's dinner parties: 'Milner is much after my heart – he has three faces, and all are good, and one is very solemn and fine.' Three faces was a good description, as Milner seems to have been an enigmatic character, reserved and hard to fathom. But he had a brilliant mind, and was supportive to his friends. So I drove to Oxford, not expecting much, yet hoping that anything written by May would reveal something about her puzzling troubles.

When you are unfamiliar with them, such institutions can be intimidating. But the Bodleian was a beautiful building to be in, and I found a smiling and helpful young man in the splendid manuscript room. Apart from my whispered queries it was absolutely quiet. A handful of young academics were bent intently over their books.

The letters from May to Milner were all on many reels of microfilm, and it was the first time I had used a microfilm reader. When I pushed the reels on and off a loud clanking noise shattered the studious hush. But as soon as I began reading the letters I forgot this, as I realized almost at once that I had made an unexpected breakthrough. I had to stop myself from shouting out in the silent room, 'Look what I've found!' A young German opposite me, to whom I had already apologized for the noise I was making with the machine, obviously sensed my bursting excitement and asked, 'What is it you are looking at?'

'I have found what no one else now alive knows,' I answered.

And as if to make the moment even more dramatic, the sky darkened outside and there was a deafening clap of thunder.

In one of the first letters to grip me, May's usually small, neat writing looked less controlled, as if she had dashed the letter off in haste. It was written in May 1896 from the Seabrook Hotel in Hythe, where May had gone to regain her strength after her usual spring visit to Beaumont:

> In some ways I am better, but the intolerable wretchedness of my
> Beaumont time has quite broken my spirit. I have been bullied into an
> acquiescing dazed creature. I didn't think anyone could be so cruel – and
> it is going on still here. You would not like to see a letter he wrote me
> three days ago – it isn't nice to read – and I cannot throw these things off
> now. Society, exercise, merriness – all things that took my mind away
> before are debarred from me by my health – and now I can't read or sleep
> much. The hopelessness and dreary suffering of the life in front of me
> completely breaks my heart.
>
> It is no exaggeration dear friend. Amy came to me after Beaumont and
> said I must get a separation as the life was killing me before her eyes, and
> no woman ought to be subject to it for a day. She would stick to me and
> go with me anywhere. But I can't you see dear – for her sake – my little
> Daphnes and Hals. No – it must be endured to the end – which will be
> sweet not bitter. I think he must be mad. I try to think so, for I know he is
> not bad.

I gasped aloud when I read this, and the German opposite looked at me and smiled understandingly. It was an astonishing thing for a Victorian daughter to urge her mother to seek a separation from her own father, and indicated the seriousness of the problem. The letter told me so much and yet prompted even more questions. It confirmed my guess that May's misery and sufferings were caused by her husband. I knew that there appeared to be a genetic trait among the Gaskell men of becoming silent, unresponsive and reclusive with age. But what exact form of cruelty did Henry Brooks exercise on his wife May, what kind of bullying? Could it have been linked to his dislike for his father, Henry Lomax, who had been so cruel to his own sweet wife Alice that it could be said that he drove her to an early death? Could Henry Brooks have inherited his father's alcoholism, and the terrible temper which drinking would only have exacerbated? I could find no hint of physical abuse, but withdrawn gloom and silence can amount to mental cruelty.

Later that year, May and her family were back at Beaumont for their customary late-summer, early-autumn visit for the shooting. It was particularly warm for the time of year; an Indian summer. May's health, after long periods abroad, was much improved. She wrote to Lord Milner:

> *It is very nice here – very very domestic – the children tumble in and out all day, Hal, Daphne and the dogs, but alas! alas! I fail to please him, probably never again shall I be anything but an irritation . . . Amy is here – she is most helpful to me. I wish you could see her in the sun, her hair all down and a sun bonnet perched on the top.*

Alfred Milner was obviously not just a close social acquaintance of May's, but someone to whom, like Burne-Jones, she could confide her secrets. Unlike Burne-Jones, he had not burnt her letters. And she was still writing to him long after Burne-Jones was dead, up to and after her daughter Amy's tragic and mysterious death. Despite Milner's brilliance and prominence, he was sympathetic and approachable, and women trusted his judgement. Another friend of May's, the Liberal politician Herbert Asquith, described Milner as 'a man of great personal charm'. He was a bachelor, and appeared to keep himself at a certain distance. He never revealed much about his personal feelings, but he liked to have close women friends who, like May, felt that their confessions were safe with him.

For two days in the Bodleian Library I read through scores of May's letters to Lord Milner. They were emotionally but evocatively written, discussing literature and politics, as well as her private life and mutual friends. It appears that Milner used to send May books:

> *The books came safely, and I am very much enjoying them. Also, having*
> *hesitated on the brink of 'The Growth of English Policy', and admired*
> *you for being well on in the first volume, I have found to my surprise how*
> *delightful and easy it is to read. What a gift is style! You have it too, and*
> *gild your pills in an equally fascinating way.*

During the summer of 1895, when May was recuperating from one of her weak spells at a spa in Switzerland, she told Milner she was reading some French novels:

> *They make me wish that the question of 'sex' didn't exist . . . Bah! I wish*
> *they knew how little 'la question du sexe' interfered with most lives. I*
> *think* most, *don't you?*

I read on voraciously in the quiet library. Through the tall windows of the manuscript room the skies remained dramatically black and stormy. In my first attempt at detective work into a long-forgotten past I could not believe my luck; the letters, which continued well beyond both Burne-Jones's and Amy's deaths, gave me vital glimpses into May's life, and her character. I was discovering clues that I'd never thought I would find. But at the same time, mysteries deepened.

As I walked back to my car at the end of the second day the rain had stopped, and sharp sunlight flooded through the cleared air onto the dampened walls of the ancient, honey-coloured buildings. Still half in another world, I almost imagined I saw the tall figure of David Melville with his little Emma Hill, walking closely together down the street in front of me during their courting days in Oxford.

When I went back to the Burne-Jones letters, it became clear to me that although Burne-Jones had frequently sounded euphoric with happiness during the first three years of his friendship with May, by 1895, faced with her continual ill health and troubles, he was increasingly worried, as much about himself as about her:

I want one thing only – for you to be getting strong – it kills me to see you ill – it destroys my life, breaks my heart – makes ashes of the world – you must live more carefully if you want to keep me alive, to play with – I know you would soon find another, nicer friend but never one to care more – never.

Two years later, in 1897, when May was yet again spending unhappy days with Captain Gaskell up at Beaumont, Burne-Jones wrote to Frances Horner, who must also have known of May's difficulties. Now he sounded almost exasperated:

. . . a desolate sad letter this morning from May who is ill and bullied . . . the perpetual story of misery makes the gentlest heaven numb out of self defence.

Burne-Jones had always wanted to be May's knight in shining armour, but as May's troubles worsened, he began to see that he could not transform her life in the way he had initially promised he would. He appeared to counsel her to avoid outright confrontations with her husband. After receiving what must have been an anguished letter from May, Burne-Jones wrote:

I can't bear you to have to go through scenes, or have any heavy weight like that – and if one difficulty, this one, were over, are you sure another should never be? Should you be strong against fate and the arrows of it ever after. Then it might be worthwhile to make a huge effort – but if one day afterwards suddenly you were in the coils of fresh trouble it wouldn't be worth having had this fight would it? Whatever befalls you are not to give in, nor be made ill – you look as if a little more would just kill you straight away – Snatch at anything that brings reprieve, that lightens the hour, and beguiles with some change, however trifling – and don't think too long, or take solitary half mad walks.

At the same time Burne-Jones himself sounded insecure, as if he really felt the 'holy' friendship, which he had always said was for life, might be coming to an end because May could not cope with it as well as her health problems and her troubles at home. He was also increasingly aware that his own life might not last many more years:

> *Should you miss me very much now? You haven't said it for a long time –*
> *you have been too ill to think of that or anything – but presently I shall*
> *want to know if you would miss me much – I hope you will never forget*
> *me – what can I do that you will always remember me? And how can I*
> *rest in your heart always – I want to look at you so dreadfully – I want to*
> *see your face.*

Between 1895 and 1896, with May abroad for long periods, Burne-Jones saw her much less than before. Did the melancholy that surfaced increasingly in his letters change May's feelings for him, I wondered, or could she still feel comforted by his tenderness? Often, he was plagued by nightmares:

> *. . . the night nearly over, but sleep difficult because of the storm, how it*
> *blows still – nightmares all night and dreadful ones. What appalling*
> *things they can be – as real as life itself, with an added horror and terror,*
> *not of this life even at its worst, but of the abyss and space and chaos – a*
> *worse one I had last night than ever man had.*
> *   No climbing with you into serene heights, but a lonely descent into*
> *unfathomable pits, black shiny shafts and tunnels, and gloomy with a*
> *mirror so that I could see my face, scared and lost for hours and hours it*
> *seemed – wish dawn would come.*

May returned to London, where a much more robust letter arrived from Fulham. Burne-Jones had been to the theatre with Henry James:

> *The play last night was such execrable folly that I had to behave badly, so did*
> *Henry James, quite badly – and people in front turned ferociously upon us –*
> *and a man glared at me – and I returned the glare with that demon look that*
> *I know I have when I want a row . . . And all was silly, ugly, a cursed folly,*
> *and went on in just the very place where it ought to go on – underneath and*
> *far below that main drain of Piccadilly in a hole called the Criterion – where*
> *we went and sat for hours, as if we had been condemned for a crime to*
> *descend into it . . . We won't go to the Criterion will we?*

In another letter he fantasized about a very different kind of outing with May:

> Let us have a long drive some evening to Hampton Court and back – starting from town at six – dining at Hampton Court at nine – leaving at eleven – getting back at two or three – shall we? I should like postilions and relays of horses!

But unresolved relationships have to change, and so it was with Burne-Jones and May. He seemed finally to realize the reality of this friendship, though he was not above trying to make May feel guilty about it:

> Sometimes of late I look at myself in a glass – and then I understand some things that have puzzled me – I couldn't love him – no – I couldn't – I should keep him always at work and out of sight and wish him well in a benevolent sort of way . . . How good you have been to me – in all the darkest hours you kept a look of welcome for me always – you pretended I helped you . . . No – I did you very little good – but you have filled my life . . . this is a debt I owe to happy Fortune, this that I am paying now – for I had you so much, saw you so often, grew bright and happy in your delicious company so many times – and I knew the empty days would come – they are just what I knew they would be – a hunger of heart – hunger hunger – pacified by little sops of letters – but hunger always – hollow gnawing at the heart . . . I should be a cur to grumble – and you are wonderfully good to me because it is so difficult – always your E.

Burne-Jones was missing another friend too. By the middle of 1896 his Sunday mornings with William Morris had to be called to a halt. He wrote to May:

> Yes – isn't it sad about the Sundays. Never any more – never even once again – I know now, and sad will be my comings and goings.

Morris, who had had diabetes for years, was growing weaker and weaker. He was now confined at his London home, Kelmscott House, on the Upper Mall at Hammersmith, slowly dying. Burne-Jones had often told May about the conversations that he and his old friend used to have as they worked together, and about Morris's funniness, his rages and outrages, his wise and wild sayings, and his wonderful stories, which never sounded as good when told by someone else. Now Burne-Jones longed for the sort of Sunday they used to have together, as he had described to May:

> *Morris walked about all morning, up and down the room shaking and disturbing me terribly . . . in a great and mighty rage he was because they were cutting down a hornbeam wood in Epping Forest – 'The biggest hornbeam wood in Europe – the fools.'*

May must have commented that she felt a bit left out of his thoughts on these occasions, so devoted was Burne-Jones to his old friend. But he was quick to reassure her:

> *No you don't lose a bit of me on the Sunday morning – not one moment – if ever Morris says some fine thing, and says it with his Titanic simplicity, I say to myself 'How I wish she had heard that, but how impossible to convey it in any other words or manner than his' – indeed when the tale is done no image of him at all can ever be made – to repeat only word for word his conversation would carry no impression of it – the moment of saying, the murmur, the march up and down the room that accompanies it, the rough gesture, the simplicity and faith of it – all incommunicable. And he must get out without a due record – that is certain . . . And when he dies it will be like the going out of the sun.*

By the end of September 1896, Morris's sun was finally setting at Kelmscott House. Georgie and Burne-Jones took turns to go and see him every day. On 2 October Burne-Jones wrote to May at Beaumont:

> *It is a dark day, almost a fog, and cold, but go I must to Kelmscott House. He is much weaker and a change for the worst has set in, haemorrhage and a deadly look about his dear face. If I don't write, it means I can't write, can't write about other things, and can't write about that. Georgie was there all morning, and I go now. I doubt if he knew me when I went last. Take care of your dear self, and send me good news.*

May obediently, but somewhat apologetically, sent him gossip about some neighbours at Beaumont, and Burne-Jones swiftly replied:

Oh no, I liked to hear of the Smiths and the sons and daughters, and anything else you write – life has to go on just the same – at least externally – so write anything, and all will be welcome. The loss is so irreparable and immense that there is only silence for it. I wish the sun would shine a little – they are such grey days.

But then at this point his letter finishes abruptly and poignantly with:

– one o' clock, a telegram just come and all is over.

The large and sorrowing funeral took place two days later at the Morris family home, the other Kelmscott – Kelmscott Manor in Oxfordshire; also, like the London Kelmscott, beside the river Thames. Burne-Jones described the welcome simplicity of it to May:

The burial was as sweet and touching as Leighton's and Millais' were foolish – and the little wagon with its floor of moss and willow branches broke ones heart it was so beautiful, and of course there were no Kings there – the King was being buried, and there was no other left.

Canon Melville wrote at once to commiserate with Burne-Jones, who thanked him for sending him such a 'comforting and touching letter', but said that at the moment he was simply 'stunned and in a way stupefied'. May wrote to her father:

It is hard to realise the lonely suffering of dear BJ. There is a Holy of Holies in the heart of his art where no one went but Morris. It must have been a wonderful thing to listen to the talk of those two great ones every Sunday morning. Nothing but absence ever interfered with the Sunday. Morris stumped in from Hammersmith to an 8.30 breakfast, and afterwards they went to BJ's studio and drew, and Morris walked up and down discussing, arguing, pouring out his huge stories of knowledge in a mighty flow of eloquence. I once went with Amy to see Morris with Burne-Jones – he was quite gentle and kind – showed me his great treasure of illuminated books, and then sat down and talked with us – at one moment using the characters in Dickens as friends, perplexing me with his intimate knowledge of the most obscure, and twinkling with delight. Then suddenly teasing Burne-Jones, who purred under it and led him on with the delight of a parent showing off a child. Later came most wonderful stories of Norse tales – and told with such a rushing mighty power of words and humour that left one breathless.

Burne-Jones's broken heart was also a sick heart. Previously he had said little to May about it, except to complain often that he didn't feel well. Earlier in their friendship, when he had been to the doctor, he told May that he had been reassured that there was nothing wrong with his heart. Later, when his irregular heartbeat was still troubling him, the doctor told him again it was nothing to be worried about:

Promised I did to tell what the Dr said. And it's alright about the heart throbbings – they may hang themselves about as much as they like – the heart is alright, only some mechanical difficulty that will go when more strength comes – like nothing, and not worth thinking of. And may come again and again, and probably will – and will not matter. So that affair is settled – I had some little fear there might be mischief – why fear? It's an easy death and a desirable one – but I love my life – and would do all I can to prolong it.

However, the grief and loneliness he suffered after Morris's illness and death can only have affected his own health. He wrote to May:

Oh if I could have got your love how wonderful it all would have been – but it isn't given to any mortal to have so much – the crown of his Kingdom, and the Queen of his heart together – besides the shadow is near – the man with the scythe – it's too late to matter – but it is nice to love you – ah there lies the better part and there I can win – and a fresh morning hope comes blowing over my world as I think of that – at least I can love her, and with all my life and soul, with tired heart, sick heart, and hands eager to hold her, I love her – but if the scythe man came now – that mower of lives – should I mind? No by heaven, not one bit.

CHAPTER SIX

THE MAN WITH THE SCYTHE

AMY GASKELL WAS IN LOVE. SHE HAD FALLEN FOR A YOUNG SOLDIER, Lionel Bonham, a lieutenant in the Grenadier Guards. He was the eldest son of Sir George Bonham, a diplomat, who, though he was not considered truly rich, owned a substantial house and estate, Knowle Park, near Cranleigh in Surrey, which Lionel would eventually inherit. Lionel had fresh-faced good looks and the perfect figure for a guardsman: tall, slim and erect. He looked immaculate in his uniform. When I showed a photograph of Lionel in his casual clothes – a straw boater and flannel trousers – to the oldest living member of his family, Sir Anthony Bonham, he said, 'How debonair,' which was exactly the right description. His wavy fair hair, blue eyes and rosy skin were unmistakably English, in contrast to Amy's more Irish looks, with her thick dark hair, navy-blue eyes and ivory skin. There is hardly a photograph of Lionel without a cigar between his rather full lips. But he was not a Philistine; he was a sensitive man who loved reading, and May was later to remark that he wrote some of the best letters of anyone she knew, which, considering her other correspondents, and her own talent for writing, was high praise indeed. Sadly, I can find no trace of Lionel's letters, and I suspect May could have destroyed them later in her grief for Amy.

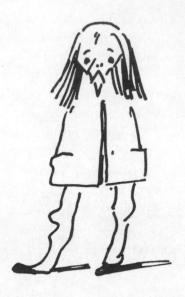

Burne-Jones liked to present a forlorn image of himself and told May that his love for her was celestial, but at the same time sent her drawings such as this one of her luxuriating in a bubble bath, which suggests that his thoughts about her were not always ethereal.

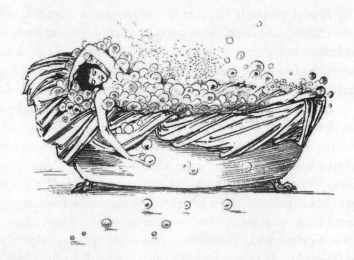

May's friend Sir Alfred Milner was far away in South Africa. He had been appointed British High Commissioner in 1897. Fervently committed to imperialism, Milner worked hard in Cape Town, but he was lonely. May wrote him long letters, full of social and political gossip. He answered them whenever he could find the time. One of her letters started: 'My heart quite jumped for joy when I saw "Government House, Cape Town" on the envelope, dear busy man, how kind of you to write.' She talked of Amy and Lionel and their 'felicity', but intimated that Lionel's parents Sir George and Lady Bonham were not as pleased as the Gaskell family about the proposed engagement. She told Milner that they had finally 'given in', but that 'Lady B swallows it like a pill and can hardly bear to see her Lionel absorbed in another woman'. May said that she herself loved watching the young couple, 'both in that blissful state of the world being just you and me'.

May went on to tell Milner that: 'my dear BJ has lost heart over a huge picture of King Arthur's sleep'. This was the great work, and ultimately the most significant to Burne-Jones himself, of King Arthur's last sleep on his deathbed at Avalon, surrounded by his mourning queens. Burne-Jones had started the painting years before, in 1881, just before his friend and mentor Dante Gabriel Rossetti died tragically of chloral addiction. The vast canvas had been in Burne-Jones's studio for many years, and he was determined not only to finish the painting before his own death, but to make it worthy of the king he had idolized since his student days. Yet now he felt a kind of block, and was uncertain how to continue. His assistant Rooke noted daily changes of design and colour, and Burne-Jones told him that people who saw the work did not seem to like it. He consulted May about it, even changing some rocks to flowers on her advice, though he felt there were many things still wrong with it. So immersed did Burne-Jones become in the problematic world of this particular picture that he began sleeping in the same position as the dead king, turned to one side and slightly raised on his pillows.

But there were still happy moments between May and Burne-Jones. May described later how at the South Kensington museum, now the V&A, they had admired an embroidered German quilt. Dated 1580, it was from a period Burne-Jones loved. The quilt represented the five senses – Tactus, Vissus, Auditus, Gustus and Olfactus – shown in female form. May wanted to reproduce this lovely work herself, so Burne-Jones gave her two little notebooks. 'He used to go to the museum with me in the evenings,' May wrote, 'and draw the designs for me whilst I copied the very intricate stitches to work.'

These outings were precious to May. In one letter to Cape Town, May describes how:

> One very delicious day in London I spent buying a new dress (very pretty) and wandering from one lovely thing to another with BJ in South Kensington. It is one of the most instructive and heavenly things I know to go round with a man who sees Beauty – clearly and simply Beauty. He is much better under the care of a new doctor. His nephew Rudyard Kipling has taken a house near him at Rottingdean which brings him great pleasure.

Burne-Jones was very fond of Rudyard, who was the son of Georgie's sister Alice. Rudyard was now thirty-one years old, and had quickly achieved fame as a writer, poet and journalist. After living for many years in India and America, working prolifically, he was now back in England with his wife and young family, and had chosen to live in Rottingdean mainly in order to be able to see his uncle frequently.

May promised Milner that she would send him a photograph of a painting Burne-Jones had on show at the New Gallery. This could possibly have been 'The Dream of Launcelot at the Chapel of the San Graal', which shows an ethereally beautiful angel standing in the doorway looking down on the sleeping Sir Launcelot on the ground outside. May said she found the painting exquisite, and felt that it was the sort of thing Milner would like to be reminded of:

> . . . you want a little romance out there. I think the Cape sounds material, and hard heeled and strong hearted . . . But it will never die in you, the love of lovely things and simple things is part of your being . . . Poor dear – the ceremonials and publicity of life must try you.

Milner told her that he often longed to be back in London, at one of May's dinner parties, and that Cape Town was 'socially quite detestable'.

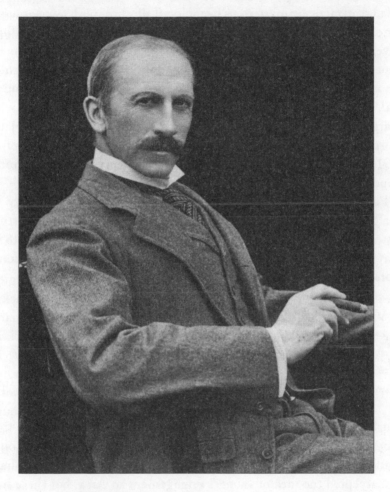

May's supportive confidant, Sir Alfred Milner

Both in South Africa and in England, Alfred Milner was much in demand socially, especially among the Souls. He was a clever, powerful and attractively mysterious bachelor. Tall, slim, with a penetrating gaze, he was now in his mid-forties, the same age as May, and had never been married. However, he enjoyed the company of women, kept a secret mistress in London, and had several close female friends, among them the Marchioness of Londonderry, Lady Desborough and, of course, May Gaskell. He was known to have been in love with Margot Tennant, an important member of the Souls who had later married Herbert Asquith; Milner had proposed to her in Egypt in 1891, but had been rejected. Now his work seemed to be the most important thing in his life.

For May, as Burne-Jones himself became increasingly dogged by ill health and melancholy, Milner must have seemed an uplifting distraction as well as a support. Writing to him in Cape Town in 1897, May implied that her husband's hurtful moods had only become worse:

> My life grinds on, it sadly wants the oil of kindliness in its wheels. It sometimes seems too hard to be grinding along trying to recover strength under the gloomiest of tempers, and for days not spoken to. Sometimes I think life will beat me yet. But if I am allowed peace, physically things are better.

Much of May's news now revolved around Amy's romance. The first time Lionel Bonham appears in one of Amy's photographs is on a family trip to Brittany at the end of April 1897. By then Lady Bonham had accepted the idea of Lionel's engagement to Amy, but there had been no official announcement and there was to be no indication for another year of when they would be married. In the autumn, May wrote to Milner:

> Amy wears herself to fiddlestrings over her Love. Lady B is an ass for a whim to insist on a long engagement and allow Amy's superb health and strength to be impaired.

Amy's Brittany photographs show a late-nineteenth-century

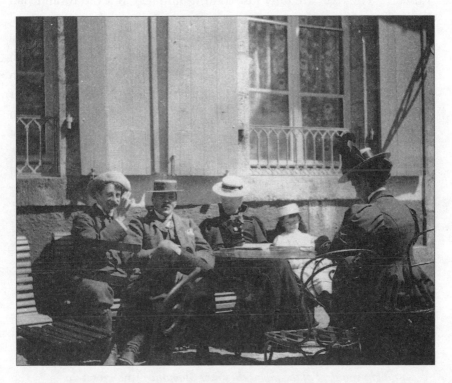

Holiday in Roscoff, Brittany, April 1897. Left to right: Hal, Amy's fiancé Lionel Bonham, May, with a veil over her face, little Daphne and her governess Miss Neurotsos

Roscoff where all the locals wear clogs, with the women and children clad in white cotton caps and aprons. Under a photograph of a group of barely thirty children, Amy has written: 'Most of the children of Roscoff'. The trees are only just coming into leaf, but the sunlight is brilliant, and all looks peaceful and relaxed. In one of several group photographs, May sits on a bench outside the Hotel des Bains de Mer, wearing a straw hat and a veil over her face. To protect herself further from the sun she also holds a black umbrella. Grouped around her are Hal, mischievously laughing, little Daphne in her pinafore, Miss Neurotsos, the governess, Boyne, the nurse, and Lionel, the future son-in-law, all wearing straw boaters. Lionel smokes a cigar contentedly. 'Digesting Dejeuner,' Amy has written underneath this photograph.

While they were away, Burne-Jones continued, as ever, to write to May, and, as so often before, sounded somewhat abandoned:

> . . . but I'm sure Brittany is sad – like Wales and looks dissenting – looks, but is not . . . The apple blossom is out in the garden and all the end of the studio looks finely white. It comes as a fresh surprise to me every year, first that I am here to see it, and then that there should be blossom at all in this stuffy London.

A few days later he wrote:

> Last night you slept at the inn of the great Monarque [the Hotel du Grande Monarque in Chartres] – so old world it sounds . . . I am sure that after you have seen these solemn kings and queens you will never again like nasty tawdry pictures and Renaissance shallowness will you? Surely you will experience conversion, which I was never strong enough to effect. And tonight you sleep by the sea, and look towards the land of Lyonesse.

May was cheered by the trip to France with her children, by the warmth of the sun, which she always referred to as curative, and by watching Amy and Lionel's happiness. On her return to England she went down to stay at Mells in Somerset, where Frances Horner lived with her husband John and their children. The beautiful house and estate were the 'plum' given to the original Jack Horner for services rendered during the dissolution of the monasteries, and features still in the children's nursery rhyme. May wrote to Alfred Milner:

I rushed off to Mells where Frances Horner and I talked the days and nights through. We laughed a lot, and we went to a Ladies' Liberal Association where she made a first rate speech, and because I giggled behind her she got up and said 'My kind friend Mrs Gaskell will now sing to you.' Mean wasn't it, but I did, and one woman said with tears streaming down her face that she had not been so happy for years. Sometimes now I can sing again, only sometimes.

It was fine and warm in the middle of June 1897, the sixtieth year of Queen Victoria's prodigious reign. Londoners were preparing themselves for their queen's Diamond Jubilee celebrations. As the *Illustrated London News* put it, it would be a celebration 'not only of the most glorious reign, but also the growth of the greatest Empire that the world has ever known'. On 21 June, the day before the triumphant procession was to pass through London to a service of thanksgiving at St Paul's Cathedral, the Queen, now eighty-eight years old, travelled from Windsor to London by the royal train. She arrived at Paddington in the afternoon, and was taken to Buckingham Palace to prepare herself for the rigours of the following day.

That afternoon, from the top windows of their house at Marble Arch, the Gaskell family could see the crowds building up all along the route she would take down the Edgware Road from Paddington, through Hyde Park towards Grosvenor Lodge and Hyde Park Corner, on her way to the palace. Amy, happy with Lionel at her side, had her large Kodak camera ready to record the events of both days. Because of her pictures I am able to see the historic event through her eyes. For these photographs of people, unlike the static group portraits of the period, are refreshingly alive. People are running excitedly along the streets in order to find a good viewpoint, the women picking up their long skirts, almost all wearing straw boaters in the bright sunny weather. Cumberland Lodge, the building to one side of Marble Arch which was dismantled in 1908, when the present traffic island of Marble Arch was formed, is covered with spectators on both levels of its roof.

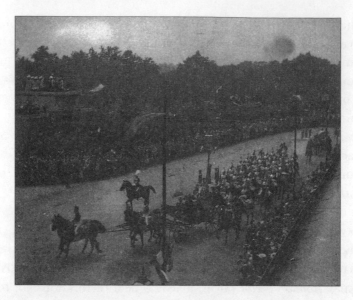

From the top windows of the Gaskells' house at Marble Arch, Amy took this photograph of Queen Victoria in her carriage on the eve of her Diamond Jubilee.

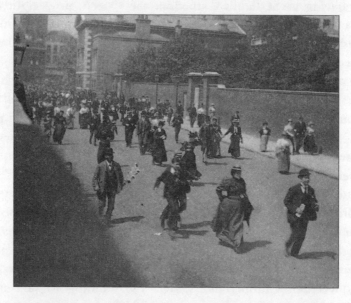

The next day Amy photographed the crowd running through Marlborough Gate to catch a glimpse of the Jubilee procession.

The street in front of 3 Marble Arch was crammed full of horses and carriages, hansom cabs, horse-drawn double-decker omnibuses and milling pedestrians, but somehow they were cleared in time for the imminent arrival of the Queen's procession. Her Majesty's delicate little open carriage was drawn by four dark horses, and followed by a large retinue of mounted lifeguards. Through a magnifying glass I can make out the small, round figure of the queen empress, dressed all in black, under a black umbrella to shield her from the bright force of the sun. After the Queen had passed, the crowds surged forward again until they completely covered the whole area from the Gaskells' house right down through the park, as far as Amy's camera could see from a top window. Jubilee Day had almost begun.

The next morning started cloudy, but before long the sun shone once more, surprising no one because, the *Illustrated London News* reported, it had 'shone always before on occasions devoted to Royal progresses in which the Queen has taken part'. Amy, dressed in summery white cotton, clutched her camera. Lionel Bonham looked immaculate in his uniform of Lieutenant of the Grenadier Guards: deep-blue trousers, rich scarlet jacket and silk sash. At his side he carried a long sword in a glittering sheath. The Grenadier Guards, who had recently been part of a Royal Review, were not to be part of the Jubilee procession through London, but they were to line the route. Amy and Lionel made their way through the thronged streets to St James's Street, which was beautifully festooned with criss-crossing ribbons of fresh flowers and declared by the *Illustrated London News* to be ' far and away the most profusely and tastefully adorned street in all London'. In Pall Mall, above the heads of the dense crowd, there were faces crammed together at every window of the gentlemen's clubs on either side. The entire processional route was described as 'decorated out of all recognition'.

London's 'Pageant of Imperialism' must have been an astonishing sight. From all corners of the Queen's empire massed military forces in their varied and splendid uniforms, emperors and empresses, kings and queens, princes and princesses, dukes and duchesses, lords and ladies, ambassadors, politicians; all were there. They were on horseback, on foot, and in glittering carriages, accompanied by brass bands, drums, pipes, and an awe-inspiring train of weaponry. *The Times* remarked that the impression they conjured up was of a sunlit river of scarlet and gold.

When the simple open landau of the Queen herself passed, drawn by eight cream-coloured horses with trappings of gold and bright ribbons, the cheers of the onlookers reached fever pitch. 'God Bless Your Majesty!' they shouted adoringly, and the little queen was reported to have had tears in her eyes as she repeated over and over again: 'How kind they are to me, how kind they are.'

When the procession had passed, Amy and Lionel were able to relax together away from the crowds in the peaceful gardens of St James's Palace, where May's old friend, Valda, Baroness Gleichen, a relation of the Royal Family, had an apartment. The engaged couple photographed each other in different poses. In one picture Lionel sits back on a chair, smoking a cigar, looking at Amy with a quizzical smile. 'Lionel sitting at ease,' wrote Amy under the photograph in her album.

The pictures give the impression that these were happy days for Amy and Lionel. They went on several outings that summer: punting on the Thames at Henley on a Sunday; swimming together in the sea at Bognor; enjoying themselves on the lawns of country houses with friends, or with Lionel's three curly-haired sisters, Lily, Edith and Evelyn. Together they visited Canon Melville in Worcester, and Amy's uncle Frank Gaskell at Cambus O'May in Scotland. They appear carefree, even though Lady Bonham was insisting that they should wait at least another year before getting married.

To Burne-Jones, who never had a good word to say about marriage, and who had reacted to his daughter Margaret's marriage as if it was a tragic personal loss, the idea that May was also to 'lose' her darling Amy was appalling. He wrote to May's son Hal, now aged eighteen, telling him that although his mother was 'making the very best of things ... you and your father and Daphne – and in my humble capacity I also – must spoil her to make up for this time. We must buy her things – make pretty plans for her, give her treats, bonnets, ribands, books, drawings, do all she bids us without a murmur – to make some atonement for this horrid time.'

He also wrote to Canon Melville, reminiscing nostalgically about the happy times he had had with his daughter Margaret before she was married, and adding resentfully, 'but they marry, these daughters, they marry and leave us'.

The death of Morris and an increasing preoccupation with his own mortality seemed to act as a watershed in regard to Burne-Jones's feelings for May. His love now was as deep as before, but calmer, less frantic. It was as if he knew that he had little time left, and his letters were now often at their most poignant:

> *I have thought of you always as a girl in a field – I have told you that – in a white frock, in a green field, where you once told me in one of your letters the garden of your life had been trampled on, and its flowers crushed. I knew it, and vowed I would build such a wall round the garden that no trampling should ever be again, and once I thought my task was failed and could never be, and now I know the wall is rising fast – such a warden of it I will be – if I can – if I live . . . And so here tonight I lie, and think over my strange history – the sorrows – the drifting – the chagrins – the deep waters – and I lie in a meadow tonight with my head in your hands, safe and content.*

This moving letter seems to encapsulate Burne-Jones's vision of the life he longed for. Behind a high wall he imagined an enchanted world of perfect beauty, of which he would be the guardian, the protector of the woman, or women, he worshipped and adored. What appears to us as a fantasy, shown in his paintings, was to him reality. His personal life was idealized in his work, and the women he loved during his life can be identified in his paintings. May is recognizable in his illustrations for the Kelmscott Press edition of the Canterbury Tales, and as one of the women in his painting 'The Wedding of Psyche', both of which he was working on during the time he knew her. His portrayal of Merlin, the wizard, was clearly based on himself, and now, not expecting that he would live many years more, he identified with King Arthur in his monumental painting of the king's last sleep at Avalon, started fifteen years before, which he was determined to finish in the time he had left.

Like King Arthur, Burne-Jones wanted beauty around him when it was his turn to die. He wrote to May:

I do love you with my whole soul and life – I want your face to be the last sight my eyes will look upon – nay it doesn't matter so much for that – the thought of you will be my last waking thought.

He could not stop thinking about the end of his life, but had to apologize to May:

Oh innermost soul of my very soul, did it hurt you that I spoke of death – I fear it less than ever now, for I have lived to know and taste what perfect love is – but if it hurts you I will never speak of it again – I also never so much longed to live.

For months, battling with fatigue and illness, Burne-Jones worked obsessively on his epic painting 'The Sleep of Arthur in Avalon'. He wrote to May:

How tired one can be and yet still go about . . . to think that I have but to will it, and say it, and I could today end my vexatious life, and go into some other place and work placidly until death comes – and yet I can't – that would be the life for me, not to move among living creatures but live in the world I could make . . . we are all sacrificed all of us – we are all wasted – greatest and least alike – none can live as he would.

But in another letter he commented:

Death won't come when it is wanted – likes to wait until we are happy – and did you ask your papa why it is so hard to see the new moon with the old moon in her arms – and shall I make you a silver picture of it one day – shall I?

In her old age, May would start copying down, in a small blank-paged commonplace book, her favourite extracts from the hundreds of letters she had received from Burne-Jones. It was as if she wanted something that she could keep by her bedside and dip into at any time. The book she used was special to her too; it had been a present from her favourite daughter, her long-lost Amy. On the front page Amy, aged fifteen, had inscribed in her round young handwriting:

'H M Gaskell from her best beloved daughter. Christmas 1889.' Apart from copying out the letters, May had added the odd little note or observation of her own. From one of these notes I learnt that in February 1898, May had taken Amy on an Italian tour because of 'a hitch' in her daughter's engagement to Lionel Bonham. The engagement had still not been officially announced. I wondered what this hitch could have been. Was there indecision on either Amy or Lionel's part? Could Amy have found out something about Lionel? Was there the slightest possibility that Amy had become pregnant? Amy was unwell, her mother said, and anxious. It may have simply been that Lionel's mother, Lady Bonham, was being difficult again. Whatever the case, May clearly thought that taking Amy away for two months might help solve the problem.

Before their departure, Burne-Jones, who had not been to Italy for over twenty years, reminisced about his travels through France to Italy in the company of friends, who had included Ruskin and William Morris. He had often been ill but was continually enchanted. He urged May to take Amy to a church they might not be told of at Genoa:

> Outside Genoa towards the east is an ancient church that I used to love above anything else in Genoa. I think it is called St Ambrogio – I am not sure – guide books are such fools and know nothing. They tell one of bad pictures amply enough, but of God inventing architecture they say nothing. See it if you can, I think it was called St Ambrogio, it is very ancient and beautiful, and touching, how I loved it . . . it must have been near the sea wall for suddenly I came out into a little cloister and saw the blue sea just below me.

Far less impressed by the house of Christopher Columbus, who was born in Genoa, Burne-Jones continued jokingly:

> I don't care for Columbus for he discovered America, and I hate discoveries and he made a mess with an egg, and I hate that particularly.

Shortly before her departure in February 1898, May visited Burne-Jones, who was not well, at the Grange. He handed her a letter he had written to her the night before, and on which she noted years later: 'He knew then, but I did not, that he was doomed with heart disease.' When Burne-Jones wrote this letter on a foggy Sunday morning he must have seriously doubted that he would still be alive when May returned from Italy two months later:

Supposing such a thing were to be that we should never meet again – you would have courage wouldn't you? The wonder is, in my life that is always perilous – that we have had six years of the most beautiful friendship that ever was. Six long years of it without a flaw, and without a thing to repent of – why do I write this? My mind is so full of it I must rest from the thought of it – I dare say God will lead you back in safety to us – and keep me alive until you come back – but if it were not so take courage – and remember how beautiful you made my last years. You shall laugh at all this if you like, and put it all down to the melancholy of unwellness. But it isn't all that – it comes from something in my mind that never leaves me.

If you are at all ill travel back if you can at once – in the agitation of misery of any alarm I could never reach you I know, I should break down somewhere. If I should be so very ill that the Doctor thought there was any immediate danger I would telegraph to you. If we missed that woeful goodbye it wouldn't matter – say it wouldn't. It would be part of the duty we have set ourselves to do – you are going away because you feel it is your duty – and I think you right – even you can hardly know the price I pay for it. If it were not that it would so hurt Georgie I would go with you – all that you know. I wonder if you can come tomorrow. Goodbyes half kill me but I want to give you this. I looked across the table at Amy and wondered if she would ever know, or if trouble would ever make her understand this heartbreak I feel these days – whilst you are by I keep up, for your wonderful nature supports me – and when that wonderful strength is removed from me I sink into an abyss – in knowing you I have known the best in this life – I have had it – none can take it from me now, I see you are right to go – but there is some injustice somewhere. Tell me always the truth – most truthful of women – don't say you are well if you are ill, and happy if you are not happy. Tell me the truth always – and now I can write no more for tears stop me, and I shall make you unhappy. Such a nimbus of Love all round you will travel with you as not

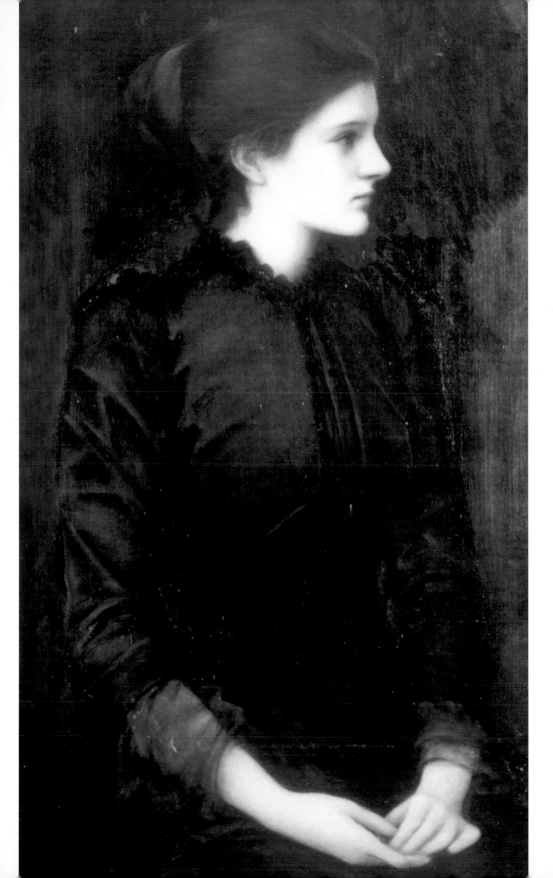

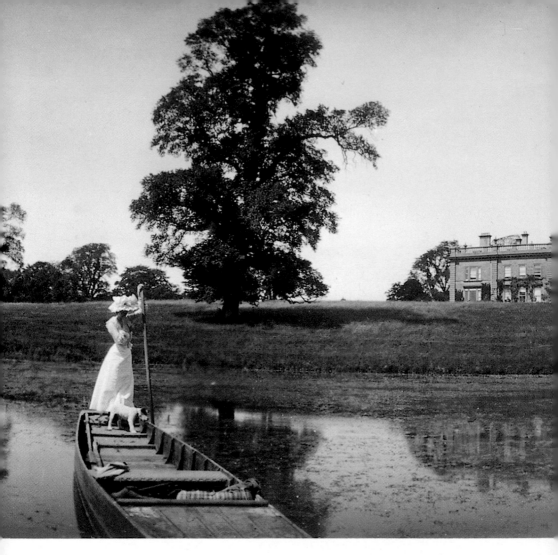

Above: The lake at Kiddington Hall, with the house in the background; one of many pictures taken with Amy's revolutionary Kodak 'Panoram' camera. For this one she must have posed in the punt while someone else pressed the shutter.

Previous page: *Portrait of Amy Gaskell*. As a special present for May Gaskell, Burne-Jones painted this haunting portrait of her favourite daughter Amy, aged nineteen. Everyone who sees the painting today is captivated by it, as people seem to have been by Amy herself in the 1890s.

Right: Amy and one of the Kiddington dogs in a punt on the lake. Although Burne-Jones chose, inexplicably, to dress Amy in black in his portrait, photographs invariably show her all in white.

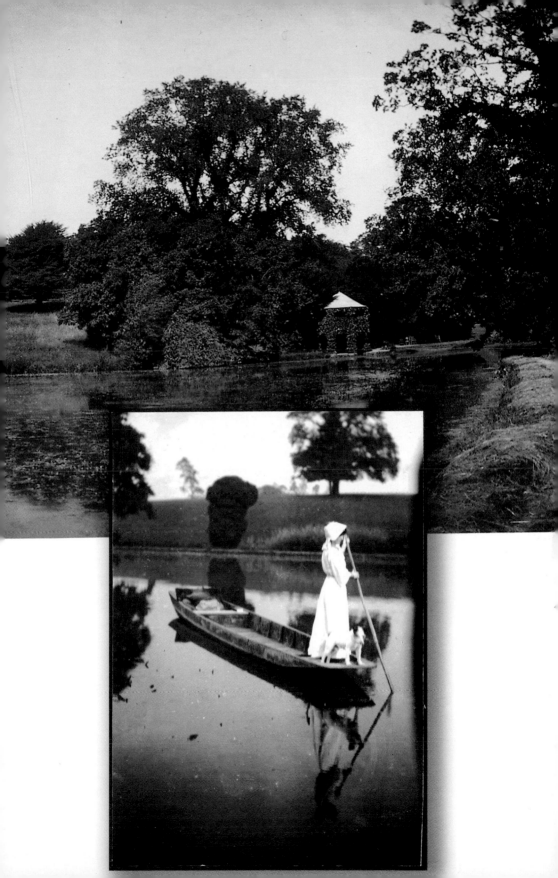

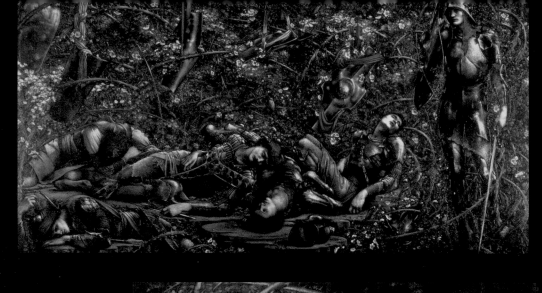

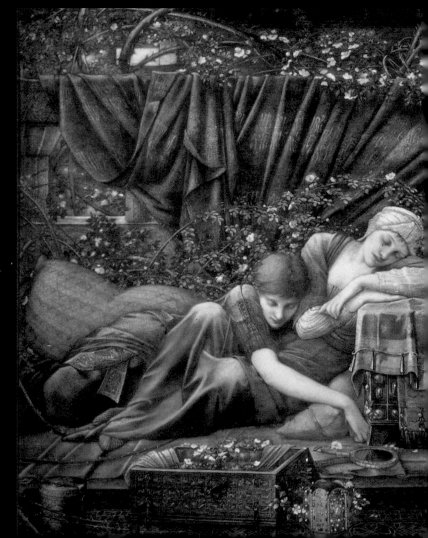

Left: *The Briar Wood*: the first of Burne-Jones's pictures which tell the story of the Sleeping Beauty. Here the prince penetrates the tangle of briar roses which have grown up around the castle, and discovers the sleeping knights.

Below: *The Rose Bower*: this shows the sleeping princess soon to be revived by the prince's kiss. May had photogravure reproductions of the Briar Rose series in her bedroom at Marble Arch; her daughter Daphne, who eventually married Frank Rose, named her second daughter Briar, thus re-creating the memory of Briar Rose for her mother years after Burne-Jones died.

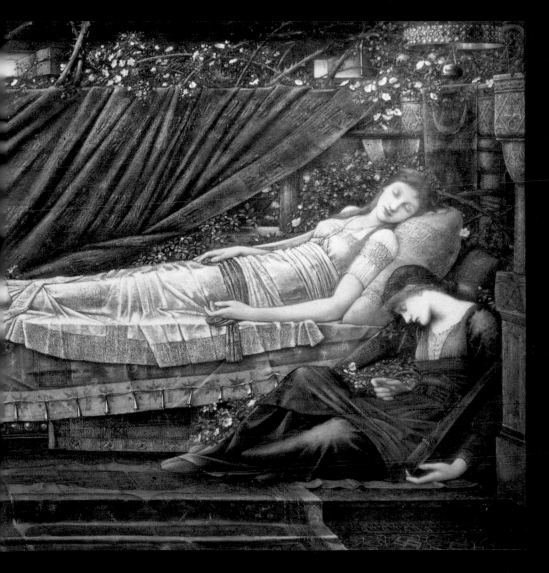

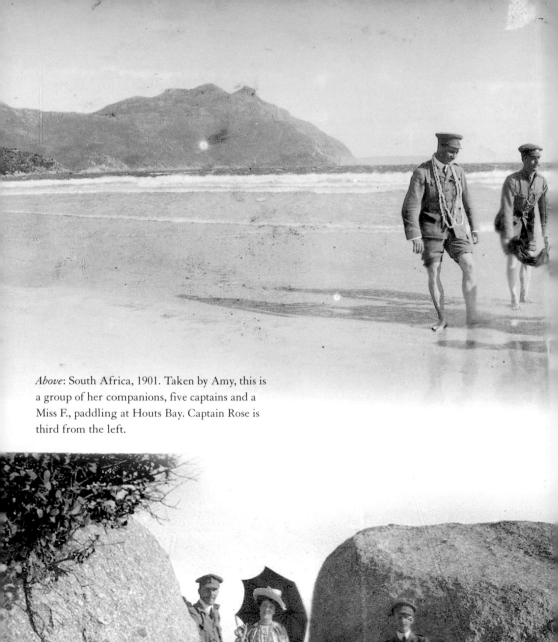

Above: South Africa, 1901. Taken by Amy, this is a group of her companions, five captains and a Miss F., paddling at Houts Bay. Captain Rose is third from the left.

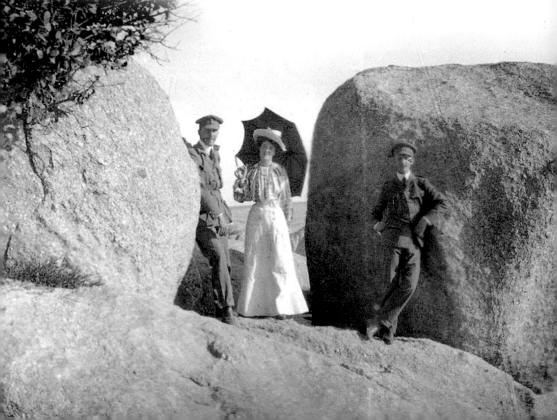

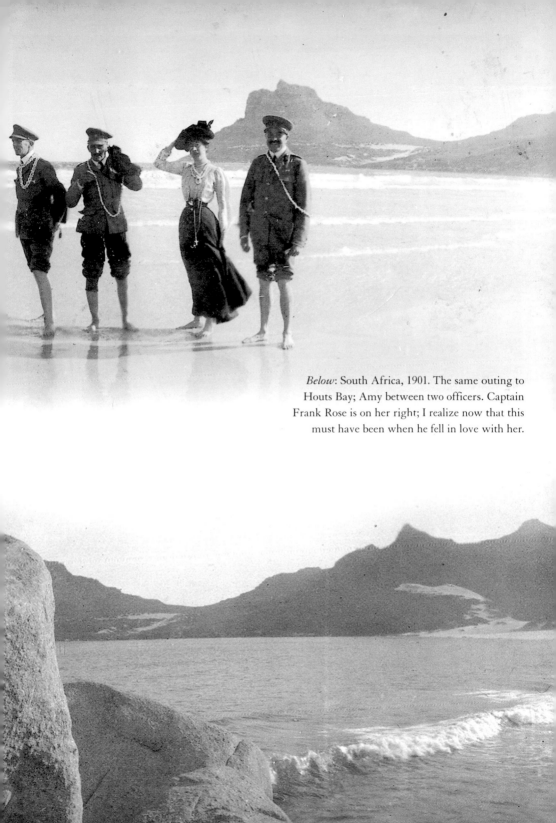

Below: South Africa, 1901. The same outing to Houts Bay; Amy between two officers. Captain Frank Rose is on her right; I realize now that this must have been when he fell in love with her.

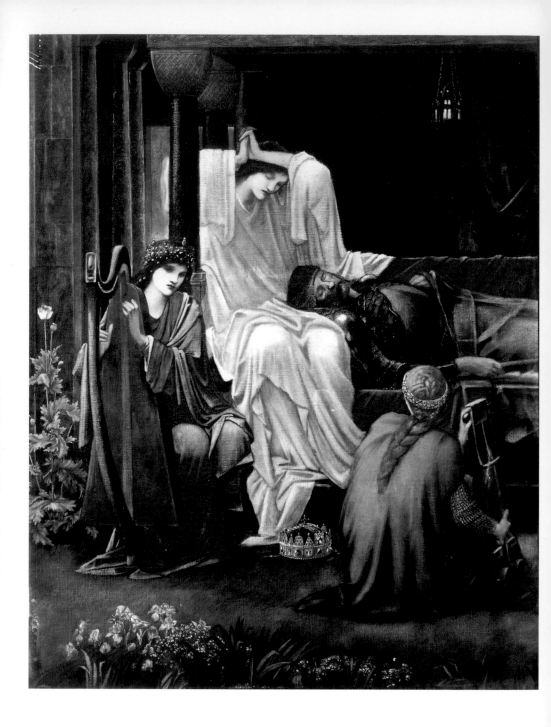

The Last Sleep of Arthur in Avalon (detail): the great painting of King Arthur's death which Burne-Jones started in 1881 and was still working on the day he himself died in 1898. By this time he had become so involved in the image that he slept in the same position as the king, with his head slightly raised.

many women before has had about them. This is the real adieu. God bless
you. E.

Just before leaving, May sent a small bunch of lilies of the valley
round to the Grange. These were the delicate, sweetly scented little
flowers that Burne-Jones associated entirely with her, and which he
showed pinned to her breast in his last drawing of her, the one I had
first seen as a child. Burne-Jones used the Victorian language
of flowers as messages in his paintings, and had invented a more secret
flower language of his own; lilies of the valley meant 'Return to
Happiness' or 'Love Revived'. Only a few months later, May was
to send a little wreath of them to his funeral, although it had been
requested that no flowers should be sent.

Burne-Jones continued to write to May at the hotels she and Amy
stayed at, seeking solace. She was so far away, and he still missed
Morris:

> *I read the book of Job last night but it sounded like splendid words and*
> *brought no comfort . . . I thought lovingly how Morris one night sat up all*
> *night with me when I was unhappy and read Job to me – neither did it*
> *comfort me then – But how he used to sit up with me and read and talk in*
> *wild times – no one ever will again – it all came back so vividly last*
> *night.*

Burne-Jones's fears that he might be dead before May returned from
Italy proved unfounded; he managed to keep 'the man with the
scythe' at bay, although he was always lurking in the wings. The time
abroad seems to have cured Amy and smoothed over any trouble
between her and Lionel, and apparently with Lady Bonham, for soon
after their return, on 11 May 1898, it was announced that their
marriage would take place on 11 June at St Margaret's, Westminster.
May, with her artistic eye and acknowledged good taste, was in her
element choosing silk for Amy's dress and for her nine bridesmaids,
and making sure the fittings went well. But the first thing she
did when she returned to London in April was to give one of her
dinner parties, at which Burne-Jones was a guest. May's friend Alfred
Milner wrote to May from South Africa that he had had a letter from

Burne-Jones saying 'that he is going to dine with you – happy man'. Nostalgically, Alfred hoped that all was 'going on in the old way in that delightful world, in which I once moved myself in a quiet way'.

At the beginning of 1898, Burne-Jones had written to Milner introducing his nephew Rudyard Kipling, who was coming out to South Africa. Although still young, Rudyard had health problems, and his doctor had advised him to work less, and spend the winter in a better climate. This visit to South Africa, with his wife and children, was to be the first of many. Rudyard was, like Milner, fiercely patriotic, and Burne-Jones repeated to May:

> . . . of course Ruddy liked him greatly – they are both Jingoes you see, and hate the Boers deeply. Ruddy says it is a hardship that Milner may not run backwards and forwards to London – a thing easily done now, but they abide by the rule that was made when journeys took long – an hour's talk at headquarters would be better than often a hundred of dispatches, but pedantry holds sway, and there he must abide, very lonely in life, says Ruddy.

Milner told May that he wished he had seen more of Rudyard Kipling during his time in South Africa. He hoped that Amy was now well and happy 'and that her future is clearing', and said that he was 'so glad to hear you see so much of BJ and that he is as ever as I know he must be, such a delightful and sympathetic friend'. He looked forward to the time when he himself and May could have 'another of our long talks as in good bygone days' and he ended affectionately with: 'keep a place in your heart for me – mine is ever yours'.

Burne-Jones had often told May that his work was everything to him: 'I don't care how much I work, I should like to kill myself with it – it would be the nicest of endings.' But although he was now working harder than ever on 'Avalon', his physical deterioration made his work less satisfying than in former days. His eyes, which had troubled him for a few years, were getting worse:

> For eyes are not what eyes were – such eyes they were once, and could look at the sun, and see the grass growing, and now they blink and ache,

*and are hot, and the lids of them creak as I open them, and grither as I
shut them — grither is a good word — I don't know if there is such a word,
but there had better be.*

But he still felt pleasure when he looked at his lovely spring garden
at the Grange:

*There are tiny apple trees planted last year full of blossom — little
precocious wretches — they look very pretty and make one smile whether
you will or no — so bubbling over with merry pink are they. But Mounter
[the gardener] has forgotten to raise tulips for which I could beat him, for
I love them with fury, and cannot have enough of them. No, in a garden,
tulips I must have (and lilies and roses of course) and poppies and sun-
flowers else I won't play and I want them as thick on the ground as they
will grow, like cottager's gardens which are always perfection . . . and for
poppies I want hundreds and millions of them, and chiefly black ones —
the black ones are like hell poppies, but the white ones are the poison cups
and herein lives a parable.*

Burne-Jones was constantly thinking of the nearing end:

*It's hateful to sit and wait for death — I should like to go out into a battle
and meet it . . . It must end very soon, and it has been a fruitless life really
— I have only begun to do the thing I want, for the art is very difficult — I
have thought of it, and worked for it only, for many years, but only begin
now to see my way — but I have loved it — that art.*

He often implied that death would be a relief:

*All these days I have lain long and thought what I would be if I heard the
tinkle of the scythe, and the dark one was coming along the passage —
wouldn't it save me many an intolerable hour — the summer's afternoon
hours, hardest to live through — and I always say 'Yes, it would be rather
nice' — life does hurt so keenly, and I was never equipped for it.*

On 2 June 1898, Alfred Milner wrote to May from Cape Town:

To think that before this reaches you Amy will actually be married. Well.
I am so glad, on the whole, both for her sake and for yours, for I know
these have been anxious years for you, and I do believe she will be happy.

Why, I wondered, still not having found any clue as to what the 'hitch'
in Amy's engagement had been, was he only glad 'on the whole'? And
was May's anxiety during the past few years, when she was herself
apparently suffering bullying and unkindness from her husband,
partly caused by her worry about Amy's complex temperament and
melancholic tendencies? May wrote later that Amy 'dipped deep into
the emotions of body and soul'. Could she have worried also whether
her eldest daughter's mysterious charisma would present problems
when she was married? Long after Amy had died, May hinted that all
the adoration her daughter had inspired had not brought either of
them happiness; she wrote that Amy had been 'given the fatal gifts of
beauty and charm' and that she was 'a woman that loved and suffered,
the daughter that lost me more tears than all else'.

Amy and Lionel were married at St Margaret's, Westminster, on 11
June 1898. Amy was twenty-three, a year younger than Lionel. May
wrote that they were known as 'Soul and Body', but she realized that
Lionel might be annoyed to be admired merely for his body. In a letter
to Amy she explained that people didn't really mean it like that, 'but
you see your body is not very big and his is not very small'. For several
days before and after the wedding the weather in London was either
overcast or raining, but in the meteorological records 11 June is identified as being 'a perfect June day' with uninterrupted sun. *The Times*
described it as 'a pretty military wedding'. Standing at attention down
the entire nave of the large church was a company of the second
battalion of the Grenadier Guards, making a brilliant border in their
scarlet uniforms. Lionel's father Sir George Bonham, tall and handsome with aquiline features, had come from Rome where he was at
that time First Secretary at the British Embassy. Lady Bonham must
have been filled with emotion at having finally to relinquish 'her
Lionel'. Lionel's younger brother Eric was best man, while Henry
Brooks Gaskell, in his captain's uniform, gave his daughter away. Sir
Edward Burne-Jones played his part in the family event by being a
witness at the signing of the register.

Amy's dress, closely fitting her slim figure, was made entirely of finest ruched white silk chiffon, embroidered with pearls and silver. She wore a simple pearl necklace, which held a diamond heart given her by Lionel, and a delicately pretty diamond and pearl tiara given her by May. Through her thin chiffon veil Amy's voluminous dark hair could be seen piled up elaborately. In a photograph taken with the veil removed she looks very young, dreamy, and slightly sad. Nine young bridesmaids, including her little sister Daphne, now eleven years old, flanked her. Their dashing outfits had been chosen by May and Amy together: the lightest white silk dresses with pale-blue chiffon sashes and wide Medici collars. On their small heads they wore black picture hats with pale-blue rosettes. Lionel gave all the brides-maids an enamel and semi-precious-stone brooch, each one a different colour, with the initials A and L elegantly intertwined in the centre.

After the newlyweds left for the traditional honeymoon 'on the continent', May felt bereft. She immediately departed for Beaumont. Burne-Jones, left behind in London, wrote to her the next day, as if he wanted to remind her that she was still needed by him:

My soul had left by the one-thirty train and gone north and there it is – and it hovered round you all night through and was at your waking and watched every mouthful of your little breakfast and is there now – so don't move too quickly or you will tread upon it – for it lies nestled at your feet and quite happy there – I don't think it wants any other life than that – indeed I know it doesn't – just to lie there always. And it would think it very kind of you not to shake it out by the folds of your dress too hurriedly when you spring up to go away.

On 16 June, five days after Amy's wedding and May's departure for Beaumont, Burne-Jones worked on 'Avalon' for most of the day. He was feeling better than he had done for some time. He then enter-tained teatime visitors, showing them some of his paintings in the upstairs studio of the Grange. When they had gone, he settled down to some letter writing. He wrote to his nephew Rudyard in Rottingdean, arranging to visit him on the following Sunday. He then wrote to May at Beaumont:

*Well I worked away till four – and then I thought of something that will
improve the picture I hope a great deal, and I felt well and getting hourly
stronger – and Harvey* [his doctor] *would be jealous to find how much
quicker your remedies are than his.*

*Also Harvey came today and sounded me – but as I have been getting
better ever since seven o'clock last evening there was no backsliding to
explain away – A nice wholesome tiredness has come upon me.*

*And tomorrow I shall go back to Avalon and try that experiment for
bettering a weak place in the picture. And on Saturday week I will go and
see Ruddy for the Sunday and have some refreshing talk with him, and
come back on the Sunday evening perhaps to dine with you – who knows
– there is no knowing in such a wonderful world.*

Burne-Jones's errand boy took his letters to the post. Many years
later, in the small leather notebook that Amy had given her, May
copied out this letter. At the end of it she noted: 'His last words.'

Burne-Jones spent a quiet evening with Georgie. They played
dominoes and then Georgie read aloud by lamplight, as she often did
now that her husband's eyes were so bad. Finally they went up to their
separate bedrooms. Burne-Jones undressed, settled himself on his bed
into the position of King Arthur in his painting, and waited for sleep
to come.

Between their bedrooms was a speaking tube. In the early hours of
the morning, Georgie heard her husband cry out that he had a pain in
his heart. She hurried to him. It was, as Burne-Jones had anticipated
so often during the last months, a fatal heart attack. The man with the
scythe had finally come to him. Georgie could do nothing; within a
very short while Sir Edward Burne-Jones, great painter, skilled and
witty draughtsman, lover of beautiful women, but an endearing,
modest human being, was dead. He was sixty-five years old. A deeply
spiritual man, Burne-Jones had always felt his painting provided, like
a transcendental experience, a link with another world. Dying as he
did, after working all day on the death scene of King Arthur at
Avalon, it was as if he had finally entered the world he loved most, the
legendary world of his paintings.

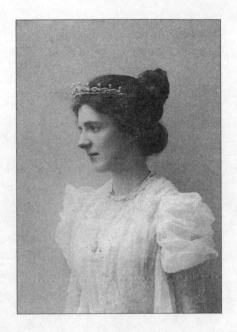

Amy in her wedding dress, with her typically pensive look. She is wearing May's tiara, and a diamond heart from Lionel hangs round her neck.

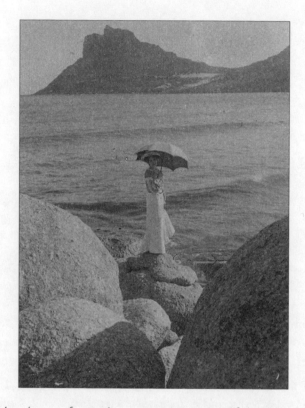

This lovely picture of Amy in Houts Bay, South Africa in early 1902, was taken by one of the British officers with whom she socialized.

CHAPTER SEVEN

A SOLDIER IN SOUTH AFRICA

IN JULY 1899, A YEAR AFTER THE DEATH OF BURNE-JONES, MAY WROTE to Sir Alfred Milner in Cape Town. As Britain's High Commissioner in South Africa, determined to bring about British domination of the gold-rich Boer republics, he was now a leading player in the quarrels and diplomatic stratagems that seemed to be leading inexorably to the outbreak of war in South Africa. But despite the immense strain he was under, Milner still found time to read May's long letters to him. She said she would quite understand if he had no time to write to her as often. After Burne-Jones's death, he had written to sympathize with her 'terrible blow' and 'unsupportable loss', telling her that he knew 'how much he was in your life . . . and how great a blank will be left'. Now, over a year later, May told him:

> *I am very lonely now – the loss of BJ's vivid personality – the perfect openness of everything with him – the daily intercourse with his mind – such a mind – leaves life quite arid – I can only struggle on as best I can – loving much, hoping much, believing little. And yet hardly that. I never hope for myself – there is nothing to hope for – but it is boundless for others and I try not to forget – for in remembering is one's best hope and power of living.*

The memory of her friendship with Burne-Jones was to remain vivid to May for the rest of her life. Perhaps it did give her the 'power of living' as he had so wished, for despite her numerous bouts of illness May did not die young. When she was in her eighties she admitted that re-reading the letters she had been sent by Burne-Jones still gave her comfort and strength, and it was towards the end of her life that she pencilled in the little remarks on his letters which, when I first read them, gave me such a sense of how she felt about him.

May expressed boundless admiration for what Alfred Milner, the closest friend and confidant she now had, was attempting to achieve in South Africa. She sympathized with his determination to extend British rule to the whole of South Africa, including the Boer republics of the Transvaal and Orange Free State, but knew it might involve war. When he had first gone out two years before, she had written to him:

> When I think of the life you are going to lead – the long nights between longer journeys – the heart breaking difficulties, the constant abuse, the uncertainty of health, the loneliness of mind – I long to help even by a moment's smile, or sigh – or thought that belongs to the life you have left.

May told Alfred she was glad to hear that a young friend, Violet Cecil, was staying at Government House in Cape Town with him. Violet had travelled out to South Africa with her husband of four years, Major Lord Edward Cecil, the son of Lord Salisbury, the Prime Minister. Shortly after reaching Cape Town, Edward Cecil left for Kimberley to join his commanding officer, Colonel Robert Baden Powell, and help him recruit a local defence force to stop the Boers moving up north from the Transvaal to threaten Mafeking, the most northerly town in the Cape Colony.

Violet was nearly twenty years younger than May, who had probably met her through Burne-Jones. Violet and her older sister, Olive, daughters of an unusual quixotic character, Admiral Maxse, had been taught to draw by Burne-Jones, and were among his favourite young girls. Violet wrote in her memoirs that to her the painter was 'deep, true and unselfish . . . full of humour . . . a real imaginative senti-mentalist'. In her letter to Milner, May commented:

How delicious for you having Violet Cecil, isn't she a fascinating young creature – loveable – and just the pleasant womanly sweet intelligence with humour that charms and rests a man! So I hope she is doing so to you.

May seemed to sense that the Cecil marriage was already drifting apart. It was clear that Violet admired Sir Alfred Milner and was attracted to him. She was not alone. By that time Milner was one of the most eligible bachelors in the Empire. Women flocked round him. But in fact this was the beginning of a special friendship, and an enduring relationship only admitted openly many years later. A few weeks after Violet Cecil's arrival in Cape Town in 1899, as the problems and agonies of war pressed in on Alfred Milner, May wrote perceptively to him again: 'It must be a comfort for her to have you – and you to have her.' Could May have felt a twinge of jealousy at the idea of a younger woman getting so much attention from a man she herself considered such a close friend?

In the late summer of 1899 the crisis between the British and the Boers deepened. The Boers were sure Britain meant to take away their independence and refused to be cowed. Transvaal's President Kruger was on the point of declaring war first, in the hope of defeating the British before they could get military reinforcements from England. May wrote to Milner:

Well you wanted responsibility and you have got it with a vengeance. And you live in a rush of intense work, and blame, and praise. And the very difficulties are intensified by acute personalities around you – and you are a man of peace, yet might cause war.

She reassured Alfred that 'if you require soldiers' her son-in-law Lionel Bonham's battalion would, she hoped, be coming out before long. Lionel was then stationed in Gibraltar, where he and Amy had a pretty little house with a garden. When he came out to South Africa, May told Milner she thought Amy would follow him: '. . . and would you be very kind to my little Amy? But I know "yes" without asking.'

On 11 October 1899, war was declared by the Boers, with skirmishes near Mafeking leading to the Boers' long-drawn-out siege of that town in the early stages of the conflict. Among the officers holed up in the town was Violet's husband, Lord Edward Cecil. On 20 December May wrote to Milner that London was in a state of high tension, and there was a 'fervour of military ardour'. Even her husband Henry Brooks had left his beloved garden at Kiddington that day and gone up to London to volunteer, together with other Oxfordshire landowner friends and neighbours. May herself had just sent out eight chests of clothes for women and children to Alfred Milner's refugee fund in South Africa:

> *I think constantly of the burden of destitution you have on your hands at Cape Town. There never was a stranger time of dark anxiety than we are living through. Perhaps the constant telegrams, the driblets of authentic news, the oceans of letters and reports make it more difficult than in times when no news came. I almost wish all the wires were cut. About twelve o'clock when the morning papers are over, shouting boys make one stop in the street to buy news. About five they begin to shout again. Every man that comes in has something to say. Every woman is nervous.*

May's one joy at this time was that Amy and Lionel, back from Gibraltar, were staying with her in London; 'They are very happy and she so pretty.' But Lionel was 'sick at not going out' yet to South Africa. His battalion, the second battalion of the Grenadier Guards, 'the healthiest and strongest battalion seen for years – two thousand eight hundred reservists', were bitter at being left at home. Yet the government was calling on the militia (non-professional soldiers, yeomanry and volunteer cavalry) and volunteers to go out for active service. May remarked, 'the grumbling is running very high against the War Office and Hicks Beach' (Sir Michael Hicks Beach was the Chancellor of the Exchequer, who, May insisted, was 'execrated by man, woman and child'). But it was Joseph Chamberlain, the Colonial Secretary, she said, who was now 'alienating all sorts of people by his flippancy and indiscretion', having voiced his opinion that Milner and the military authorities had exaggerated the risks of the campaign at Mafeking.

One person who was not volunteering to fight in South Africa was Hal Gaskell. He was now twenty years old, and since leaving Eton had spent every possible moment of his time painting. As long as he was painting he did not seem to be as vulnerable to the family depression that May had already recognized in him. He told May that he was at his happiest out in the fields with his palette, 'revelling in paint and my own company'. He had been all over England in order to sketch and paint, staying in country inns. In the family today there remain scores of small, skilled watercolours from this period. Hal had also travelled in northern France, walking and painting, always alone. Just occasionally, after weeks spent by himself in unfamiliar places, he would become lonely. In one letter to May, who worried about his being too solitary, he wrote from rural France:

> *You will be glad to hear that I admit that I do wrong to be alone. I have felt it greatly the last fortnight. My nerves, which at my age ought not to exist, have played havoc and I have worried at this and worried at that and my digestion went wrong, the weather went wrong, the world went wrong, and above all the work went hopelessly wrong. I even became afraid of people looking at me.*

By the time the war in South Africa started, Hal had a studio in Paris and lodged by himself in the Rue St Jacques. He studied with Burne-Jones's ex-assistant Thomas Rooke. May had given her son a copy of Malory's *Morte d'Arthur*, the book that had shaped Burne-Jones's life and work. Hal told his mother that he was reading it 'studiously and lovingly'. He was trying to work hard in the studio, he said, but yet again he felt lonely:

> *The work goes on with much biting of lips and a good deal of depression, but what do we live for but to fight and hope and fight and hope again . . . the studio is still very empty so I must put on a bright face and learn what I can, and do as the birds who sing in spite of the cage and a hot dusty room . . . but I do fret and worry, worry, worry – and that is why I am so grumpy and cross and stupid.*

In Hal's letters to his mother at twenty you can still hear the voice of the introspective little prep-school boy, prone to wallowing in his own troubles. He continued to suffer from homesickness, as he had when he was a young boy, and he still fretted about his mother. He fantasized to May:

> *I would like to walk into the drawing room and see you lying resting on your sofa and have a long talk, but I daresay I should not be able to say anything at all, and should get hot and worried. Now the best thing in the world for me would be to take Daphne to school, entertain Lionel and Amy and look after Father's lunch ... Winter has set in swiftly and hard here and when I run through the Luxembourg Gardens in the morning the grass is all white, and the few people scurry along with turned up coat collars and red noses ... and don't forget we are going to spend a good old world Christmas up at Beaumont and have a good old time together.*

But that Christmas, even though Hal came home and May had all three of her beloved children with her, she had to conceal her own loneliness. It was only when she wrote to Alfred Milner that she was able to talk about Burne-Jones and admit that 'the void and loneliness he has left is as aching as ever'.

Despite his happiness with Amy, Lionel, now promoted to the rank of captain, had been impatient to leave for South Africa. Finally, early in 1900, not long after the 'old world Christmas' at Beaumont, the orders for departure came: Lionel was to set sail for Cape Town with his regiment in early March. May was in Rome at the time, staying with friends. She started a letter to Daphne on the morning of 12 March, the King of Italy's official birthday, and the day on which Lionel's ship was to leave Southampton. May knew that Amy would be at the docks to say goodbye to him.

In Rome, the sun was shining. From a balcony on the top floor of the house she was staying in, May watched the marching soldiers and military bands in the crowded street below, and saw the King, known as 'Umberto the Good', mounting his horse in the palace gardens, ready to join the procession. In her room once more, she continued the letter to Daphne which she had started when she woke that morning:

> *And whilst the bands are playing here – and the drums beating, my heart is far away today with Lionel and Amy – where the drums are also*

beating, and the bands playing – but so differently – in one it is in grim
earnest, and in the other play.

As it turned out, this was to be the last celebration King Umberto I would enjoy; four months later he was assassinated by an anarchist, to the horror of most of his subjects, who loved their good-humoured, generous king. But May did not feel involved with the colourful festivities in Rome. Later in the afternoon she returned once more to the letter she had been writing to Daphne:

I wonder if Lionel's ship has started now. I have been thinking of him and
Amy all day.

By April, Lionel was taking part in operations in the Orange Free State. For the moment Amy remained at Holdhurst, a small gabled house with extensive views over the Surrey countryside, which she and Lionel had been lent on the estate at Knowle Park, near Cranleigh, which belonged to Lionel's father. At the beginning of May, Amy's mother came to keep her company. It was a particularly fine spring that year, but both women's thoughts were in South Africa. May wrote to Alfred Milner:

My dear friend, the difference, but the difference here to where you are.
For two long hours no one has come near me. I am sitting writing in a
little summer house, for a warm spring rain is falling, which helps the
buds to burst, the blossoms to smell, the birds to sing – indeed the whole
earth is a chorus of spring love and colour. I can see a nightingale's throat
throbbing with its song as I write, and last night there was a nightingale
festival in a full moon and we sat out until after ten o'clock. No county
beats Surrey for flowers and birds, but in spirit how I should like to spring
across and see you, and just gather with my own eyes how you look, and
my ears how you sound, and my heart how you feel. It seems to me a very
different Alfred Milner will come back and that such deep waters must
change the man, yet deep down I know much will always remain
unchanged – the scholar, the lover of books . . . how nice it would be to
give you one whole idle English Sunday on the edge of a primrose
carpeted wood. So shall we go for a walk you and I? Oh my dear, 'makers

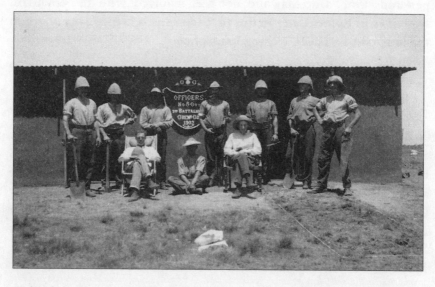

Lionel Bonham, seated left, and fellow officers in the Transvaal in 1902 when Amy came out to see him.

*of nations' don't go walking in primrose woods with nightingales singing
to them, no – they slave in cities, and write dispatches, and play large
games with men and armies. I often wonder if you had chosen the scholar's
life, and to be a maker of books instead of history at the turning of the
ways – would you have been happier?*

When I first read May's letters to Alfred Milner, I was surprised by
how much they could sound like love letters. She obviously had a soft
spot for her friend, yet I am convinced it was the love of an intimate
yet platonic friendship. If only, I thought, if only Burne-Jones had not
destroyed all her letters to him, burning each one up in 'a blue flame'.
If May wrote like this to Milner, for whom her love and dependence
were not nearly as deep rooted, what could she have poured out to
Burne-Jones? Feeling, as I did by now, that I had been allowed to
share the secret of their relationship and the pleasure that they gave to
each other, the fact that not one of May's hundreds of letters to Burne-
Jones has survived seemed to me a tragedy.

I was still perplexed about the family legend of my great-aunt Amy,
whose letters May had burnt, perhaps because they contained things
she did not want anyone to know. It is strange how often people seem
to see into the future. Amy had posed herself as dead in her bed for a
self-portrait photograph. And May, staying with her beloved Amy in
the unbroken peace of Holdhurst while Lionel Bonham fought on the
veldt of the Orange Free State, told Milner:

*Amy is looking a most lovely little woman – very pale and anxious but not
showing it a scrap in daily life, and severe on those who do. She is the most
delicious gentle loving little daughter to me – and so happy in her married
life that my heart stands still with fear lest some bitter sorrow should cloud
it.*

It seems almost as if May had a premonition of what was to come.

The Siege of Mafeking ended when the British forces relieved the
town on 17 May 1900, after 217 days. Lionel had been active in the
Orange Free State for the past few weeks. On 29 May he was wounded
by a Boer bullet during the Battle of Biddulphsberg, which was

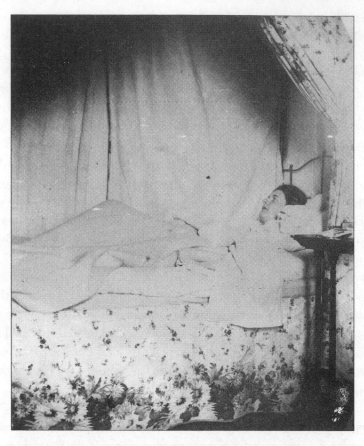

*Amy's prophetic self-portrait of herself in bed,
which she entitled 'Dead'.*

near Senekal, a small town of about twenty-five houses and a church.

As the Grenadier Guards advanced on the morning of the battle, they could see no sign of the Boers, but they soon came under a hail of bullets. They lay down on the ground but, still visible on the open veldt, were an easy target for the enemy. With many men already wounded, the long dry grass suddenly caught fire behind them, probably as a result of a dropped match, though to this day no one knows for certain. The wind quickly fanned the flames and produced a high wall of fire and smoke. Faced with a hail of gunfire from the unseen Boers in front of them, the Grenadier Guards were forced to retreat through the flames, carrying their wounded, with the result that many of the men were badly burned. Any wounded men who could not be carried were horribly burnt to death where they lay.

The Grenadiers lost over forty per cent of their men that day, more than in any other battle during the entire war. In the circumstances, Lionel was lucky not to have suffered any burns, and to have been shot only in the arm. At the end of this horrific day the Boers came out of their trenches and helped the British surgeons and orderlies to carry their wounded off the battlefield. Although the Boers would frequently steal the wounded or dead soldiers' personal possessions, they showed Christian charity at the same time, giving the wounded water, and wrapping them up to keep them warm. In the words of one of the Grenadiers who was both badly burnt and wounded at the Battle of Biddulphsberg, 'The Boer to the wounded is a true hearted being.'

Lionel spent a month in the Dutch Reformed Church in Senekal, which the British had turned into a hospital. On hearing the news of her son-in-law's wounds, and the horrors of the battle, May, who had recently gone through an illness which she said was 'made bearable by books', suddenly knew what she must do: she would send some books out to Lionel and his fellow wounded soldiers to distract them from the miserable hospital conditions. She felt that reading would provide an escape from their pain and memories of battle, or simply from the boredom of lying there day after day. This instinct was the first seed of a personal mission that would change May's life. She filled three cases with books, specially chosen to revive the soldiers' spirits, she hoped, and shipped them off at once to South Africa. When the cases arrived in Senekal, Lionel wrote back to May gratefully:

*If I lived to be a thousand no words could ever tell you what your books
are to us in the ward. We have cut up the Rudyard Kipling volumes into
numbered parts, and we pass them down the beds, for a volume each is too
precious.*

As May explained in her old age: 'I never forgot this.' Thirteen years
after she had sent Lionel and his fellow soldiers those first cases of
books, after a time of great personal grief, the memory of her son-in-
law's appreciative letter was to revive May's own life, giving her a new
direction and purpose.

When he was well enough to travel, Lionel Bonham was sent back
to England for a month's leave, and was reunited with Amy. Both
mother and daughter now saw him as a hero. 'Although his arm is
quite stiff he looks the picture of a fine young Englishman,' remarked
May to Alfred Milner when, after just a month of massage treatment
and his young wife's company, Lionel was fit for action once more,
and ready to set sail again for Cape Town. By this time scores of wives,
sisters, and even unattached young women had followed the soldiers
to South Africa. Some of them helped relieve the suffering in the hospitals and amongst the refugees, but mainly it seems they were there
for a new experience, to enjoy the warm climate during the English
winter and a more stimulating kind of social life, charged by the
wartime atmosphere. Amy was tempted to do the same.

But Queen Victoria voiced her disapproval of this 'hysterical' aspect
of the war in South Africa, caused, she said, by too many women going
out 'where they are not wanted'. In a message to Alfred Milner via
Joseph Chamberlain, the Colonial Secretary, she pointed out that the
'unusual number of ladies visiting the seat of war' interfered with the
work of the men, as well as taking up valuable hotel accommodation
which was needed for wounded officers. Although Milner published
the queen's objections, it did not stop Amy deciding that she would
definitely go out to South Africa to see Lionel. May's friend Rudyard
Kipling, whom she had first met through Burne-Jones, was to travel
back to Cape Town with his family at the end of the year. The Kiplings
had begun to spend their winters at the Woolsack, a house on the slopes
of Table Mountain lent to them by Cecil Rhodes, the financier and
empire-builder. May suggested that Amy should sail at the same time

as the Kipling family, who invited Amy to visit them at the Woolsack, which they said was a haven of peace, while she was in South Africa.

During the autumn before she left, Amy assembled her hot-weather wardrobe, and looked forward to the diversions of social life in Cape Town, where she knew she would find many friends. She would be proud of her Lionel too, who had just been awarded two medals for the part he had played in the Battle of Biddulphsberg. Her mother's thoughts, however, were often with the suffering caused by the conflict on the battlefields. She was also worried about her friend Alfred Milner, and the responsibility he bore for what had become a far longer war than he could have expected. The war was supposed to have ended in June 1900, when the British believed the Boer offensive had been broken, but the Boers had regrouped and an ugly guerrilla war continued. In England and abroad there was a fierce division of feeling between those who were pro- and anti-Boer. 'Tired and sick we all are of your war,' May told Milner, 'and who so weary as you I expect, my dear, dear friend. Hatred and vengeance seem to flourish as rampantly as ever, and my heart sinks to think of the years it will take to soothe the inheritance of hatred.'

But the war did not prevent May from telling Milner about her own troubles. She complained to Alfred that she had lost much of her vitality recently, and now found it 'an effort to face parties', as instead of finding them exhilarating they made her depressed. Most un-characteristically, she said that she had lost her interest in people, felt inferior, and that 'home difficulties absorb most of my energies'. Clearly she found Henry Brooks no easier to live with since Burne-Jones's death; her husband's gloomy silences were just as hurtful and hard to bear. She was concerned about the effect the atmosphere in the house could have on her children, even though it was only Daphne who lived at home permanently. May wrote to Milner:

I do so want to keep it a happy place for the children, and it all depends on me. Amy is a very sweet beloved little daughter to me now – repaying the anxious years. Hal is going through most difficult times in his character – and turns to me – but I have no one now to turn to except as you see, poor long suffering friend, to you – by a page of personal complaint! Forgive me.

Family letters show that there was a clear bond between Daphne and her father. She was now a tomboyish thirteen-year-old, and had for some time shown an interest in Henry Brooks's passion, the garden. She loved outdoor life, the horses, and the many dogs and cats both at Kiddington and at Beaumont. May would criticize Daphne for her untidiness, her 'love of dirt', and the way she had of 'fighting every order'. Governess after governess left because of Daphne's naughtiness, but May observed that she was 'the sunshine of her father's life'.

Henry Brooks never scolded his youngest daughter; he teased her affectionately and called her 'the queen of dirt, the empress of all blackness'. When Lionel was wounded her father wrote dismissively to Daphne, who was up at Beaumont with her latest German governess:

> *I hope you have found plenty of people to kiss and have had fun – you know that Captain Bonham has had fun, and got shot in the arm. I have not heard if any more dogs and cats are dead at Beaumont.*

Some of my great-grandfather's odd remarks show an unmistakably Gaskell turn of mind, familiar to me from all the male Gaskells I have known.

In mid-December 1901, Amy boarded a Union Castle Liner, the SS *Kinfauns Castle*, bound for Cape Town. Her photographs make life on board look rather like a house party in a large English country house, although the food was apparently far worse. There were plenty of people on board whom Amy knew socially in England, as well as her travelling companions, Rudyard and Carrie Kipling, with their two young children, five-year-old Elsie, known as Birdie, and little John. After several voyages to and fro between Southampton and Cape Town, the Kipling children now thought of the ship as another home which belonged to them, stewards, sailors and all. Since the end of the war was finally in sight there were a number of officers returning to South Africa, some accompanied by their wives and families, to be there for the final moment, as well as diamond and gold prospectors, businessmen and politicians. There were also other wives like Amy, going out to see their husbands as the war drew to a close, in anticipation of an enjoyable social life, still with the added buzz of war.

The close group of passengers on the *Kinfauns Castle* stopped for what appears from Amy's photographs to be a very jolly Christmas day in Madeira. Rudyard Kipling wrote that he particularly liked the Christmas part of his voyages, when the stewards on board would write seasonal messages on the cabin mirrors in soap.

They arrived at Cape Town on 7 January, in the middle of a heat-wave. Although Lionel remained with his company of Grenadiers near Bethlehem, in the Orange Free State, Amy had plenty of male company at the Mount Nelson Hotel. This impressive hotel, still lovely today, had been recently rebuilt on a grand scale. It opened at the start of the war, and provided a haven for officers' wives, off-duty officers, journalists, and other camp followers. With its neatly planted gardens and spacious terraces, life there, and on the many excursions and convivial picnics shown in Amy's photographs, looks extremely enjoyable. The hotel was set in the pine forests under the shadow of Table Mountain; luxuriously modern, with electricity and hot and cold running water, it seemed far removed from the hardships of war.

Before long, Amy visited the Kipling family at the Woolsack, which was not far from Cape Town, between the Liesbeck River and the lower slopes of Table Mountain. Cecil Rhodes, who lived on the neighbouring estate of Groote Schuur, had rebuilt the gabled Cape Dutch house two years before. He wanted the large bungalow to be used by visiting writers and artists, as he thought the beauty and grandeur of Table Mountain would inspire them. The first person he offered this refuge to was his friend Rudyard Kipling. The Kiplings would spend five to six months in South Africa when it was winter in England and summer there, every year from 1900 to 1907.

The Woolsack was a cool, peaceful house set beside a heavily scented grove of eucalyptus and pine trees, in the shade of some old oak trees. Rudyard described how 'in the stillness of hot afternoons the fall of an acorn was almost like a shot'. After the social bustle of the Mount Nelson Hotel, Amy must have found the Woolsack very quiet. She used to sit on a basket chair on the colonnaded stoep, or veranda. At the centre of the house was an inner courtyard. The

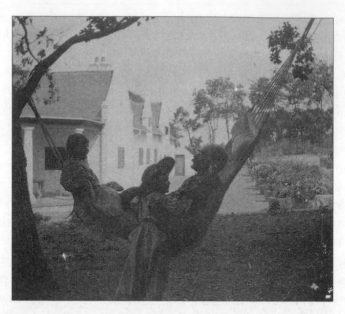

Amy's photographs were taken when she was staying with the Kipling family at The Woolsack, under Table Mountain. Above: Rudyard in a hammock with his children John and Elsie.

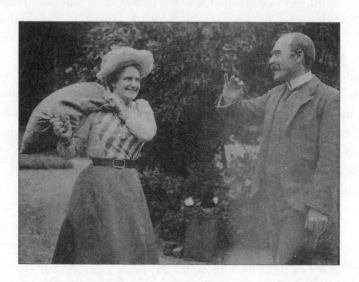

In this photograph Rudyard's wife Carrie appears about to attack him with a cushion; it is an unusual image as she was not known for playfulness.

walls of the house were thick and whitewashed, the shutters and windows made of teak. All around it was a well-laid-out garden, with paths through wide flower borders, and hedges of powder-blue plumbago. Another path through a ravine in the flank of Table Mountain led to Cecil Rhodes's house; the path was edged by a mass of intensely blue hydrangeas, which looked, Rudyard remarked, 'like a blue river'. With her huge camera, Amy photographed the garden, the house, Rudyard's teak-panelled study, and Rudyard, the family man. In one picture he sits in a hammock with his children, in another his wife Carrie beams uncharacteristically as she jokingly attacks Rudyard with a large cushion. Carrie was a large, plain woman who was thought to be stern and sometimes neurotic, but she said that the peace of the Woolsack calmed her nerves.

Amy seemed never to be without attentive male company. In her photographs, whether standing on a rock at Houts Bay looking out to sea, or sitting in the Mount Nelson garden, there is always at least one man at her side. Occasionally it was Lionel; at the Vineyard Hotel, near Cape Town, an old house set in beautiful parkland with spectacular views of Table Mountain, he and Amy must have spent a short time together. They took photographs of each other, which show that for some reason Lionel walked with a stick. But he was clearly recovered enough to be spending most of the time with his battalion, taking part in operations in the Orange River Colony. Meanwhile, in Lionel's absence, I noticed one officer in particular reappearing in Amy's photographs, firstly on the sands at Houts Bay, and thereafter in many of the other pictures. He was a mild-looking man, not handsome, but with a gentle expression and fine pale eyes; his name was Captain Frank Rose. I was to discover that his family lived not far from Kiddington, at Hardwick House, beside the river Thames. This man's life, I came to understand later, was to be profoundly affected by those days in South Africa with Amy.

After six months in South Africa, shortly after peace had been proclaimed on 1 June, the SS *Kinfauns Castle* brought Amy back to England again. The peace document signed by the Boers was being carried back to England on the same voyage, and Amy photographed it on deck, being held up proudly by a Colonel Hamilton and a

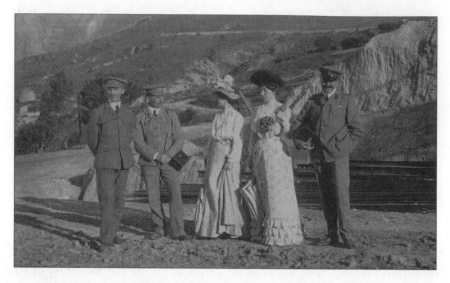

An expedition to Table Mountain. Captain Rose is
on the far left, Amy in the middle in the pale hat.

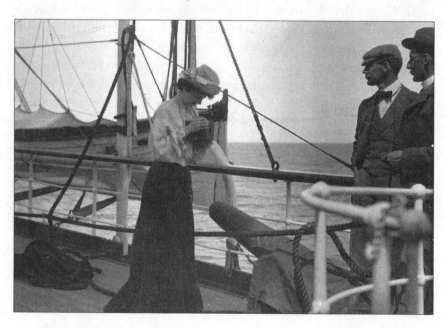

Amy on board the SS Kinfauns Castle on her return journey. She is
photographing Colonel Hamilton and Captain Marker, who were
carrying the peace treaty signed by the Boers back to England.

Captain Marker. She had said goodbye to Lionel once more, as he was not due to return home with his battalion until late autumn.

On her return, Amy found England agog with Edward VII's imminent coronation. It was now high summer and the country, having got over the shock of Queen Victoria's death the year before after sixty-three years on the throne, was now excited about the change.

Henry Brooks could not tear himself away from his garden at Kiddington for the festivities, but May and Amy went to London. There May found 'the world in a turmoil'. As she watched the procession from her seat in Whitehall, her curiosity about far-off places and people attracted her to the foreign troops. In a long description of the day that she wrote to Henry Brooks, she told him that she found the soldiers from Fiji 'quite delightful to look at with their beautiful bare bronze legs and feet and tiny tight petticoats of white linen – very short'. They had, May remarked, 'such faces – great brown eyes like a stag, short noses and small pouting mouths. My heart went out to them. Especially when they felt tired and sat down on newspapers which they evidently thought were made for the purpose.' May was also sympathetic to the Samoans, who had 'hats like china plates turned upside down, and who were so frightened when the King passed and "Present Arms" was shouted that they held each other's hands tightly and shivered'. This letter, apart from the ones May wrote to India in the very early days of her marriage, is the only one I found from May to her husband, kept because of its historic content.

King Edward was still recovering from the acute appendicitis he had suffered two months before, at the time first set for his coronation. The appendectomy had been performed by Queen Victoria's court physician, Sir Frederick Treves, best known for having presented Joseph Merrick, the Elephant Man, whom he had found in a freak show, to the medical world. The king's simple operation had been successful, but for the coronation ceremony in Westminster Abbey he wore a metal corset to make it less tiring for him to stand up straight. The King, May observed:

looked years older but all smiles and radiantly cordial – the Queen one blaze of jewels – she seemed to be entirely dressed in pearls and diamonds

— her face was working with emotion as she flung out her hands to the cheering people.

May went on to describe how:

... everyone choked back their tears when the whole congregation rose and shouted with the Westminster Boys 'Long Live King Edward'. There was a bit of consternation however, when the poor old Archbishop of Canterbury knelt to do homage after the very long service, and then fainted away and had to be carried out. The King remained upright while this went on, but before processing out of the abbey he passed behind the altar and had food and ten minutes' rest, the only sign of his being an invalid.

The King was not the only person in the Abbey who was tired and hungry. At the end of the service, May, who had evidently been invited to one of the official luncheons, possibly in the House of Lords, told Henry Brooks:

... there was almost a stampede of the Abbeyites to get to the House of Commons or other luncheons and refresh themselves. The scene was too funny — men and women fell on the food, anything that came first, jelly, bread, fruit, meat — higgledy piggledy. After bearing such a weight for eight hours, peeresses were tearing off their mighty tiaras, leaving the feathers anyhow and looking perfect scarecrows — the peers in their silk stockings and their coronets awry were stalking about hunting for carriages and scolding footmen.

At the end of her letter, May asked her husband to 'keep this account for your children's children'. Well, here am I, one generation further than my great-grandmother had envisaged, smiling at the idea of the greedy, inelegant peers and peeresses of a distant era, and wondering if there could be similar scenes at the next coronation.

Some of Amy's most striking photographs, for which she used her innovative Kodak Panoram, were taken at Kiddington during that summer of 1902. The pictures are truly panoramic and sharply focused, with great depth of field. Amy herself may not have pushed the button for the most romantic photographs herself, as she features in them, dressed all in white, in a punt on the glassy lake. But she must have set them up. It was these photographs that I noticed as a child, which captured my imagination, and which stayed in my mind.

Kiddington was looking its best. At the very end of the nineteenth century May had completely redecorated the house, showing the assured good taste which later led her to helping others, such as Alfred Milner, to decorate and furnish their houses. Nowadays she would no doubt have been a professional interior designer. Until he sold the house in 1953 her son Hal never changed anything she had done at Kiddington, and refused to install gas, electricity or a telephone. So it was May's house, with the thick silk curtains under ornate pelmets, the William Morris wallpapers, the hand-painted hall and drawing room, that I came to know when I stayed there with my grandparents as a young child. As my uncle wrote later: 'Time stood still at Kiddington.'

On my childhood visits, I realized that my grandparents' house belonged to another era. I found it then – and the memory of it still – absolutely magical, but a bit frightening too. Once or twice my grandfather met me at Hanborough station, then drove to Kiddington at a snail's pace in his beloved vintage Daimler. But at other times it was Mr Coote, the chauffeur, who drove, not much faster, in a black Sunbeam Talbot. I must have stayed at Kiddington first in the early summer, because one of my most vivid images is of the cow parsley on either side of the road, its lacy white flowers backlit by the sun. My grandfather had a passion for anything on wheels, the older the better. He would have thought the Sunbeam Talbot and even my grandmother's 1935 Morris Tourer, with its discoloured glass, too modern.

Hal had bought the Daimler in 1911, even though he had lost the sight of one eye in a shooting accident two years before. He continued to drive it well into old age, in spite of not being able to judge distances, and he never had an accident. Inexplicably, he also remained a good shot. The Daimler was Hal's pride and joy; it was called Silent Knight, and he had paid £110 for it. A handsome car with a soft top and side screens, it still had its original khaki-bronze-coloured paint when I saw it in the 1940s. My grandfather would drive very slowly, never more than twenty-five miles an hour, to the

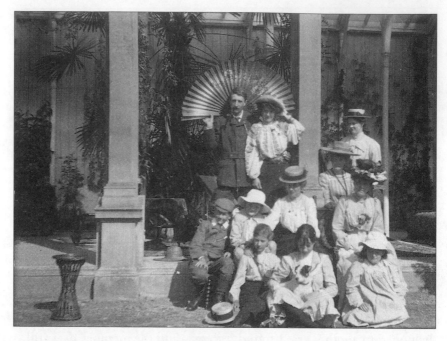

I love this group taken at Kiddington in the summer of 1902 when Amy was back from South Africa. Hal and Amy stand at the back with one of her fans. May, in characteristically large hat, sits on the right, and Daphne is on the ground with a beloved dog. The others are cousins and aunts.

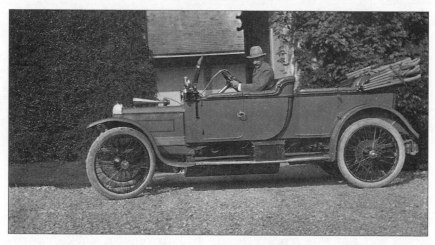

Hal in the Daimler, which he continued driving for years, but never at more than twenty-five miles an hour

constant irritation of other motorists on the Oxfordshire lanes, who could not get past him. He told Mr Coote the chauffeur that if he drove any of the cars faster it would wear the machinery out.*

My grandfather also still kept two prized closed carriages, which even retained their carriage lamps. One was a grand Victorian brougham, lined with blue damask, the other was much bigger, described in the sale catalogue as a 'two-horse station bus or wagonette with removeable top'. They had both belonged to his own grand-father, Henry Lomax Gaskell. I remember seeing them being lovingly polished in the stable block, together with the Daimler. There was also a governess cart, which my aunt Diana knew well during her child-hood, when her father insisted she should go to dancing classes in Woodstock by pony and trap, as it was 'too far for the car'.

My oldest cousin Robin was frequently driven in the Daimler during the war, when he was evacuated from London to Kiddington. He shudders at the memory of how cold the car was, but adds that the house was no refuge afterwards, being almost as bad. Even on my childhood summer visits I felt that chill in the house, and can still see the flickering oil lamps at night, and what seemed to me like miles of long dark corridors, which scared me. There was one bathroom in this house of about fifty rooms, and the bath was a deep copper one with a plug in the centre. The enamel had worn off and the copper tarnished to black. Having to use that bath was one of the horrors of my child-hood. It was so deep that once I was inside I could not see over the edge. The low level of dark, tepid water trickled away as I sat there shivering, waiting to be helped out.

Kiddington was certainly spartan, but because of the large plate-glass windows the main bedrooms and reception rooms were light and welcoming, and the food, something already important to me, was good; it was cooked by the kindly Mrs Busby, who still used a vast Eagle range, reputed to consume sixty tons of coal a year. There were wonderfully fresh fruit and vegetables from the kitchen garden, and

---

* When Hal sold Kiddington and most of its contents in 1953, at a very low point in the post-war market, the Daimler, perfectly preserved, still in running order, and with an incredibly low mileage, went for the same price Hal had paid for it in 1911: only £110. It is now in Switzerland and must be worth a fortune.

of course my grandfather would never use anything as modern as chemical pesticides or fertilizers. I particularly remember the thick cream and dark yellow butter from the farm, strong tasting and oozing tiny drops of water. Meals seemed dominated by my grandfather's silence; only once during a meal, when my grandmother told me off for clumsily dropping a plate, did he look up and roar with laughter, which naturally made me like him much more. Of course for me as a child, the greatest pleasure when staying at Kiddington was playing outside around the lake and in the lovely grounds that Amy had photographed on a shimmering summer's day so many years before, happy and confident, unaware of her fate.

I knew from a list in May's will that the Ashmolean Museum in Oxford held a substantial collection from the hundreds of drawings Burne-Jones had given her during their six-year friendship. Although photographs show that May hung several of his drawings and paintings in the house at Marble Arch, Burne-Jones told her he preferred the idea of them being at Kiddington or Beaumont. It was more discreet, he said, for them to be further away from those who might gossip; 'else they will make deductions and come to conclusions and be otherwise horrid'.

Entitled 'The Helen Mary Gaskell Bequest', the drawings at the Ashmolean are kept in the print room. I wanted to try and identify a drawing Burne-Jones gave to May as a special present when she visited his studio on her birthday one year. The story of that birthday drawing was told in her obituary in *The Times*. May was visiting the painter in his studio at the Grange, as she did often. As it was such a special day, he said he would let her choose any of the drawings in his portfolio. Burne-Jones valued May's artistic judgement, and had changed details in several of his pictures because she had expressed a view. On that birthday, May studied the drawings in his portfolio carefully before decisively bringing a silver-point drawing to him. Burne-Jones is said to have remarked, 'Ah, my dear, you have chosen the finest drawing I have ever done. You shall have it, but I should like you to leave it to the Nation.'

It may have been as a result of this that she decided to leave such a large bequest of the best drawings Burne-Jones had given her, including a large book he had had made for her, containing forty-eight drawings and paintings he had chosen specially for her. And probably May chose the Ashmolean because it was a museum she often used to go to when she escaped from Kiddington to seek culture and conversation in Oxford.

It was very quiet in the print room at the Ashmolean Museum, with that wonderfully evocative smell of old paper. It all looked just as it might have done in May's day; even the two curators, living with such a wealth of old masterpieces, did not seem quite part of the modern world. My own voice sounded to me very loud. Then I noticed something that brought me back to the present day: a young girl sitting at a laptop computer. She brought out a large folder for me, and the album Burne-Jones had made for May. I put on the protective white cotton gloves I was given. There were some wonderful drawings of women, several in silver point, one particularly dramatic one of a woman rising out of a tomb, 'The Raising of Tabitha', in gold point. This method is a true test of drawing skill as it is indelible. Paper is prepared with a coloured plaster mix and feels like fine sandpaper. The artist then draws on it with a pure silver, or occasionally gold, pencil. The smaller drawings in the album were exquisite, and interesting in that many of the women were not idealized in the familiar style of Burne-Jones, but had irregular features and very real expressions.

Finally I came across what must almost certainly be the silver-point picture which Burne-Jones had told May was the best drawing he had ever done, and had given to her on her birthday. It was a nude of Antonia Caiva, a well-known Italian model used by several of the Pre-Raphaelite artists, in silver point, the body pale, on grey prepared paper; a truly beautiful picture. What a birthday present!

As I showed the curators some photocopies I had brought of Burne-Jones's last drawing of May, and his dark portrait of Amy, the girl who had been at the laptop came over to look too. She admired the one of May and asked, 'Isn't there another woman called Amy Gaskell?'

'Yes,' I replied. 'She was May Gaskell's daughter. Here she is,' and I pointed to the reproduction of the haunting portrait of Amy.

The young girl said, 'Amy Gaskell was my great-aunt.'

I thought I had misheard, and looked at her enquiringly. But she repeated emphatically, 'She was my great-aunt.'

I was now completely puzzled, as this girl was at least thirty-five years younger than I. I exclaimed, 'But she's *my* great-aunt.'

It transpired that Flora, as I learnt she was called, was one generation out, but was indeed a relation I had not been aware of before: a great-great-granddaughter of Amy's sister Daphne, whom I could now see she resembled, although prettier. We both exploded in amazement in the still quiet of the print room. For Flora did not work there permanently; it was by pure coincidence that she was in the print room at the very hour of the same day that I visited the Ashmolean to see May's bequest. This followed another coincidence soon after I began working on this book, when a friend mentioned my project to some people she was staying the weekend with, and it turned out that the husband was another great-grandchild of May Gaskell, and had two trunks of May's letters and papers in his attic. And my meeting with Andrew Lloyd Webber at that London party was also sheer chance. Fact is stranger than fiction. 'To those who come after,' May had written. I left the Ashmolean that day feeling more than ever that my quest was meant to be, and that through the strength of her will, May was orchestrating it.

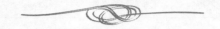

CHAPTER EIGHT

FAMILY AFFAIRS

MAY REMAINED DEVOTED TO HER FATHER, CANON MELVILLE, throughout his long life. At eighty, he was described in a newspaper as 'a commanding personality even in advanced age', and remained exceptionally active for another decade. When he preached from the pulpit of Worcester Cathedral, his melodious voice remained unfailingly strong, and was audible from every corner of the great building. A cathedral chorister at that time, Albert Bibbs, commented later in a personal memoir that no one could ever forget 'the scholarly sermons of Canon Melville', and that he had been particularly struck by the old man's definition of conscience: 'Conscience is a lantern within the soul to light us on the way to Eternity.' David Melville did not want to stop preaching; he was not to resign his position of canon and sub-dean until he was ninety, and then refused to take a pension. In the early spring of 1898, since the canon, by then eighty-seven, did not travel to London any more, May had taken Burne-Jones back to Worcester to visit his friend, who, although twenty years his senior, was to outlive him.

During that last visit, Burne-Jones, who knew perhaps that he would never see this charming, erudite man again, did a silver-point drawing of him, which he completed in two hours. It survives today and is unusual in that it is not idealized, as we are used to with

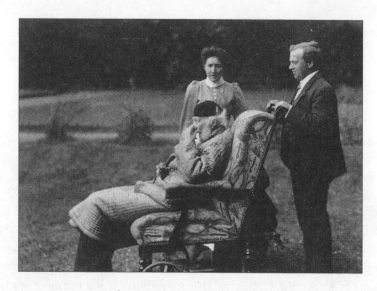

Summer 1903; one of Amy's photographs of Canon Melville, aged ninety-one, in his garden at College Green, Worcester, with his devoted nurse Mary and her husband. He died a year later.

Burne-Jones. It is a brilliant drawing, and clearly true to life: the strong bone structure, deep-set eyes and fine nose which made David Melville such a handsome man in his youth remained impressive in old age. It was at this time that the local paper recorded an incident in Worcester, when their oldest and best-loved canon 'showed his remarkable retention of physical vigour when, seeing two men fighting in the cathedral close, he threw himself upon them, separated them and made them desist'.

In the summer of 1903, in his ninety-second year and still living on College Green next to the cathedral, age finally took its toll on Canon Melville. Reluctantly, he took to a bath chair. During that beautiful summer, Amy, back in England after a visit with Lionel to her uncle Willie in the Argentine, visited her grandfather, the old canon. She brought a new camera with her to Worcester and took some touching photographs, including the one I knew well of her grandfather reading in his bath chair. In another picture he sits back against the patterned upholstery of the bath chair, looking pensively straight ahead. By his side are his nurse, Mary Collins, and her husband, who look down at him affectionately; the couple were apparently devoted to their ancient employer.

While she was staying with her grandfather in Worcester, Amy went back one day to see May's childhood home, Witley Rectory, taking her camera with her. Here she photographed every aspect of the house and garden to send to her uncle Willie in the Argentine, to remind him of his Worcestershire childhood. Amy had her own memories of times when she had stayed there with her grandparents as a young child, so in the album she sent to Willie she labelled pictures she found specially evocative from that time, such as: 'The chickens' paradise'; 'The frog corner'; 'The cherry orchard'; and, inexplicably, 'My crying tree'.

With Amy and Lionel back in England, May was enjoying summer at Kiddington, from where she wrote to her friend Alfred, now Lord Milner. He was still High Commissioner in South Africa, absorbed with the huge and divisive task of regeneration there. A team of clever young men from England helped him, and became known as 'Milner's Kindergarten'. One of these young men was John Buchan, the novelist, who lived near Kiddington and was to become a close

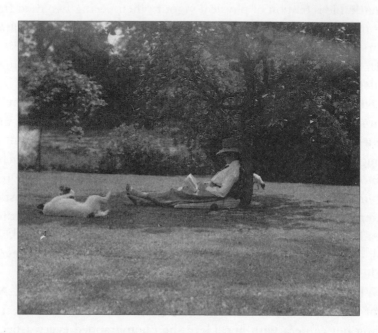

*Daphne on the lawn by the lake at Kiddington in 1906, with the
dogs she and her father loved. May titled this picture 'Daphne
enjoying herself.'*

friend of my grandparents Hal and Dolly Gaskell. May wrote to Alfred from Kiddington:

Oh! It is such a divine English summer morning, misty, a tremble of sunshine giving promise, the mowing machine whirring down the grass – a little ripple of wind, green, deep peaceful green closing in round one . . . The heart of friendship continually remembers you. As I stood looking out in the early morning I remembered a day in just such another leafy June which we spent on the Oxfordshire river – and I thought how you had been pulling against stream ever since. I thought of that bare highlight glare, in every sense, which you are living in now, and wondered if you would ever care to linger by the Windrush and look at old grey houses again.

May talked about Amy, and how pretty she was looking that summer, 'leading hearts by her dainty apron strings – but her own is safe I hope with her Lionel'. Could she perhaps have already had doubts about Amy's feelings for Lionel? At the end of her letter she mentioned her father, whose loss of strength after such a long forceful life she was finding hard to watch:

Father lingers – so old – oh dear friend, great age is the most pathetic thing alive. Goodbye – your country friend May.

But Daphne was the real country girl; May told Milner that, while writing, she could observe a dejected Daphne outside, leaving the garden reluctantly to go to her German lesson. Daphne wanted most of all to be riding her horse, or playing with the dogs on the lawn. Apart from the animals, Daphne had another passion: God. She told May she loved God above all others, and that he had comforted her 'more than any human ever could'.

Daphne's religious fervour was one of the things that led to rows with May, who particularly disapproved of what she considered her youngest daughter's unsuitable obsession with a local clergyman, Mr Philipps. Daphne had tried to explain to her mother in writing that he had done more for her than any of the family ever could, because he had made her 'love religion more than anything in the world'. She

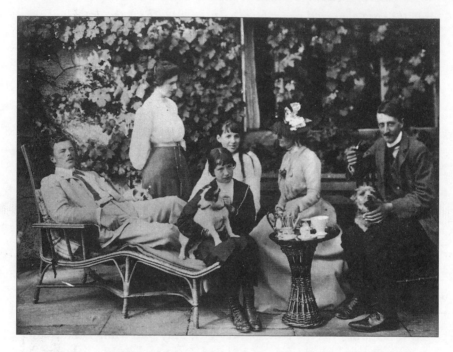

Autumn 1903; the family at Beaumont. Left to right: Lionel Bonham, Amy, Daphne, Dolly Bagot, May and Hal

wrote that she knew she and May would 'never agree about religion', and that May's teasing her about going to church twice a day and 'liking clergymen and parish things' only made her feel 'further away from you than anything'. Mr Philipps was a 'fine man', explained Daphne, 'I have not been absorbed with him personally, nearly so much as you think, though I own I like him <u>very</u> much.' She ended by dismissing something that May, in a letter I have not found, had apparently expressed concern about, regarding an incident in Mr Philipps's past: 'he was very young then and I'm sure he is forgiven'.

May and Daphne were going through a phase familiar to many mothers and headstrong teenage daughters. Daphne wrote a letter beginning affectionately 'Little Mother', and left it in May's room, to 'try and clear away a sort of barrier between us'. She confessed that she had begun to think that May did not love her: 'for the last three months you say I've been abominable to you, never thinking of you or anybody but myself'. She admitted there might be some truth in this, that she did get cross when May asked her to do things, but she felt she had reached an age 'when I think you order me around too much'. She realized she was 'selfish and very jealous and most things bad' and she tried to explain to her mother:

> When you are kind and loving like you used to be, I love you more than I can say, but sometimes mother you are so unkind and hard and even unjust . . . if you had a difficult nature like me you'd understand all this, but your nature is so much easier to manage than mine because it's not got such a cursed temper . . . remember I am fighting myself all the time . . . In years to come you will see that this is true, though you may not believe it now.

Daphne marked the envelope simply 'Mother'. May, sorting out and re-reading her letters towards the end of her life, had added in pencil: 'Poor little darling'.

That autumn the Gaskell family went up to Beaumont as usual. They were photographed in a group, the only notable absence being Captain Gaskell. The result was the kind of picture that people say 'speaks volumes'. Lionel, shortly to leave for Asia Minor, reclines on a chaise-longue, a cigarette holder in his hand, staring into the distance with a nonchalant air. Amy stands with her back to him, looking at her mother. Between them is a cheerful-looking young girl, about sixteen years old, with long dark hair and a straight fringe. May, who sits by the tea table in the kind of large stylish hat for which she was to be known until old age, is gazing intently at the girl with the fringe. In front of them is Daphne, holding a dog, her large nose clearly visible; she is looking cross. Daphne is also sixteen, but appears younger than the other girl. On the right of the picture sits Hal Gaskell, a curved pipe in his hand, holding another dog. His straight dark hair is parted far to one side so that a long lock crosses his forehead; he has a small dark moustache and looks straight at the camera, with a characteristically teasing expression in his eyes.

The young girl with the long dark hair was called Dolly Bagot, and she was to become my grandmother. Her family owned the historic and famously haunted Levens Hall, not far from Beaumont, near Kendal in Westmorland. Her father was Captain Josceline Fitzroy Bagot; once called 'the handsomest man of his time', he was also a politician and writer. And her beautiful, spirited mother, Dosia, was one of the women who had raised a few eyebrows when she went out to the Boer War in the kind of thrill-seeking way that had earned Queen Victoria's disapproval. The Bagots were close family friends of the Gaskells, and Dolly, their oldest daughter, shared a governess with Daphne, both at Beaumont and at Kiddington.

May had always loved to listen to her father's stories, and often repeated what she called his 'witty retorts', such as 'Common sense is uncommon sense.' At the beginning of the following March, in 1904, May went to visit her father for a few days. Canon Melville talked of his early days at Durham University. He told her the story, which she had often heard before, of when he had been seated next to Prince Louis Napoleon, nephew of the Emperor Napoleon Bonaparte, at Lord Londonderry's dinner table in 1848. Lord Londonderry had said of the prince, 'He is rather a bore I am afraid, and we would be most grateful if you will help her ladyship entertain him.' It was indeed hard going. But during dinner a messenger from France had arrived with a letter summoning Prince Louis to Paris to be offered the presidency of the French Republic, the prelude to his being elected emperor, as Napoleon III. The Prince had departed at once, leaving a relieved David Melville in the easier company of Lady Londonderry.

May returned to Kiddington feeling reassured because her father had seemed well. But the day after she left he caught a chill, which quickly turned to influenza. May received a telegram asking her to return to Worcester as soon as possible. She wrote later:

> *His heart was failing – he knew this, and fought Death vigorously for two days. But I was not sorry when the end came, and his spirit, that indomitable spirit, was clear and bright once more. I was alone with him. We buried him in the graveyard inside the cloister of his beloved cathedral, and on his stone is carved his own motto: 'Denique Coelum'. Heaven at last – at the age of ninety-two, what words could be more suitable.*

In the following week's edition of the High Church journal *The Guardian*, William Griffiths, a former Hatfield College pupil of David Melville, remembered the forceful character of the man he had known for over fifty years:

> It seemed as if his thoughts came out too thickly; not one patiently following another, but all in a bunch; averments, inferences, limitations, accentuations, alternatives, concessions, all flashing forth in one rich volley, like the storm of simultaneous shots from the broadside of a great ship . . . [there was] probably no man upon whose keen intellect, shrewd wisdom, and unprejudiced judgement it was more safe to rely. Peace to his ashes, good old man!

The casket containing Canon Melville's ashes was placed in a brick grave in the cathedral cloister, near to the Miserimus door. The grave was lined with moss, in which hundreds of bunches of snowdrops had been inserted. Even the banked-up earth was decorated with trails of ivy, snowdrops and yellow jonquils. There were a large number of people present at the funeral of this man whose remarkable personality, it was generally agreed, would be impossible to replace. The finely robed clergy included the dean, an archdeacon, eight canons and three minor canons. Accompanying May were her husband, her three children, and her younger brother, Beresford Melville. Lionel was unable to accompany his wife as he had just left for Salonika in Asia Minor, where, seconded from the Grenadier Guards, he was to train the Macedonian gendarmerie for a period of at least two years. So, at the same time as losing the grandfather she loved, Amy was parted from her husband once more.

Although young Hal Gaskell had lodgings in London, he much preferred to be in the country at Kiddington or Beaumont, or exploring provincial cities. He had thought of becoming an architect when he was a schoolboy, and still remained interested in buildings. But painting was what he enjoyed most, and during the spring and summer months he often wandered through the north of England, painting buildings and landscapes. Always alone, he was sometimes melancholy, but also revealed his odd humorous view of life in his letters to May. From the White Hart Hotel at Lincoln he wrote:

> *Here I have launched into a fine place they call a 'family hotel', where a young lady with a smirking face meets you at the door in a black lace gown, and the family part consists of many old maids and their companions, who have good appetites and don't seem to know what to do with themselves except wander about from one hotel to another.*

Hal enthused about Lincoln's fine cathedral, which overlooked the surrounding countryside, and the city itself, which had, he said:

> *... wonderful architecture of different dates from the Romans up. But after passing many marvels you finish with the gems of modern architecture, including 'Belle Vue', looking out onto a corrugated cow house, 'Suntrap', slightly windswept and looking north, 'The Laburnums', conspicuous by their absence. All these houses have a tin stork, or owl, painted white, in their gardens. This is what the guidebook calls modern progress. What is modern progress, can you please tell me?*

Hal was only twenty-four years old when he wrote these letters to May, and joked about his hair, which was already thinning:

Can you or Father tell me of any man in London learned on bald heads
and loss of hair as I fear the last three months have made sad ravages on
my head, and the fine forelock you were so proud as being like that of the
ticket collector at Lancaster is fast disappearing.

Amy never stayed in England long; she had inherited her mother's
urge to travel. A few years later, a friend of Daphne's wrote: 'It is a
pity Amy hates England.' In the early summer of 1904, while Lionel
was setting up a new training school for gendarmes in Salonika, Amy
was feeling bored and restless in England, where she could find no
inspiration for her painting and drawing. So she set off for Venice.
From the photographs in her album it looks as if she had no travelling
companions. She stayed at a pensione in Venice and spent time with
friends of May's, Mr and Mrs Eden, at their large villa nearby. The
villa was surrounded by a lovely garden, known as the Garden of
Eden. The only person who appears in her photographs, other than a
gondolier called Antonio, is an Englishman who, I learnt from one of
May's later letters, lived in Venice – a Mr Ker. From the two small,
distant photographs Amy took of him it is hard to see how old he was,
but it is just possible to make out that he had high cheekbones, a good,
straight nose and a rather stylish dark beard, and that his clothes and
Panama hat gave him an artistic air.

I found a reference to this Mr Ker in a letter written by May to
Daphne much later, four years after Amy's death, when she was in
Venice herself, shortly before the war started in 1914. She had seen
much, she told Daphne, of 'Amy's great friend Gervy Ker, who was
very fond of Amy'. It seems that he was so fond of her that 'he carved
a little A in stone over his garden door, which pleased her very much'.
Gervy Ker showed May the pensione on the Giudecca where Amy had
stayed, and pointed out her window. 'I like to look at it,' wrote May,
'she used to paint and sketch and drift about in a gondola all day and
every day, dining with him generally at a little restaurant we often go to.'

Was Ker just an older gentleman friend innocently looking after
Amy in Venice? Even though Amy was a married woman, she often
appears to have dined with him alone. This did make me wonder
about their relationship.

I have been able to follow some of Amy's movements over the years from a sort of birthday and autograph book, in which she asked friends and acquaintances to write the date and place they had seen her in the space provided for their own birth date. She took the book with her wherever she went, and often added small photographs of the signatories. Some wrote her poems. On April Fool's Day in 1896, when Amy was twenty-one years old, her grandfather Canon Melville had written:

> *A fool and his folly 'tis said are soon parted*
> *If so the fool simply becomes single hearted*
> *But this for myself I decline if so may be*
> *As my folly asserts itself – weakness for Amy.*

While she was in South Africa in 1902, a Mr Lewis wrote verses in French, envying Lionel for having such a sweet wife, and ending:

> *a ton mari la gloire*
> *seulement de t'avoir*
> *et de t'aimer – la bien aimee*
> *Thus my homage sweet Amy.*

In the same year at the Woolsack, Rudyard Kipling wrote out a verse from one of his long poems, 'The Native Born', in Amy's autograph book:

> *To the home of the floods and thunder*
> *To her pale dry healing blue –*
> *To the lift of the great cape combers*
> *And the smell of the baked Karroo –*
> *To the reef and the water-gold –*
> *To the last and the largest empire*
> *To the map that is half unfurled.*

Over three-quarters of the entries are from men, particularly when she was on her travels. Edward Burne-Jones, on an undated visit to Kiddington, had simply drawn a charming cherub sitting on a tree-topped hill.

*

I have always remembered a story my mother told me about my grandparents' engagement. Who told her the story remains a mystery, as no one alive in the family today remembers. What is known is that Dolly Bagot's mother, Dosia, was a vain woman. She was certainly striking, though I have never liked the slight sneer of her full, down-turned lips in photographs and portraits. The story goes that Dosia had a horror of being thought anything other than young and beautiful. She had three daughters; when her oldest, Dolly, was seventeen, people began to notice what a very pretty young girl she was, with her heart-shaped face, sparkling eyes, neat features and thick dark hair. Dosia did not like the idea of being thought of as the mother of an attractive grown-up daughter. One day when the Bagot family was staying at Kiddington, as they often did, Dosia walked into the conservatory to find Dolly sitting on Hal Gaskell's knee. 'Congratulations on your engagement,' she said without any hesitation.

According to my mother, Dosia was keen to marry Dolly off as soon as possible, so that instead of having to introduce a grown-up daughter at parties she could just say 'Do you know Mrs Gaskell?' Though this story may not be entirely true, the fact remains that all of a sudden Hal Gaskell, not the most decisive of men, was engaged to his younger sister's playmate, who was only seventeen. In fact Hal had started to befriend little Dolly two or three years previously, and used to write to her from all round the country when he was painting and sketching. As early as 1902, when Dolly had not yet turned fifteen, he wrote to her from Pembrokeshire:

You see I have started on my lonely summer tour across hill and down dale, squatting in front of rivers, castles, trees and odd things, scratching away on a dirty bit of paper. It does seem senseless rot doesn't it? But isn't it more useful than putting and taking off dresses all day and lacing yourself up so tight that there is hardly room for the seven cups of poisonous tea some people pour into themselves every afternoon.

These were still the days when girls as young as twelve wore tightly laced corsets.

At the start of spring 1904, a year before Hal and Dolly were married, Hal prepared to set off around England once more with his palette, paints, pencils and sketchbook. He wrote to Dolly:

> How old Hal relishes the idea of spring coming on, how he longs to be always among the things he loves best in the world, sunning himself, with his pencils always going. There is no joy in the whole world so sweet as the love of natural life of which poor worn out man was originally wholly part – so may we in time get nearer to what we were meant to be: happy, free, healthy, peaceful and contented.

Although in jest, Hal often ended his letters in the familiar plaintive tone of his childhood, 'Pity me' or 'Your poor old Hal'.

In January 1905, Hal was staying up at Levens just after his engagement to Dolly had been officially announced. In her old age, Dolly told her eldest grandson that Hal used to climb up the drainpipe to visit her in her bedroom at night. Hal wrote to Daphne, for the first time referring to Dolly by the Bagot family's pet name for her, Dar:

> Dar is very pleased with reams of correspondence coming in every morning full of congratulations to her. I fear it ought to be more the other way round. Dar looks and is simply delicious, and there can't be two people better off than we are at present.

But poor Daphne told May she felt she was losing her closest friend.

With his passion for quiet rural life, Hal must have been put out by the fact that owing to a recent fire at Levens, Dolly's mother Dosia had arranged a large, smart wedding in London. On 9 May, hundreds of distinguished guests filled the Holy Trinity Church in Marylebone. Eighteen-year-old Dolly looked angelic in her white satin dress trimmed with old Brussels lace. Significantly, May had given her new daughter-in-law a bouquet of the flowers Burne-Jones had assigned to her – lilies of the valley, tied with long white satin streamers. Daphne was one of six bridesmaids. Amy was unable to be there; she had gone to Salonika to visit Lionel, a reunion that was to be their last time together. *The Times* listed an incredible collection of luxurious presents. The elaborate wedding must have been quite an ordeal for such a private person as Hal, but when it came to the honeymoon he had his own way. Not for him the traditional tour in grand hotels on the Continent; instead, after their reception, he and his young bride set off for the depths of the English countryside he so loved.

Hal wanted to show Dolly a place that was particularly special for him: Great Witley, in Worcestershire, where he had frequently stayed with his Melville grandparents as a child. He took Dolly to the Hundred House Hotel, still there to this day, which had seen the festivities on the eve of his own parents' marriage. Soon after they arrived, Hal wrote to May:

> *We are staying here a fortnight as we are both so very happy and Dar loves the place. We spend our whole time on the hills and in the woods . . . Dar and I are simply brimming with happiness, and the new life has thrown us into the seventh heaven.*

Hal was horrified to discover that the new vicar had felled most of the fine trees his father had planted at the Rectory, his grandparents' old home. But Witley still held its magic for him in his newly found bliss with Dolly. Hal told his mother:

> *You have no idea how happy we are, everything seems to join in with us, the sun shines, the birds sing and all the old Witley flowers and blossoms come out to their full. We even heard a nightingale singing in the place where I used to come and listen for them . . . Thank you so much dear mother for all you have done for us, and I know you will see what a solid foundation stone you have laid for our future happiness . . . I would go through all the years waiting, again and again, for Dar.*

On 27 May Hal brought Dolly back to Kiddington. They were to live at Kiddington Assarts, a farmhouse on the estate, as well as renting a house in London. Many years later Susan, Lady Tweedsmuir (John Buchan's wife), published a charming photograph in her memoir *The Lilac and the Rose*. The picture was titled 'An Oxfordshire Squire brings home his bride in the 1900s', and it showed Hal, Dolly and a dog entering the village in a carriage. But a horse did not draw the carriage; in harness instead was a grinning local, while

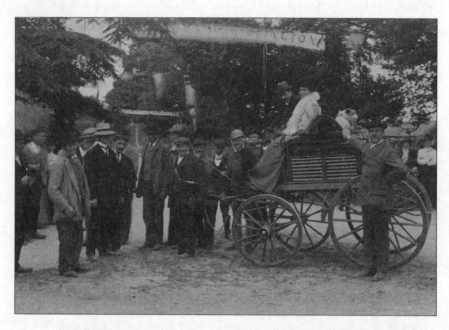

May 1905; 'An Oxfordshire Squire brings home his bride'; Hal arriving back at Kiddington with his new wife Dolly after their honeymoon in Worcestershire. Note the grinning estate worker 'in harness' at the front of the carriage.

all around spectators were seen smiling wryly. Above the happy scene a banner read: 'Welcome back to Kiddington'. Hal, who spent the rest of his life resisting anything new, looked dapper in a smart trilby hat with a ribbon round it. He wore this hat well into old age, refusing to throw the tattered thing away, but grudgingly allowing Dolly to put a clean piece of ribbon on it each Christmas, taken from a box of chocolates.

By the end of 1905, May was feeling troubled. Her huge collection of letters from Burne-Jones was still a great source of strength and comfort, but she could not forget that he had always told her to burn them. What would happen to them if she died? She wrote to Lord Milner, whose advice she respected so much, and told him of her dilemma. After he replied she wrote again:

> When your letter came agreeing with my own longing about the letters *I was very glad*. If your advice had been different I should have followed it – such faith have I in your understanding affection. I shall put those which are the most precious to me now into locked books and leave them to Amy in my will to destroy after my death. She may read them all if she likes – but then the love that prompted them must cease to be known.

As I read this I had a pang of conscience. The letters had not gone to Amy because she had died before her mother. By the time she left them to Daphne many years later, May had changed her mind about asking for them to be destroyed. But she did say that they were 'not for the eye of the casual reader'. So what was I doing putting them into a book? Yet I feel certain that through her correspondence, left carefully labelled for all to see after her death, May did ultimately want 'those who come after' to know about the love she had inspired in Burne-Jones. In old age she even had many of his letters beautifully bound in leather, showing her intention to preserve them for posterity. Much time has passed, and there is no one left who could be hurt by anything they reveal. Of course May would have felt sensitive about the famous painter's most intimate letters being seen during her lifetime, but I hope that my disclosing the depth of their friendship now will be a tribute to both of them, and something they would each have wanted. A friend of mine told me that he feels that the dead wish to talk to us. He may be right.

In the same letter to Milner about Burne-Jones's precious letters, May wrote: 'I sent the most likely to be misunderstood to you – I have many like that.' This suggests that May had sent Milner some of the most intimate letters. She explained:

> I knew *you* would understand what they are to me – how they were possible and beyond all that even, the exquisite pleasure they are to read ... I don't think this life would be possible if I couldn't enter into my chamber and be still, and read, and remember about all that the past has been to me. Then peace comes and the past seems the reality, not this worried present.

If only, May wished, Burne-Jones could know how he supported her still: 'I often think how glad he would be to know his help is still with me, strong and good and giving happiness.'

To add to her previous ills, whether they were a psychosomatic reaction to her unhappy marriage or not, May, now fifty-two years old, was beginning to suffer from bad arthritis. She wanted, as often before, to go somewhere warmer and drier than cold, damp Kiddington that winter. Though she said she was reluctant to leave Daphne, or Hal either, particularly as Dolly was pregnant with their first child, she justified her proposed escape: 'I see more harm in gradually growing useless without a struggle to improve.'

So far, as I had followed May through her life I had admired her in many ways, but now her confidences and complaints to Milner seemed full of self-pity. Why did she leave her family so often? How bad were her ailments really? How unbearable was her marriage? How close was she in truth to the children she said she loved so much? I did not want to turn against my great-grandmother, for I felt she had admirable strengths, and I was to find that in later life she achieved much through her compassion for others, but at this point I wondered about all these things. In a letter to Milner she observed that women 'are not supposed to have individual lives'. Perhaps her journeys abroad, even if they were 'for her health', simply gave her a life of her own.

So May did travel to a restorative warmer climate in early 1906, despite the fact that her first grandchild was expected at the end of February, and that her husband Henry Brooks had not been well for some time, though he never complained. She left him in Daphne's care: Daphne was a more caring companion for her father than May would ever be.

Once she reached Sicily, May sounded far happier, her pain apparently forgotten. In a letter to Dolly's father, Josceline Bagot, from the Grand Hotel Villa Politi in Syracuse, she wrote:

> *The sun is as warm as June, birds singing and all the sounds and sights of sweetest spring ... Before me is lovely Syracuse with its piled up island town floating in the bluest of seas ... I fear Daphne cannot join me, Captain Gaskell's long illness has been a great anxiety, and it would never do for her to leave him.*

Why would she imply that it was his daughter rather than his wife who could not leave Captain Gaskell when he was ill? Was May being ironic, or was she feeling guilty? And could Captain Bagot, who had a somewhat flighty wife of his own, have known about May's marriage difficulties?

On 1 March 1906, Dolly Gaskell, just nineteen years old, gave birth to her first child at their London home, 21 Chester Terrace. She insisted on walking about until the very end of her labour, and then produced a nine-and-a-half-pound boy. This was my father, whom they called Tom, the first Gaskell heir for five generations not to be named Henry. Amy, who was in the house at the time, was asked to be his godmother. The baby was said to look exactly like his grandfather Henry Brooks, with the large Gaskell nose already in evidence. Secretly May had hoped the baby would be a girl, with a neatly shaped nose like Dolly's. When Dolly had first become pregnant, May had remarked that she hoped the baby would not inherit the nose that, she said, 'has been too much for me'. If she heard remarks like this, it is not surprising that Daphne, who had certainly inherited the nose, felt unloved by her mother.

The news of Tom's birth reached May in Syracuse by telegram the same day, as she was watching 'the afterglow of the sunset' from her hotel room. For some reason the telegram was worded in French:

'GARCON TOUT VA BIEN'. May was of course delighted, and wrote to Hal the next day:

> *I am so happy. I do trust with all my heart that Dolly had a good time,*
> *and is now lying pale and lovely with her little Prince Royal beside her –*
> *and you feeling more tenderness in your heart for the mother of your child*
> *than ever you felt for your wife. It is a time never to forget.*

May talked about Amy, now preparing to make the long journey to Ceylon, and remembered the joy of her birth. She must have longed for her firstborn daughter to have a child of her own. But May was pleased to be a grandmother, and imagined how the news of the baby's arrival had been received in Kiddington:

> *I expect the bells rang finely, and father smiled grimly in his bed with*
> *them clanging away close by, and was really as pleased as anyone about*
> *the son and heir.*

May's husband Henry was now sixty. Despite his ill health he was still a local magistrate, gardened energetically at Kiddington, and went shooting regularly. He had only recently given up occasional pruning work at Kew Gardens, which he had done voluntarily, because he loved being amongst the rare plants and exotic trees. Because of increasing chest problems he would sometimes go abroad for 'cures' during the colder months, probably because May encouraged him, though even if they went abroad at the same time they never chose to travel together, and were always in different countries. Henry Brooks would frequently write to his 'little Daphne' while he was away. In the spring of 1907, when he was staying at the Hotel Bristol in Gibraltar, he wrote a misanthropic letter to Daphne, who was in Spain with May:

> *Awful noises have been coming from the cathedral next door, and now*
> *they are howling dreadfully. There are an awful lot of old women here*
> *who bag all the newspapers, block up all the doorways, and never go the*
> *Ladies Salon, which is specially provided for them. I have not spoken to*
> *anyone.*

In early December of that same year, Daphne met her father at the local station after he had been shooting in the north of England, and they drove back to Kiddington together. Hal and Dolly had given up their London house and were living permanently in the farmhouse nearby with their little son Tom, now a toddler, as Hal learned about the management of the estate. Amy, they heard, had reached Ceylon and settled down at the Galle Face Hotel in Colombo. I can find no record of where May was at this time, but perhaps she was abroad once more. Five days after his return to Kiddington, Henry Brooks, walking the dogs he and Daphne loved so much, began to feel unwell. A chest cold had developed into pneumonia, and a week later, on 20 December 1907, he died in his bedroom, with Hal and Daphne at his side. Daphne was heartbroken, and left Kiddington at once to stay with some friends. Hal wrote to her the next day:

The little gold ring from his little finger you certainly must have, and anything else you would like, to help you in the future, or anything you think he would like you to have. He left me a letter, at the end he said 'Take care of little Daphne', and it shall be so, as far as Dar and I can give you lifting hands and pleasant moments. Poor little girl I do understand it.

Amy wrote from Ceylon, sympathizing with her sister on the loss of the father she herself had not been close to:

I am dreadfully sorry for you because I think it means more to you than anybody – I do understand how frightfully you cared – and how he was everything to you – but he said so often that he dreaded a long illness so I know you will be glad for his sake . . . I wish I was there to help you, I understand so well how very, very bad it is for you. Keep this letter to yourself – your very loving Amy.

It seems that I shall never discover how May reacted to her husband's death, or if she was even in the country at the time, because I have found nothing that mentions her, and no letters for that period amongst those she wrote to Alfred Milner. Perhaps this is telling in itself.

Henry Brooks was buried in the graveyard of the little church

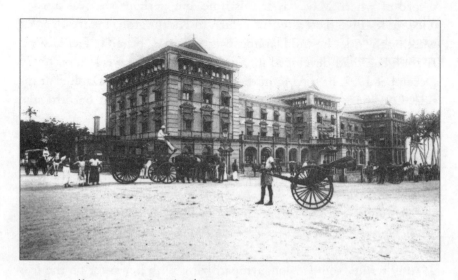

The Galle Face Hotel, Colombo, c.1900, where Amy stayed when she first arrived in ceylon in 1907.

adjoining Kiddington. He left the legacy of his expert planting of trees, shrubs and roses; a cedar tree that he planted can still be seen from the church at Kiddington. On a marble slab within the church is a memorial to him with an inscription taken from I Kings:

> And he spake of trees, from the cedar that is in Lebanon even unto the Hyssop that springeth out of the wall.

When May chose this epitaph for her husband she must have remembered a letter that Burne-Jones had written her early on in their friendship. He had observed:

> *How we do agree together about everything that is – from the Cedar of Lebanon to the Hyssop on the wall.*

She may also have regretted that this compatibility could not in latter years have been applied to herself and her husband.

In early 1908, May and Mrs Iles, her devoted, long-standing personal maid and by now her closest companion, prepared to move out of Kiddington to make way for Hal, Dolly and their baby Tom. The Gaskell house at Marble Arch had been sold a few years previously and Beaumont was now let again, so May was moving temporarily to a rented house in London, 10 Victoria Square, but planned to travel abroad even more than before. Hal did not want to change any of May's tasteful decoration at Kiddington, and never did. As a result of his refusal to install electricity, there was still a lamp boy amongst the staff in 1950. In 1949 he was finally persuaded to allow electricity to be installed at Kiddington's home farm, but, although he knew Dolly wanted it, he still would not hear of it in his own house. May left most of the furniture and pictures behind in the house, but she took all her Burne-Jones paintings and drawings with her.

At this point she decided to lend a very large gold chest, or cassone, decorated by Burne-Jones, which stood in the hall, to the Ashmolean, from where it was moved to the Birmingham City Art Gallery, where it remains today. A cassone is a Renaissance marriage chest; it may have been a significant choice of gift to May, considering that Burne-Jones's work often contained secret meanings and messages. In giving

May this chest, could he have intended it to signify a kind of mystic betrothal? It is a beautiful piece called 'Feeding the Dragon in the Garden of the Hesperides', and recalls Burne-Jones's famous painting 'The Garden of the Hesperides'. The wood is covered in gesso and gilt, with elaborate mouldings at top and bottom. The front shows the tree that bears the golden apples, entwined by a vast winged serpent. On either side are two lovely women, the beautiful Hesperides, who were nymphs of the setting sun, the daughters of Hesperus, the evening star. The Hesperides guarded the Garden of the Gods on the very edge of the world, where the tree with golden apples grew in the centre. To steal these apples and to kill the serpent, Ladon, was one of Hercules' final labours. The verses inscribed at each end of the cassone are by William Morris, taken from one of his long poems, 'The Life and Death of Jason', and end with:

> *But since the golden age is gone,*
> *This little place is left alone,*
> *Unchanged, unchanging, watched of us,*
> *The daughters of wise Hesperus.*

There is a photograph taken by Amy in 1905 of the cassone in the hall at Kiddington, and an earlier one at Beaumont, taken about twelve years previously. Today another chest is in its place at Kiddington, but the hall remains unchanged, still retaining the Chinese-style wall painting which May commissioned when she moved in ten years before the end of the nineteenth century.

In 1908, having organized her own departure from Kiddington, May turned her attention to Daphne, who was still extremely upset by her father's death, and sad too at having to leave her beloved Kiddington. The only time she looked happy now was when she was on her horse, Ditchley, who had been frequently mentioned in her father's letters. May decided that they should go to the Argentine to visit her brother Willie. Amy, on hearing of this plan, wrote from Ceylon that Daphne would like South America; 'the ponies, sun and outdoor life', she told her sister, would be distracting and enjoyable, though she added, 'but I do not see Mother there'. She had observed before that Daphne and May had 'diametrically opposite natures', and

May had always been more stimulated by culture and civilized places than by wild open spaces. Amy, accustomed to years of admiring attention from her mother, which was sometimes overwhelming, now seemed somewhat put out that May had only written to her once since Henry Brooks's death: 'so I know nothing about anything or anybody – only my friends write, those who do not know any of you'.

Daphne's sister-in-law Dolly, her childhood friend, also wrote to her:

> *I felt so sad saying goodbye to you, and how I thought about you that afternoon when you went away – I know how much you loved Kiddington and what a dreadful wrench it must have been for you ... you have been so good and sweet to me, I must seem a most horrid creature taking what ought to be yours, and I shall never forget all the kind things you have done for me and all the fun we had at Beaumont and Kiddington.*

Hal, in his way, had clearly been concerned about his little sister, and now that he was head of the family felt he should offer her some fatherly support. He too wrote her a note, in his odd but affectionate style, which may well have reminded her of her father:

> *My Dear Little Woman – As I was not able to say a proper goodbye today I take this opportunity to wish you luck in your future journey through life, and may you find a husband, and a jolly good one too, and don't flirt too much, it doesn't suit you. You will always find a helping hand and willing hearts at Kiddington. We mean to make the sun shine, as healthy nature would wish, so you mustn't leave us too long. Take the advice of one who has never succeeded. Keep your eyes and thoughts on the present, don't pry into the future, or look back into the past, and above all keep your mind smiling. Your sincere plaguey old Prophet, Hal.*

Hal's droll remark about his lack of success was not really a joke to him: he suffered from a great lack of self-esteem. Since he was a young boy, when Burne-Jones had given him his first lessons in drawing and painting, and encouraged him to pursue painting as a career, Hal had longed above all to be a great artist. He had proved by now that he had real talent, and he had even been accepted as a member of the Friday Club, which Vanessa Bell had started in London in 1905, hoping to create the kind of artistic circle she had found in Paris café society, where artists could come out of their lonely studios, meet each other, exchange ideas and see each other's work. The Friday Club's occasional exhibitions, which included work by young artists of talent, drew much comment from the press.

One of these exhibitions had taken place at Clifford's Inn Hall, in one of London's Inns of Court, in 1906. Hal, aged twenty-seven, showed six of his watercolours in a mixed show, which included works by several other members who were, or were to become, illustrious artists, including Vanessa Bell herself, Wilfred Scawen Blunt, Henry Lamb, Neville Lytton and Roger Fry. Even though Hal was young, his painting style was in no way modern, unlike that of many of the Friday Club members; he belonged firmly to the classic English watercolour school. The painters he most admired were Thomas Girtin, who died in 1802, and John Sell Cotman, who was dead by 1842, both of whose work some of Hal's early paintings can almost be mistaken for.

However, even though young Hal painted in the style of a former generation, a review of the exhibition, stuck proudly in May's album, observed that 'Henry Melville Gaskell's six watercolours will seem to many the most remarkable achievement of the exhibition. Their perfect execution, delicacy of colouring, and admirable restraint, deserve the highest praise.' Yet despite this encouragement, Hal would within a few years cease showing his work to anyone, and although he continued painting prolifically in private, he destroyed hundreds of his paintings. This regrettable situation may have stemmed from the first time his paintings were ever shown, in a local exhibition; only his family and friends bought them, and Hal hated the idea that they might have felt obliged to buy simply to support him. He said he never wanted it to happen again. Coupled with his odd, withdrawn character, this may have prevented him from seeking the wide recognition he had dreamt of.

After his first hard and dangerous years in the Argentine, May's elder brother Willie had risen, May wrote, to become 'one of the most prominent settlers in the Argentine Republic'. He was much loved out there, and his 'splendid physique and charming personality', inherited from his father, were admired by all. He always kept in touch with his beloved Worcestershire by reading Berrow's *Worcestershire Journal*, which was sent out to him, together with clothes and boots, which he still had made for him in Worcester. In 1908 Willie was fifty-seven years old, but was still manager of the Estancia Drabble, where he had both built the house and established the vast farm for the absent owner. The house had deep verandas, and was painted in the traditional style of the area: cream whitewash and brown woodwork. There was a well-tended garden, and the heart-shaped leaves of a large catalpa tree gave dappled shade to the lawn.

Willie had worked so hard during his years in the Argentine that he did not marry until middle age, but his heart was finally won by a beautiful young girl, Celestina Cantaruti, with flashing black eyes and raven hair. She was the youngest of six daughters of a nursery gardener of peasant stock and Italian extraction, who provided trees and plants to the new homesteads being set up in the area. Willie sent Celestina to Buenos Aires for a year to learn English, and then 'kept her under wraps', not taking her out into the local 'stuck up' Anglo-Argentine society until two years after their marriage. Their Pygmalion-like story is still remembered in Argentina today. Apparently Celestina underwent a transformation, and 'lived and behaved like any duchess would', becoming in old age a true 'grande dame', to whom everyone in the district deferred.

May, who only wanted her favourite brother to be happy, had no reservations about Celestina's humble origins, but Amy, who had been the first of the family to meet her, had told Daphne that she could 'make things difficult', which may have been a reference to Celestina having developed, with her rise in station, a rather imperious manner. Amy and Lionel had visited Uncle Willie, Celestina, and their baby son, Berry, at Estancia Drabble in the autumn of 1902, shortly after Lionel's return from South Africa. At that time, Willie had written enthusiastically to May about the visit of 'little Amy and her glorious Lionel'. They had stayed with him for four months. Soon afterwards Celestina gave birth to another son, Tinito, who astonished everyone by never crying, until it was found out from the smell on his breath

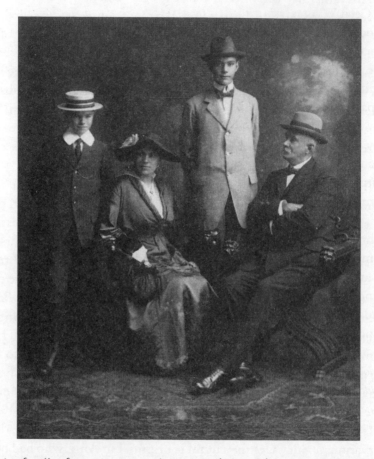

The family from the Argentine: May's beloved brother Uncle Willie,
and his wife Celestina, with their two sons Tinito, left, and Berry,
in the centre.

that his nanny had been giving him a little brandy to keep him happy.*

Very soon after May and Daphne's arrival in the Argentine in the autumn of 1908, Daphne became engaged to a man she had only just met, Cecil Wynter, who worked on an estancia near Drabble. Perhaps she took her brother Hal's advice rather too literally, or perhaps it was a reaction to the death of her father and the loss of her childhood home. It may also have struck her that with Amy abroad for an indefinite period, her mother might start relying too much on her company. The engagement was welcomed; friends and family, who knew how attached Daphne had been to her father, were full of sympathy for her. Although her vitality was attractive, Daphne could be difficult, and with her enormous nose and little face she was no beauty. She had lived under the shadow of a glamorous older sister, whom her mother preferred, for too long. This 'strong, clean young man', nicknamed Cis, who had fallen so instantly in love with Daphne, seemed an unexpected blessing.

Amy, who had left what seemed to have become her permanent base at the other end of the world in Ceylon, wrote to her sister from Peking, after visiting Japan, of her delight in hearing that 'you have found somebody to really belong to you and love you'. She thought it 'splendid' and pointed out yet again:

> *I do not think you and mother would ever have got on very well . . . I seldom was so pleased at anything as to hear you were so happy after the miserable time you have had lately.*

---

* Tinito Melville grew up to be a charming, cultured man who wrote poetry and plays prolifically, but was too shy to publish them. He had continued to live at the house his father had built on his retirement. About thirty-five miles from Drabble, on land known for its particularly sweet water, it was called El Clarin. Like Hal at Kiddington, Tinito changed nothing in the house after he inherited it. He never married, and when he died in 1983, he left no will. Some ageing cousins on his mother's side of the family, who spoke no English, were surprised to inherit the farm. An English friend of Tinito's came to sort out the English family papers and photographs to send back to May's descendants, but was told that as they were selling the house complete with its contents they would not part with some attractive pictures of two women. I have just found out that these were photogravure reproductions of Burne-Jones's portrait of Amy and his last drawing of May. They remain to this day, stained with damp, in the house in the middle of the Argentinian pampas.

Although his niece was such an outdoor girl, and although he liked and admired her young man, only Uncle Willie was not sure if Daphne was quite suited to the rough, raw life of the Argentine.

By the time Daphne got back to England, and went to meet her fiancé's parents in Yorkshire, she was not so sure herself. She telegraphed to the Argentine and asked Cecil to release her from the engagement. Being such an upright young man, he granted Daphne her freedom with a good grace, telling her that he would always think her 'such a ripper' and 'my greatest friend on earth – nothing will ever change that'. With great generosity he added that he would send her two horses he had given her while she was out in the Argentine. But his mother was appalled; she told Daphne that her decision to break the engagement after only four months had been a terrible blow:

> Colonel Wynter and I could not imagine you had ceased to love my boy (if it ever was love except in your imagination) . . . I know that he is suffering horribly – and God knows what effect it may have on him.

But their son's suffering did not last long; two years later Cecil was to write happily to Daphne, telling her that he was engaged to another 'ripping girl'.

Daphne's broken engagement precipitated a revealing sisterly letter from Amy, who was back in Ceylon. She wondered if Daphne was doing the right thing:

> Of course if you don't love your Cis it was the only thing to do – but it seems rather sad, as you really liked him and everything in him – I am not such a believer in Love – I think only one in a hundred people find the real person (the other side of themselves) – personally I have never found him.

Even more tellingly, she told Daphne that 'in nearly all things that matter' women were stronger than men, but that a woman had to make her man think himself the stronger; 'for in letting him think so lies her strength'. She felt that Daphne was searching for someone who was 'stronger, cleverer and more richly endowed' than she was, but that she might never find him. Amy recognized that 'things will be difficult for you living with mother', because, she suspected, of their very different natures, but that Daphne must not make the mistake of thinking that 'ordinary attraction to a nice looking decent man' was love. She told her little sister to 'go slow' in her relations with men and to use her head rather than her emotions. She ended her letter consolingly:

> *This looks like a sermon but it is not – it is just telling you a few things I have learned . . . darling little Daphne – if you ever worry about a man come to me – if I am anywhere about – for I shall always understand and perhaps be able to help you better than most. Your very loving Amy.*

Nowhere in her long letter, or indeed in the few others I have found, did Amy mention her husband Lionel. I sometimes wonder if she ever really loved him, or anyone. Certainly that is what is implied in this letter. But of course she had not seen Lionel now for about two years, and only sporadically for a few years before that. It was now nearly ten years since they were married, yet they had no children. And Amy's letter to Daphne suggested that she had had other relationships with men – one of whom, as I found out later, was to be the man her little sister was searching for.

So Daphne faced the return to Kiddington she dreaded, where she felt she no longer belonged, where she would no longer be her father's favourite, 'the queen of dirt'. A new generation of Gaskells were beginning to grow up there: there was little Tom with his shiny dark hair, olive skin and slate-grey eyes, and a new baby girl, Diana, who was born in the summer of 1909. Dolly had told Daphne that she would be welcome at Kiddington whenever she chose to come, even though, she added hopefully, 'things will have to be changed and different as time goes on'. But would things ever really change at Kiddington? Sometimes when I go back and stand in that familiar hall I wonder if they ever have. Since Hal and Dolly had moved there the year before, Dolly was beginning to find that Hal could at times be as silent as his grandfather and father had been when they lived there. Before they married, Hal had written to Dolly about his family: 'all of us are as funny and unsuited to one another as usual'. It appears that this situation was set to continue for the next generation.

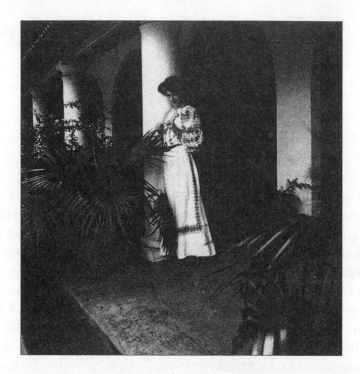

The only photograph I have found of Amy in Ceylon, wearing
her favourite peasant-style dress.

CHAPTER NINE

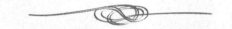

THE MYSTIC EAST

MAY ONCE DESCRIBED AMY AS 'A WONDERFUL MYSTIC CREATURE OF wayward charm'. She certainly appears to have been wayward, with her determination to live mostly apart from family and friends, and she was interested in mysticism and spiritual things. Amy had become fascinated by the Orient when, aged twenty, she read a book called *Out of the East*, by an Irish writer, Lafcadio Hearn. This compelling writer caught Amy's imagination. When he was young he had travelled to Japan and married a samurai's daughter. He became a Japanese citizen, took a Japanese name and wore Japanese clothes. He wrote books of a poetic and spiritual nature, interpreting Japanese traditions and thought for Western readers. Amy was one Westerner who became entranced by the pictures he painted, and she had resolved to travel to the East one day.

Over ten years later, towards the end of 1907, despite her father's deteriorating state of health, Amy first set off on her Eastern travels, planning to start in colonial Ceylon before visiting Japan and China. She arrived by boat in the capital, Colombo. Colombo was said then to be more progressive than any other city in South-East Asia, yet it still had open sewers, the contents of which would spread over the muddy streets during the floods of the rainy season. In the dry season the

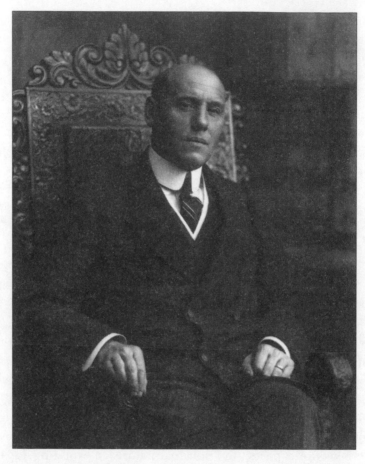

Sir Hugh Clifford, Colonial Secretary and Acting Governor in Ceylon while Amy was there. He lent her his house in Kandy.

winds sent up whirling clouds of dust, particularly along the Galle Face esplanade, where Amy stayed on her arrival at the imposing Galle Face Hotel, built twenty years before. It was, and still is today, a vast and grandiose building facing the sea, set in forty acres of grounds. At that time it vied with the splendour of Colombo's Grand Oriental Hotel, which had previously been favoured by rich visitors to Ceylon.

In British-governed Ceylon, Amy found herself in a small social circle. She had an introduction to the Colonial Secretary, Sir Hugh Clifford, who was a friend of May's. Sir Hugh's appearance was arresting: he was extremely tall, with deep-set, piercing eyes and an abnormally large, bald head, which he never protected even in the most sizzling sun. He was strong in physique, intellect and character. A couple of decades later, a young acquaintance of Sir Hugh Clifford's, Noel Coward, got the idea for his song 'Mad Dogs and Englishmen' after observing Clifford's sunburnt head and erratic behaviour. Throughout his many years as a colonial administrator, both in Malaya and Ceylon, Clifford was regarded as highly gifted, although reactionary, eccentric, and intolerant of views other than his own.

Clifford was also a prolific and much-praised writer of both novels and non-fiction, almost all relating to the Far East. As a writer about similar areas, Clifford published the first survey of Joseph Conrad's work in the *Singapore Free Press* in 1898, and the two men met and became friends after Conrad reviewed one of Clifford's books. Conrad felt that it was Clifford's fuelling of public enthusiasm for his work that led to *Chance* becoming his first successful novel. He dedicated the book to him: 'To Sir Hugh Clifford KCMG, whose steadfast friendship is responsible for the existence of these pages.'

Clifford was deeply interested in the character and ways of the people in whose countries he lived. Twenty years in Malaya had fuelled this fascination. He had mixed with the Malay rulers, eaten their food, and often dressed like the natives. He wrote several romantic novels drawn from his experiences there. He was, for that era, a champion of equality between the races, though his first non-fiction work, *Studies in Brown Humanity* – the one which Conrad reviewed – could hardly sound less PC to us today. Almost twenty years later, the president of the Ceylon National Congress remembered that when Sir Hugh arrived in Ceylon as the new Colonial Secretary, he made a deep impression on all who met him:

> . . . *he dazzled us with his brilliance. His great intellectual gifts, his high literary attainments, his unbounded energy and capacity for work, and his commanding personality, won our profound admiration.*

However, Hugh Clifford was already showing signs of the bouts of extreme behaviour and manic depression that would dog him as he grew older, though at the time Amy knew him he just had occasional 'black dog' days. He was a fascinating personality and a man of great charm, reputed to be 'a tremendous lady's man'. He had recently lost his first wife. Soon after Amy arrived in Ceylon at the end of 1907, it was reported that Sir Hugh Clifford had been seen riding in a carriage down Lady Horton's Walk in Kandy with a 'glamorous lady', described as the visiting wife of an Indian Army officer. It was remarked that 'even a brief glimpse showed that the lady had made a conquest'. Since the timing fitted exactly with Amy's visit, and she was also the glamorous wife of an army officer, it is possible that there had been a mistake about which army the lady's absent husband was in, and this could well have been Amy.

During this period the governor of Ceylon, Henry McCallum, was on leave, and Sir Hugh Clifford was acting governor. At such times Clifford liked to use the governor's residence in Kandy, a grand building known as the King's Pavilion, when he came up from Colombo, instead of his own official residence next door. Kandy, high in the hills, had been the last independent kingdom of the Sinhalese until the British took it in the early nineteenth century. The town still held the shrine containing one of the most sacred of Buddhist relics: the Buddha's Tooth. At the beginning of the twentieth century, Kandy was the capital of the planting districts – primarily tea, as well as coffee, and just recently the start of rubber plantations. Because of the town's position and mild climate, officials loved to serve there, or else arranged to come up from Colombo for prolonged holidays.

Hugh Clifford remained between marriages for the years that Amy based herself in Ceylon. As the Lodge, his official residence in Kandy,

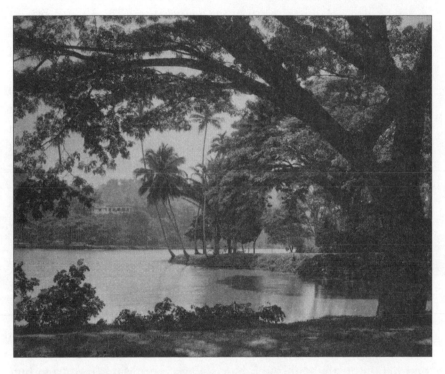

View of Kandy, Ceylon. High in the hills and set in a beautiful landscape, Kandy was a wonderful escape from the sticky heat of the capital, Colombo.

was currently unoccupied, he offered it to Amy, and it was from here that she wrote to her sister Daphne in February 1908:

> *Imagine to yourself a bungalow filled with comforts of all description, books, piano etc – set in the middle of the most beautiful scenery you can think of – a garden filled with flowering trees of marvellous colour and scent besides quantities of gardenias and huge bamboos. This has all been lent to me – and I am living in it alone. It is never more than seventy-two in the shade, and the nights are cool – each day more beautiful than the last. It is a sort of paradise on earth – from which I am afraid to wake.*

It was perhaps at this point that Amy might have written to May about the contentment she had found in the East. When May wrote sorrowfully about her beloved Amy after her death, she remembered: 'When in her wanderings she came to the East – "This is my house" she wrote, and after that she only touched the North to die.' May added that despite Amy's painting lessons in Italy and Paris when she was younger, she had 'failed in expression', and it was only in the East, during the last two years of her life, that she had found 'the power to paint, and it relieved the pent up feelings of her heart. She found herself.'

It appears that May, most uncharacteristically, had not been writing much to Amy in Ceylon. Could it be that she disapproved of Amy's wanderings abroad at this time, and the perhaps unnecessary separation from her husband? And had this caused a rift between mother and daughter; the child who had always been May's favourite, but whom she found increasingly hard to understand?

Although there was no one but Amy living at the Lodge, she can't have been alone very much. Kandy was a tremendously social place. In the hilly centre of the island, with such a beautiful setting and climate, surrounded by tea and coffee plantations, it was not surprising that Kandy was where everyone wanted to be. Leonard Woolf, who a few years later was to marry the writer Virginia Stephen, was at that time a young office assistant to the government agent in Kandy, and spoke in his memoirs of his luck in coming into contact with Sir Hugh Clifford's 'exalted circle' there. Clifford, 'a formidable man', had luckily found the young Woolf 'extremely competent', which made all the difference to his career prospects in Ceylon.

While Amy was staying at the Lodge she made friends with her neighbour, to whom Sir Hugh Clifford had lent the King's Pavilion next door, and who was a good example of the acting governor's 'exalted circle'. This neighbour, who, Amy wrote to Daphne, 'is very nice to me', was no less than the Empress Eugenie of France, the Spanish-born widow of the Emperor Napoleon III of France. The old empress had travelled to Ceylon on a yacht lent to her by Sir Thomas Lipton, who had made his fortune from tea. She was now eighty-one years old, tiny and bent, dressed completely in black, with a black straw hat and veil. But she was lively still, and very talkative.

Leonard Woolf, in his account of his official meeting with the Empress, thought that Eugenie, a renowned beauty in her younger days, was 'positively ugly', though he admitted that others had expressed the view that in old age she became almost more beautiful. He had been surprised that although the 'ex-Empress' was very affable, she received him surrounded by her retinue, with as much etiquette and ceremony as if she was still the wife of the reigning monarch, which she had not been for thirty-seven years. But Amy easily made friends with two of the Empress's retinue: a lady-in-waiting called Mademoiselle Germaine de Castelbajac, and the Comte de Clary, another young man of whom, Amy told Daphne, 'I am very fond'. Giving the impression of a much more informal set-up around the Empress than Leonard Woolf had done, Amy continued: 'So when I want people I am in there, or they here.'

By now Amy was planning a visit to Japan. Her interest in the country had been further fuelled by a forty-page letter, written like a personal guide to Japan, by Frank Rose, the young soldier I had noticed in so many of her photographs in South Africa in 1902, whose parents were friends of her parents. Frank was now a captain in the 10th Royal Hussars, stationed in India. From Rawal Pindi he wrote to Amy in Ceylon. Having himself been to Japan the year before, Frank gave Amy detailed descriptions of his route, the hotels, the gardens and the islands.

In his long screed Frank Rose recommended all sorts of things he thought Amy would particularly enjoy. Given that he was prepared to go to this trouble, I realized he must be more than a passing admirer of Amy's, and I was further convinced of this when I read that he had bought her 'some antique lacquer and other pretty things', which he had sent back to Holdhurst, her marital home on the Bonham estate in England. He explained that he had sent them there rather than to Kiddington, because 'I expect you would like to find those for yourself', by which I suppose he meant she would not want Hal and Dolly watching as she opened such generous gifts. Amy, sadly, was never to do so.

Frank had told her that at the time she planned to be in Japan the blossoms would be at their best. I found out later that Captain Rose, like Daphne's suitor Cis in the Argentine, had also sent Amy a horse from India, which she was never to ride.

Amy left Ceylon on 13 March 1908 aboard a German ship, the SS *Yorck*, bound for Yokohama. The voyage cannot have been too lonely, as several young men, whose photographs Amy took, signed her autograph book en route. She arrived in Yokohama at the beginning of April, but, apart from an entry in her book which shows that she was in Kyoto by May, no record of Amy's Japanese experiences appears to have survived. One certainty is that these experiences were not entirely spiritual. She did a lot of shopping; Kiddington was filled with lovely things that Amy bought in Japan, and China afterwards, and sent back to England. When she reached Peking, Amy wrote to Daphne and told her that she had bargained hard, and bought some marvellous jade at a very good price. Both Amy and May loved a bargain.

But it was not all shopping; the Japanese ship on which Amy was heading for Peking had been caught in a typhoon, and had to shelter in a bay for twenty-four hours. Also on the way, together with 'a friend' she did not name, she visited Seoul in Korea. Korea had become a protectorate of Japan in 1905, but Korea's last king, King Sunjong, remained in the capital until 1910, when the Choson dynasty was to end officially with the annexation of Korea by Japan. Amy felt honoured that 'by special permission' she was able to visit the splendid Changdok Palace, where the Royal Family was still living. Amy and her friend were shown round the many separate buildings of the palace by the 'Royal Master of Ceremonies', and then walked in the secret garden, originally known as the Forbidden Garden, which was reserved only for Royal Family members. The gardens were extensive, dotted with pleasure pavilions and lotus ponds. Intertwining paths linked wooded slopes filled with small game, which the king used to hunt.

From Seoul it only took two hours by train to Port Arthur, at the end of the Lin Tao peninsula in China. Four years earlier, on the night of 7 February 1904, during the Russo-Japanese war, a Japanese fleet had launched a devastating surprise attack on Port Arthur, then a Russian garrison port, in what has been described as 'a foretaste of Pearl Harbor'. During the siege hundreds of Russian warships were destroyed, or blockaded in the harbour. Amy found that nothing had been touched since the destruction:

> *... everything was in ruins, great holes made by shells in the roofs and walls of the houses, and even the houses still standing have half their windows broken.*

When Amy finally reached Peking, after a very tedious journey, it was not a disappointment. 'This is the most wonderful place,' she told Daphne. She said she had been lucky enough to catch a glimpse of the Dalai Lama of Tibet, who 'lodged in the marvellous yellow temple which has bronze and gold roofs ... he is treated as a God – even the Emperor kow-tows to him.'

That same year, after his visit to Peking, the Dalai Lama sent several small Shi Tzu dogs to Tzu Hsi, the dowager empress, often said to have been the most formidable woman in history. Tzu Hsi began life as a concubine in the Forbidden City, and rose to become known as the Dragon Empress. When Amy visited Peking in the spring of 1908, Tzu Hsi was an old woman, but still ruled as Regent to her nephew Kuang Hsu. In November of the same year she died, and her tomb was covered in diamonds. During her long reign she had encouraged the modernization of China, and changed Chinese life for ever. Amy saw the end of an era on her travels in the East, and with her passion for photography she must have taken many fascinating pictures. Sadly, none appears to have survived.

By the time she visited Hong Kong in January 1909, Amy had been on 'her wanderings', as May called them, in the Far East for nearly nine months. On 8 February she was back in Ceylon at the Galle Face Hotel, and soon afterwards in the cool air and peaceful surroundings of Kandy once more; the place which she had told May was now her 'home in the East'. It would appear from the visitors who signed her birthday book that she must have stayed in Kandy, on and off, for another year, until tragedy forced her to return to England.

In 1909, May was herself travelling as frequently as usual. Although I can find no letters from this time, Alfred Milner noted in his diary that he spent about ten days with her in Italy in March. He joined her in Perugia, in Umbria, where she had taken a room for him at the Hotel Brufani. With a shared sitting room in between, it adjoined her own. According to Milner they spent the time strolling, sightseeing and gossiping. Milner commented in his diary: 'Nobody here I care about much except Mrs Gaskell, who, however, is a delightful companion and knows a good deal about the sights of Italy.' Together they visited Assisi and Orvieto, and finally moved on to Florence, where they parted.

Increasingly frustrated by political wrangling in South Africa, Alfred Milner had resigned as High Commissioner in 1905, and returned to England. His approach to administration in South Africa had been divisive, culminating with his authorization that 'light corporal punishment' should be used to control outbreaks of violence among the Chinese labour force he had himself drafted in. This had caused outrage in England, and Alfred announced he would retire from public life. In 1906 he had bought a handsome Tudor house, Sturry Court, in the peaceful countryside of Kent. Alfred remained specially close to Violet Cecil, whose husband was stationed in Egypt, but was still loyal to his wide circle of female friends and companions, including May. Admiring her good taste, as so many people did, he had asked her to decorate his new house for him. After her time with Alfred in Italy in 1909, May spent a weekend at Sturry. During the weekend they had 'long talks', as always, and on the Sunday Alfred noted in his diary, 'Spent the whole day with Mrs Gaskell, mostly in the garden.'

Perhaps everyone lost touch with Amy during her last year in

Ceylon, or it could be that her letters were destroyed later. I feel that May must have burnt Amy's letters after her death, including her own to her. Could it have been that she also destroyed Amy's photographs of the Far East? Did they reveal something May did not want known? One other person who must also have felt cut off from Amy was her old friend from South Africa, Frank Rose. Back in England after long years abroad, he was a lonely man, and, now aged thirty-two, he felt he needed a wife. He was still with his regiment, but spent as much time as he could at his family home in Berkshire, where Daphne Gaskell, now twenty-two years old, came to stay as a house-guest in October 1909.

The Rose family lived at Hardwick House, beside the river Thames. Frank's father, Sir Charles Day Rose, had bought the house after having made a fortune on the Stock Exchange. He was an entertaining, passionate man, who was always having crazes for unusual activities such as snow-shoe running in Canada, and flying small aeroplanes. He was extremely proud of his large open car, a 1904 Mercedes Simplex Tourer. It had a six-cylinder engine and a very long bonnet. Because of Sir Charles's life by the river, his dynamic personality and his great attachment to his motor car, it is thought that his fellow banker and friend Kenneth Grahame based Mr Toad, in his book *The Wind in the Willows*, on him.

Kenneth Grahame often came to Hardwick. His marriage was not a success, and he would visit on his own. It is still said at Hardwick that he used to lie on his tummy on the river bank, with his head over the side, watching the water rats. The small, wet world he found himself in was, they say, the inspiration for his most famous book, in which he created a fantasy world that helped him to escape from his own problems. Certainly the image of Hardwick at that time is echoed in *The Wind in the Willows*: the river bank with its animals, the large, rather crazy host who was mad keen on motor cars, and even the Wild Wood just near by.

It was here that Daphne came to stay for a weekend. With her lively eccentricity, Daphne lifted Frank's spirits, and at first she was special to him just for being Amy's sister. Frank and Daphne both loved horses almost more than anything, and they went riding together. When Frank returned to his regiment in Salisbury, he began

writing to Daphne, and she wrote back. It seemed that they had much
in common, and in this new friendship they both already saw a way
forward in life. Frank wrote:

> *Your letters do cheer me up very very much, they help drive away the*
> *horrible fits of depression I get when I am alone for long. I know you too*
> *have suffered, and I know what pain is . . . I wish I could tell you all I*
> *think, but I can't – some day I may.*

Daringly, Frank told Daphne that he would love to see her with her
hair down, wearing a 'very loose' kimono, and wondered if he ever
would. 'You have brought a ray of sunshine into my life, which has
been grey for many years.'

May must also have seen the possibilities for Daphne and Frank.
She began taking Frank out to lunch, and to concerts. In a letter to
Daphne he said, 'Your mother is kind to me, and I'm very fond of her
– and as my father is fond of you I think they would both be very
pleased if . . .' and there he stopped, as if he dared not be more explicit.

When Frank broached the subject of Daphne visiting Hardwick
for Christmas, May seemed delighted. She told Daphne how much
she liked him. There was only one small criticism that she could not
resist mentioning: 'I never cease regretting the spectacles he has to
wear – they hide those kind eyes, which tell his character better than
any other thing, and are so blue.'

Daphne was now living in London with May at Victoria Square,
but despite frequent letters and meetings with Frank, sometimes even
without a chaperone, she was not yet sure she loved him. Frank told
her this would simply make him fight hard to win her: 'and if at last
I do the prize will be so splendid that nothing will ever be able to
separate us'.

In retrospect, these were rash words.

It was Frank's first Christmas in England for ten years. He had now
asked Daphne to marry him, and she had promised to make up her
mind by New Year's Day. In the end she had stayed with May for
Christmas, but Frank was looking forward to her coming to
Hardwick again:

I want you to ride my beloved Paddy – or rather he is Amy's really – I sent him home from India for her nearly three years ago.

Daphne knew that Amy and Frank had become friends in South Africa eight years before, but she might have been a little surprised when he told her now:

I am going to write to Amy and try to explain things if I can – she must know that I would not ask you to marry me unless I really loved you – dearest one – but I fear she may think I am behaving badly to her, and I don't want her to think that.

In a previous letter he had admitted that he had 'once caused a woman unhappiness and have never forgiven myself'. Did it now cross Daphne's mind that this woman might have been her sister Amy?

Frank told her that he was sometimes 'in a turmoil'. He said that it was because he knew that if she made up her mind she would 'give everything', as he would himself, and he was worried about Amy's reaction to hearing that they were such 'great friends':

I feel that Amy does not want me to marry anyone because she wants me to stick to her always – but I have begun to realize that it only brings pain, and does no good to anybody . . . Now you Daphne will always come first, and I want more than anything to make you happy.

It was not surprising that Frank was confused, or that Daphne was unsure. On the one hand, Frank was promising lifelong devotion to her:

I feel my life is being rather wasted alone, and I want to be of use to someone . . . I have found you Daphne, and you can take away all the loneliness which is in my heart.

On the other hand, he admitted that he would always remain fond of Amy: 'nothing could ever alter that'. He thought it was only fair for Daphne to know this before she decided to say yes or no:

I think you will understand – and I know you will not be jealous –
because when we are married you will always be first in everything. I will
stop writing to her if you like Daphne, only it seems such a great pity to
put an end to what ought to be a lifelong friendship.

Daphne must by now have suspected that Frank's feelings for her
sister were much more than just friendship.

Frank told Daphne that he had tried to explain to Amy that their
long friendship would be 'much healthier, open and honest' if he
married Daphne. 'I do wish Amy could see things as I see them,' he
wrote. 'I feel that if she could only see it, our friendship would give us
far more pleasure if I married you.' On the face of it, the preservation
of Frank's friendship with Amy seems an odd reason for him to be
marrying Daphne. 'She wants to keep you to herself,' replied Daphne
rather cattily, but then, astonishingly, in her next day's letter, she
regained her devoutly Christian generosity, and declared that she did
'absolutely understand', and that she was very sorry for both Frank
and Amy.

New Year's Day 1910 dawned, and Daphne still could not quite
bring herself to say yes. May did not put pressure on her daughter, but
she was certain that marriage to Frank would be the best thing for her.
Although Frank had told Daphne not to mention his friendship with
Amy to her mother, as 'it might shock her', it is likely that May knew
more about Frank and Amy's long relationship than Daphne did. May
said she thought that it would be a good idea if Daphne and Frank
went away separately for a short time, Daphne to the country to stay
with friends, and Frank to hunt in Ireland, so that they could think
things out. She also mentioned that Hal would be delighted if they
married at Kiddington. Frank told Daphne:

Your mother is a wonderful person, she understands you so absolutely in
the present case – doesn't she – and I really feel that she has made you
understand yourself.

May was right about a spell in the country. Daphne's doubts
cleared. 'I think it will be rather delicious,' she told Frank excitedly.
Finally, she decided she should write and explain things to Amy

herself. Suddenly sounding much more mature than Frank's 'funny little thing', as he had called her, she said that she felt this was the thing to do.

> *... it's rather delicate ground we're walking on. Poor little Amy, I wish she could be happier, but she won't be, I'm afraid, until she learns to give.*

Frank was full of gratitude:

> *My dearest Daphne – you are an unselfish little angel to write like that to Amy, and I love you ... I really see happiness in front of me at last.*

It is at this moment, in mid-January 1910, that Lionel reappears, mentioned in both Frank and Daphne's letters. He had been moved from Macedonia and was now stationed at Smyrna (Izmir) in Turkey. There he had been taken ill, and was bad enough to be moved to the British Seamen's Hospital in Constantinople (Istanbul), which had been established in 1855 by the British for seamen during the Crimean War, and recently built on a monumental scale in Gothic style. The doctors found that he was suffering from typhoid fever. Lionel's mother, Lady Bonham, was very anxious for her favourite son, and set out for Constantinople with his younger brother Eric. On 20 January May wrote to Frank, telling him how worried she was that there was 'no change in Lionel', but that she was delighted by 'your own change', referring to Daphne's decision to marry him at last.

Daphne wrote to Frank:

> *Poor old Lionel, how I wish we could hear something better. I do wonder what Amy is doing ... So I am going to promise to obey you am I? Well, that's what I love doing when I love. I've only obeyed one person ever – Father, and I loved him better than anyone in the world ... no more changing my mind, it's all settled, and I'm happy, and I want you, and I know I am the luckiest child in the world because you are the best person in the world, far too nice for me really ... the world must know next week, and I want them to know now.*

Frank's reply the next day was a similar mixture of self-centred happiness, and anxiety for Lionel and Amy:

> *I simply can't tell you how happy I am. I am only sad about poor old*
> *Lionel and Amy, but I do think he will pull through all right. And little*
> *Amy. What is she doing I wonder? No one seems to know where she is.*
> *This will make her nerves bad again I'm afraid. Poor Amy, things don't go*
> *kindly for her, do they.*

Poor Amy? Did she know that Lionel was ill? It seems that she must have done, because on the following day, 23 January, Daphne wrote to Frank: 'Amy is a strange little lady, I wish she had gone straight off to Lionel, she ought to have, whatever mother says.'

She went on to discuss the engagement ring Frank wanted to buy her. 'I don't mind what stone – except opal.' Opals were Amy's favourite stone.

In Ceylon, on that same day, Amy wrote back to her sister, having received Daphne's letter of about three weeks before 'explaining' about Frank and herself. As Frank had hoped, Daphne's carefully chosen words seemed to have had the desired effect:

> *Darling little Daphne, I was so glad to get your letter about Frank*
> *yesterday. It has been impossible for me to write to you openly until you*
> *took the initiative. Frank is one in a thousand and will make you the*
> *kindest and most perfect husband – I know you have so many things in*
> *common . . . also I don't think he has been very happy in life and you, I*
> *know, will make him so, and be the making of him – you can't think how*
> *delighted I am about it. As for his being a special friend of mine – I have*
> *no possessive feeling about friends – they come and go – I am glad when*
> *they are there – but when they go it is probably what is best for them.*

How different this reaction was from the one Frank had predicted. Daphne often referred to her older sister as 'strange', and May later called her 'unfathomable'. Perhaps what perplexed me most in this four-page letter was that not once did Amy mention her husband Lionel, who she must have known by then was seriously ill. His apprehensive mother and brother were already on their way to

Constantinople. But they were too late. That very evening, only hours after Amy had written to her sister telling her how pleased she was for her, Lionel Bonham died alone in Constantinople. He was thirty-six years old.

Telegrams flew backwards and forwards between the British Ambassador to Constantinople, Sir Gerard Lowther, and Sir Edward Grey, the Foreign Minister, in London. In a private letter to Lionel's father, Sir Edward called Lionel 'such a distinguished officer' and commented that he had 'rendered excellent services in Macedonia, and more recently at Smyrna'. For his part, Sir Gerard Lowther talked of Lionel as 'courageous and energetic', and admired the way that he had 'accepted service under the Turkish government in the general gendarmerie of the Empire, the organisation of which he threw himself into heart and soul'. His 'straightforward and thorough manner' of dealing with both men and officers, he added, had endeared him to all.

I found these tributes to Lionel among several pages concerning his death in the Foreign Office records. Although there were recommendations of messages of sympathy that should be sent to Sir George and Lady Bonham, there was no mention of condolences for Lionel's wife. In fact there was nothing to indicate that he even had a wife, no reference to Amy at all. Sir Gerard Lowther held a memorial service at the British Embassy Chapel in Constantinople. Several other ambassadors, attachés and prominent members of the British colony were there. Lionel's body, sealed in a lead coffin, was taken to the docks and put on a steamer bound for England, as his parents wished for him to be buried amongst the other Bonham family graves, in the churchyard of St Nicholas's at Cranleigh, near their estate.

On 27 January, four days after Lionel's death, Alfred Milner noted in his diary that he had had tea with May at her house in Victoria Square. He had found her 'in distress about Amy, who is in Ceylon, and has just lost her husband'. He stayed with May until nearly eight o'clock that evening. It must have been around that time that Amy had finally left Ceylon, her sanctuary in the East, and started on the long journey home, for the burial of a husband she had not seen for over two years.

*

Although Ceylon was much further than Constantinople, Amy arrived in England ahead of Lionel's coffin. The journey from Ceylon by steamer usually took three weeks; by sail it would have been two months. Amy must have taken the fastest route, through the Red Sea and then the Suez Canal to the Mediterranean. Boarding a train at Naples or Brindisi in Italy would have saved a week. She arrived in England on 15 February, exactly three weeks after Lionel's death. February was particularly grim that year. The freezing rain was almost constant. On the Continent it was just as bad, and there had been serious storms at sea, causing the steamer carrying Lionel's coffin to be held up at Gibraltar for some time until the weather calmed again.

May went to meet Amy off her train, and wrote to Daphne that night. I found it an astonishing letter: 'Darling. I met Amy – she isn't Amy but some strange far away creature, quite frozen.' May went on to say that, as she had expected, Amy did not want to stay at May's house in Victoria Square. She asked her mother to take her to a hotel, and said she did not wish her to remain with her. 'So I just left her,' wrote May. 'I do not think God would have chosen suffering more than I have borne today, seeing her.'

But on the next page of her letter, May pulled herself together in an extraordinary way. She told Daphne of the 'charming stuff' she had chosen at Liberty's for the bridesmaids' frocks for her wedding – 'quite cheap, and very pretty' – and how she thought the little pages should wear 'velveteen overcoats stamped with gold fleur-de-lys'. I suppose it is true that when tragedies take place, normal life has to go on, even for the closely involved, but there could hardly have been more contrast in those two pages.

Mrs Iles had been with May at the station to meet Amy. She recorded later that she too was shocked by Amy's appearance, which had changed dramatically since she had last seen her. Amy was not just thin; she was emaciated, and seemed very weak, 'clearly suffering from nervous exhaustion'. May decided that although there was still no word about the arrival of Lionel's coffin, it would be better for Amy's health if she went to the country air of Holdhurst, the house she had shared with Lionel on the Bonham estate near Cranleigh, where the funeral was to be held, and waited there.

So the day after Amy's return May borrowed a friend's 'motor', and, accompanied as always by Mrs Iles, collected Amy from the hotel and drove her down to Holdhurst, where in past years they had spent happy days together. Although Amy seemed 'very ill', it was not thought that she needed nursing. An arrangement was made with the local doctor, Dr Hope Walker, to visit her in a day or two. Amy went to bed early, in the room she had shared with Lionel. It was similar to her bedroom at Kiddington: very light, being on a corner of the house, with windows looking out on two aspects. As at Kiddington and at Beaumont, Amy had a canopied bed.

The next day, Amy got up in the late morning and had lunch with May. During the afternoon Lady Bonham came over from Knowle Park, the house Lionel would have inherited, and talked to Amy in private. Once again Amy went to bed early, at about nine o'clock. She took the medicine she had brought down from London, and gave instructions to May and the servants that she must not be disturbed until she rang. That night was black and squally, with driving rain. In the morning May could not resist peeping into her daughter's room at about ten o'clock. Amy appeared to be sleeping peacefully, lying, as she always did, on her right side, facing the door, with her dark hair spread out on the pillow.

One day I drove down to Cranleigh and found Holdhurst, the gabled house I knew from Amy's photographs – less far out of town now than in Amy's time, though there is still a farm next door. The house stands on level, elevated land, which looks out on to a remarkably unspoilt view of the gently undulating Surrey countryside. Unannounced, I knocked on the door and was willingly shown round by the present owners, who were slightly puzzled, but welcoming. I stood in the room where Amy had been sleeping that bleak February night. I could imagine May's concern as she walked back along the corridor and down the Victorian Gothic staircase into the drawing room below, which looks out over smooth green lawns bordered by long clipped yew hedges, which have grown up from the tiny bushes Lionel planted when he and Amy first went to live there. In the drawing room I could almost see May trying to concentrate on the large quilt she was embroidering; the one Burne-Jones had drawn the designs for when they saw the original together in 1897 at

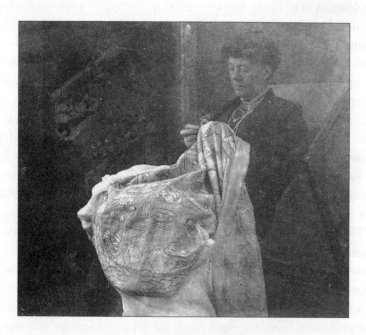

1910; May working on the last stages of the quilt she had started
in 1987, after Burne-Jones had drawn designs for her to produce a
replica of an old German one they had admired together at the
Kensington Museum (now the V&A).

the Kensington Museum. It was almost finished now. As she worked, May would have been listening for sounds upstairs as she wondered what the future held for her eldest, most loved, but most inscrutable child.

At half past twelve, when lunch was being prepared and May had still heard no sound from above, she felt she must go and check once more. She peeped quietly round the bedroom door and was surprised to see Amy in exactly the same position as before, 'of complete repose'. Her smooth, pale skin was glowing in the half-light behind the closed curtains, and her abundant dark hair still spread across the pillow. She looked beautiful, and at peace. Feeling more uneasy, May walked softly up to the bed and suddenly, with heartbreaking horror, realized that her daughter's 'sweet eyes were closed in the sleep of death'.

Dr Hope Walker was called immediately. He told May that Amy had been dead for at least eight hours. As the death had been sudden and unexpected, an inquest had to be arranged for three days later. May, Rose Iles and Dr Hope Walker spoke as witnesses. A report of the inquest in the local paper did not mention an autopsy, and since Amy's body had not left the house it seems that there cannot have been one. The paper simply stated that in Dr Hope Walker's opinion the cause of death had been 'heart failure', which of course could mean anything. However, on Amy's death certificate the cause of death was given as 'syncope of heart disease'. This is puzzling, as syncope simply means fainting, and heart disease had never been mentioned before, and was certainly never later given by May as the reason for her daughter's sudden death. I then discovered, tantalizingly, that the local coroner's records for 1910 had been lost in a fire.

Over the years there have been all sorts of suggestions in the family about the exact cause of Amy's death. May had always told the family that she 'died of a broken heart', or 'of grief'. In the God-fearing society of the turn of the century, suicide was something that would have brought great shame to the family if it were publicly known. Amy's body could not have been buried in consecrated ground. If they knew, or even suspected, that her death was by suicide, the Bonhams and the Gaskells would have tried hard to hide this. The doctor and the coroner, who would have known both the bereaved families, might well have been sympathetic to turning a blind eye.

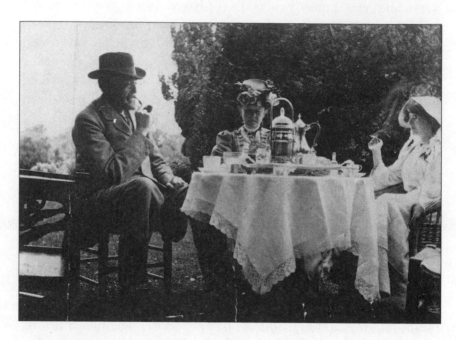

I think you can feel the tension in this photograph of Captain Gaskell, May and Amy having tea in the garden at Kiddington in 1903. The most surprising thing is to see Amy smoking openly in public; something very rare for women in conventional, upper-class society at that time.

There was even a story, told by Daphne in her old age to one of her grandchildren, that Amy shot herself, which clearly could not have been true. But it indicates that Daphne certainly believed, or knew for certain, that her sister had committed suicide. My aunt Diana remembers that about twenty years after her aunt Amy's death, she became aware of a rumour that Amy had killed herself by taking laudanum, a form of liquid opium which was widely taken as a sleeping draught and to calm the nerves. It is now known, of course, to be addictive, and it would have been easy to overdose on. It is also perfectly possible that Amy had become addicted to opium in Ceylon, where it was easily available, or even that she was already addicted to laudanum before, leading her on to the purer opium of the East. Opium was linked in the public mind of the time with art and sleep and death, and the exotic East, all of which fascinated Amy so much. When she got off the boat from Ceylon, her 'frozen', emaciated state, her secretive manner and her apparent inability to feel emotions properly could have been indications of addiction to opiates. In her weak state, she may have overdosed on laudanum accidentally.

There is a telling photograph of Amy taking tea with her parents at a table in the garden at Kiddington in 1903. May sits in the centre in one of her large hats, pouring out the tea; she is frowning and her lips are pursed. Captain Gaskell looks stiff and uneasy. Perhaps May's apparent disapproval is because Amy, leaning back in her chair and looking intently at both her parents, is holding in her hand a cigarette, from which a delicate ribbon of white smoke wafts up into the air. It was extremely unusual for women to smoke in public at the turn of the century; the habit was mainly restricted to liberated bohemian and intellectual circles, and to prostitutes. A sexual connotation lingered around women who smoked, and some cigarettes were thought to have had opium mixed with the tobacco. If Amy, from her conventional upper-middle-class background, was daring enough to smoke at that time, it could indicate that she would have been ready to try anything she was offered when she reached Ceylon a few years later.

But if Amy did kill herself deliberately, why she would have wanted to do so is still a mystery. Perhaps Lionel's death and the sudden withdrawal from her mystic world in Ceylon had brought on such terrible regret and disillusionment that she had seen no alternative but to end her life. There is a strong possibility that, on her return to England after so long, the realization that she had come back not only to bury a husband she may no longer have loved, but also to lose the undivided devotion of Frank when he married her sister, might have seemed too much to bear. And could the 'broken heart' May talked about have been broken not by Lionel or Frank, neither of whom she had seen for at least two years, but by someone else in Ceylon?

Alternatively, her sudden death does not need to have been suicide. She was ill and emaciated, possibly as a result of a tropical bug or of opium addiction, and she appeared to Mrs Iles to be suffering from 'nervous exhaustion'; a combination of these things could have caused a fatal heart attack. She may have been anorexic, although it would not have been recognized as such then, and her extreme thinness could, in itself, have caused heart failure. Or perhaps, in her weak state, and seeing no positive direction or role in her life now, Amy might have almost willed herself to die.

In a eulogy she addressed to Amy in letter form several years after she died, May claims that when she found Amy dead, she 'thanked God that your pain was over, and that you had reached Lionel, and all was understood'. But for May, the pain was only just beginning. In her writings about the family, when she came to record the death of Amy at only thirty-five years old, she wrote: 'On that same day my heart broke and the pleasure of living ended.'

Daphne and Frank were staying at Kineton, a house belonging to Daphne's cousins, the Brand family, in Warwickshire. As soon as they heard the news of Amy's death they drove to Holdhurst; Daphne said she would remain to help her mother, but would spend the nights at Knowle Park with the Bonhams. Above all she was concerned for Frank, who was distraught. As soon as they arrived at Holdhurst he went up to Amy's room, to see her body lying on the canopied bed, and spent some time with her alone. When he came down again he looked drained and white, with tears pouring down his cheeks. With hardly a word to Daphne or May, he drove straight back to Hardwick. Daphne must have written to him soon after he left:

My Frank, I understand all you feel, and my heart is very sad for you. I know you loved her, and I am glad, for I loved her too, more than I quite realised until today. But I can't help feeling that for her it is best. And that's the thing that comforts most, isn't it? Poor poor little Amy, her life wasn't very happy . . . In this last fortnight I have got to know both you and myself better. In you darling I see all that is good and pure, and true, and in myself I see a strange mixture. But in my heart of hearts I love you Frank, and I pray that I may always make you happy.

The next morning Frank wrote, apologizing for his show of emotion the previous day:

My own darling, the world has seemed a very different place the last two days – everything I suppose is for the best – and it is only our own selfishness that makes it hurt so – I'm afraid I was very weak yesterday – and you were so brave – I thought I was getting used to pain and sorrow and yet this is something far greater than I have ever felt before. I suppose it is because for nearly eight years Amy has been in every thought and action of my life. In everything I did I used to say to myself 'Would Amy like me to do this.' And now she is gone . . . I can't tell you how grateful I was to be able to see her to say goodbye – she looked quite beautiful – didn't she . . . I'm afraid this is a very selfish letter – but I do realise that others are suffering even more than I am . . . You are the most wonderfully brave and unselfish little girl in the world. Your loving Frank.

As I read this letter I remembered it was eight years earlier that Amy had visited South Africa during the Boer War, and I looked at the photographs she took then of Frank Rose with renewed interest.

It was decided that Amy and Lionel should be buried together. Despite the fact that there might be a long wait, Amy's body had not been taken to a morgue; it lay for six days in the bedroom where she died, with the windows open to let in the freezing winter air and keep the room as fresh as possible. This might seem morbid to us now, but at that time it was not unusual for bodies to lie in the house for some time, so they could be seen by all the family. Only May and Mrs Iles were actually sleeping in the house, but Daphne would come over from Knowle Park during the daytime. Many wreaths had been sent, and Daphne explained to Frank that she had placed them around Amy's body. On 24 February, when they heard that the steamer carrying Lionel's coffin was finally due to arrive at Southampton, Daphne wrote to Frank:

> *I've just been putting all the wreaths out in the rain to freshen them up. Also today they are coming to put Amy in her little coffin of plain oak, so the wreaths are getting fresh to cover her again. They are lucky flowers to be near the loveliest little lady I have ever seen. Though I didn't understand her, I felt that if ever I was in trouble I could go to her.*

She told Frank that now her father and Amy were both gone she had only him for support, as Hal was 'a real dear, but useless', and her mother, 'who I love better than I have before', now needed help far more than anyone. Amy's coffin stayed at Holdhurst for three more days, after which it was taken to the church to join Lionel's the night before the funeral.

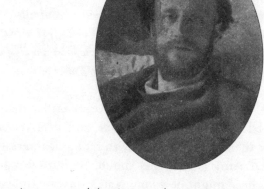

March 1910; Hal in the nursing home three months after his eye accident. With a beard and without his humorous expression he looks very different. He was unable to be at Amy's funeral.

Hal had his troubles too. He really was 'poor old Hal'. Two months before, he had been accidentally shot in the eye by a neighbour when they were out pheasant shooting near Kiddington. He was still re-covering in the Acland nursing home in Oxford, and although the doctors were able to save his eye, which still looked normal, Hal lost the sight in it. From then on he became even more withdrawn and silent. There is a strange picture of him sitting in bed in the Acland home shortly after Amy's death, his eyes clear and un-bandaged, with a look of blank sadness. Miraculously, however, even with the sight of only one eye, he was shooting again with great accuracy by September that year, and he continued painting and shooting for the rest of his life. On my visits to Kiddington as a child, I never realized that the eye behind my grandfather's clear-glass monocle did not see anything.

At Holdhurst, the crate of oriental antiques and kimonos Frank had sent back for Amy from his travels in Japan about three years before were still waiting for her, unopened. While Daphne passed the days before the funeral sorting things out, she asked Frank if she might have one or two of the kimonos, if it would not hurt him to see her wearing them. He replied that he would love her to wear them, and reminded her that he had told her early in their friendship that he would like to see her in a kimono. He said he felt sure Amy would like it too, and they both knew she was far happier now in the next world than she had ever been in this life, or would ever have been. The important thing now was to cheer up May, and he knew that their wedding would help to do that, and give May 'something to live for'.

Amy's kimonos lived on too, and with them her memory; the ones which Daphne did not choose for herself were moved to Kiddington, and my aunt Diana remembers when, thirty-five years later, my mother, who had married Hal's son Tom, was given one by her new mother-in-law. It was a rich, deep red, and suited my mother beautifully, Diana told me.

When Lionel Bonham's coffin finally reached Cranleigh, on 27 February 1910, after its difficult journey from Constantinople via Gibraltar, it was placed in the chancel of St Nicholas's Church beside Amy's. The joint funeral was to be the following day. The young couple, apart for so long, lay side by side in the dark church overnight, which was lit only by the candles that were kept burning round both coffins. The morning of 28 February dawned grey, and very cold. After lunch all the shops in the village closed, and people were seen hurrying towards the church. It began to rain.

'PATHETIC DOUBLE FUNERAL' read a headline in the *Surrey Advertiser*. Indeed, the scene and circumstances of Amy and Lionel's funeral could hardly have been more tragic. The church was full long before the service began, and the graveyard became crowded with townspeople who could not squeeze into the church. They stood 'amid general evidence of the deepest sorrow', in the pouring rain, those who could sheltering under the dark branches of the cedar tree. At the end of the service, Mr Vince, the organist, played Chopin's Funeral March, and sixteen non-commissioned officers of the Grenadier Guards carried the two coffins out of the church. On top of Lionel's coffin were his bearskin, sword and scarf.

Following immediately behind the coffins were the chief mourners: Lionel's parents, Sir George and Lady Bonham, his two brothers and three sisters, and several of the servants from Knowle Park. May walked between Daphne and Frank, with Mrs Iles just behind. Hal, still in the nursing home, was unable to be there to support his mother, and neither was Dolly, who had had a difficult birth six months before with her second child, Diana. Dolly, who had been in London for her firstborn son Tom's birth, blamed the complications she had suffered the second time round on an inexperienced country doctor, but even more on the Gaskell family, who, she said, were too mean to pay for a doctor in London. This was family history repeating itself: May had also blamed the death of her second child, the 'curly headed boy', on an 'ignorant country doctor' and the penny-pinching Gaskells.

Amy and Lionel's double grave had been lined with glossy ever-green leaves and white flowers by Mr Stemp, the Bonhams' head gardener at Knowle Park. He and Mr Wild, the gardener at Holdhurst, were among the mourners. All around the grave were the wreaths which had surrounded Amy as she lay at Holdhurst waiting for her husband's body to join her, together with many more 'beautiful floral tributes' which had arrived that day. The silent crowd, shivering from sadness and cold, stretched far across the uneven grass of the graveyard. As the two coffins were lowered slowly into the grave, the 'Nunc Dimittis' was sung. The two families gathered closer. Tears mixed with splashes of rain on many cheeks.

CHAPTER TEN

LOSS, LOVE AND A MYSTERY

AFTER AMY'S FUNERAL, DAPHNE AND FRANK WANTED TO GET married as soon as possible, to try and distract May, and themselves, from their grief. Hal had agreed that they could be married at Kiddington; although he was still at the nursing home in Oxford, recovering from his eye accident, he hoped to be back in time to give his sister away. Daphne still felt that Kiddington was her home, and she would be near her father there, so recently buried in the churchyard. The wedding was fixed for 31 March, and although they decided not to have a formal reception because of their 'deep mourning', the family, including uncles, aunts and cousins, would be able to gather together at the house they all knew so well.

There was a lot to do in a month. May had to sort out Amy's things and move them out of Holdhurst, but she was also determined that Daphne's wedding would look pretty, and celebratory too, despite the recent tragedy. She even ordered an astonishing cake: an enormous riot of sculpted leaves, flowers and birds, which looked like an ornate urn. With her assured good taste, May thought out every detail in the same way that she did when she decorated a house. Apparently still influenced by Burne-Jones, May wanted Daphne's wedding to be medieval in theme. The colours would be restricted to white and gold

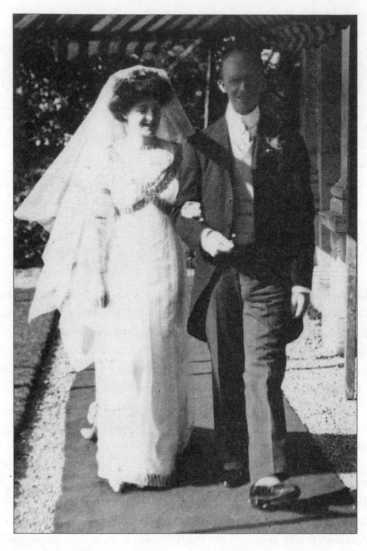

Daphne and Frank Rose walking from the church at Kiddington on their wedding day in 1910, only five weeks after Amy's sudden death. May herself was dressed in long, flowing black, medieval in style.

for both Daphne's cross-bodiced dress and the dresses of the two bridesmaids. As it was to be a smaller wedding than originally planned, May had decided there should be only one page, Hal's four-year-old son Tom, her only grandson so far. Tom was nevertheless to wear the smart white velveteen tunic May had envisaged before Amy's death, dotted with gold fleurs-de-lis, over white tights. An added touch was fur trimming on the tunic, and on some pointed silk slippers. For the bridesmaids, May designed flowing high-waisted dresses, also dotted with little fleurs-de-lis, and gold net caps ornamented by antique pendants. And of course Daphne, May decided, would carry a posy of May's own flowers, lilies of the valley. The little church, May told her daughter, would be lined with potted palm trees and tall vases of scented white lilies.

Frank wanted to put his troubled past behind him. As the wedding day drew near, he wrote to Daphne every day, and sometimes more:

I am counting the days now until the 31st when you will be all my own for evermore, and I shall be all yours. I love every moment I am with you – but I shall love it still more when I am really yours – the hours are simply crawling by, I want you so, dearest.

Poor Frank; after his wasted years of love for Amy, he confessed:

. . . there has been so much pain, anxiety and sorrow in the past that I sometimes think it has made me an old man before my time.

Decades later, Daphne told one of her grandchildren that when she had heard of Lionel's death in Constantinople, and realized that Amy would be coming back from Ceylon a free woman, she did not believe Frank would still marry her. Now Daphne was as determined as Frank to make their marriage a success by putting their shared bereavement behind them. She wrote ecstatically:

My best beloved . . . if love can make you happy then I think you may be, for I love you deeply and truly . . . Oh Franco, what a glorious game life is, and I mad with joy . . . I love – love – love til I can't love anymore . . .

*all sorts of bits of me have woken up since you and I loved each other, bits
that have slept since Father died.*

The shared grief that May, Daphne and Frank felt after Amy's
death had not only brought mother and daughter much closer, but
also seemed to have intensified Daphne and Frank's love. At the
wedding, May wore a long and flowing velvet coat, trimmed with
braid, also medieval in style, though dark and sombre. The strain
showed on her face. But shortly afterwards she wrote to Daphne:

*Ever since I saw your radiant face as you left the church with Frank, I
have been much happier. And your love, which has come to me at last, is a
wellspring of joy. I could see in a moment that Frank had touched the
depths of your deep nature. To be in love is a wonderful thing – there is
nothing like it in the whole world – nothing to compare to it. You have
been through deep waters my child – and to see your grief and loss soft-
ened whilst happiness is all around does make me happy. I love to think of
it.*

With the wedding over, May moved out of her rented house in
Victoria Square, and stayed at her club in London while she looked
for a new house she could afford. When Daphne had first become
engaged to Frank, she had offered her mother some of the money that
her father had left her, which was now invested in the Argentine and
had done well. May had told her she would not dream of accepting it;
'I could not take the money, I <u>could</u> not,' she protested. Henry Brooks,
May pointed out, had wanted Daphne to have the money not only in
case she didn't marry, but also because she was 'the apple of his eye',
and the greatest comfort to him during his 'last altered years'. May
told her daughter:

*However rich a husband may be, it is <u>everything</u> for a woman to be
independent for her personal expenses. Had I been so my life would have
been very different – some day I will tell you why.*

With all her travelling, May appears to have had her fair share of
independence, but perhaps she meant that if she had had her own

private means she would have been able to escape completely from her unhappy marriage. After Henry Brooks died in 1907, the Devil of Wigan would probably have turned in his grave had he seen his grandson's will. Although Beaumont Hall, which was rented out again, had been made over to Hal Gaskell on his marriage to Dolly in 1905, the value of the substantial Kiddington estate had decreased enormously since Henry Lomax Gaskell's death eighteen years before. Henry Brooks left all his real and personal estate and effects, valued at £23,000 – a little over a million by today's values – to Hal. He left £2,000 to May, and another £1,000 to Daphne. There was no mention of Amy, possibly because she was married. May would have been able to buy a house and live comfortably on the money she was left by her husband, plus a settlement her father-in-law had made on her marriage which provided her with £500 a year. But she could not afford to be too extravagant, which must be why she often refers to having to be careful about spending.

At times of loss, a lifelong friend can be a vital support, someone who understands the past, and always has time to talk. May had such a friend, called Eda Ames-Lyde, whom she described as 'strong, capable and tender'. May must have introduced Eda to Burne-Jones, because in one letter he remarked: 'She's a dear that friend of thine – good through and through.' Eda was another keen traveller and appears to have become particularly fond of Amy; perhaps it was Eda, who knew the East well, who encouraged Amy to read about it, and ultimately to travel there. Eda had visited Amy at the Lodge in Kandy in 1908, and may well have known more about her last years than anyone else. After Amy's death, Eda was particularly supportive to May and often had dinner with her when they were both in London. May told Daphne later that on these occasions 'we just talked for hours about Amy, always Amy – Eda told me that Amy yearned to know the Beyond of Life.'

Only four years after Amy's death, Eda herself died in Shanghai. When May heard the news, she wrote to Daphne: 'She pined for the hot sun and smell of the East . . . it was the death she would have chosen – away alone – no fuss – in her beloved East.' Perhaps it also crossed May's mind that it was exactly the end Amy would have wished to have. She pointed out that Eda was 'such a part of my old life . . . no one but I could have loved Amy better than Eda – and now there is nobody left to whom I can talk perfectly openly about Amy.'

After Amy's death, May had told Daphne that she was so tired of living that as long as Daphne was happy, and had 'a good man to love you and take care of you', she did not mind what happened to her own life: 'I want no more storms and tragedy, I want to dwell only on your sweet happiness and love.' Frank was to be stationed at the cavalry depot at Scarborough, so as their first home he and Daphne had rented a little house in the countryside nearby. Although May spent that whole summer in Germany and Switzerland 'for her health', she wrote constantly to Daphne. May's home-making instincts had been awakened, and she was full of practical domestic advice about choosing servants, fixing the right wages, and finding the right cook:

> Get a cook in the country for the country . . . enquire how they clear their soups (a very little raw meat is best), ask if they boil hams, vegetables etc in plain water – and if not what? The water should always have bones in it . . . Fish should always be filleted at home, never by the fishmonger, and you can put the bones and skin into the water which the fillets are cooked in. I think you should get the 'Common Sense Cookery Book' which taught me and Mrs Iles all we know . . . a good strong housemaid will be easy to get, and let the tweeny be in the scullery and just do the cook's, and chauffeur's and her own room.

May travelled with enormous quantities of luggage. Wherever she was she created a home for herself, draping 'lovely bits of stuff' around to cover anything ugly in her room, and arranging her photographs, reproductions of favourite pictures and even drawings by Burne-Jones all around her. In July that year, while she was staying at a hotel in Saxony, it was cold and rainy; 'I am listening to vast sweeps of a tempest downpour, that come like gusts of passion.' But May's room was a refuge. It was, she told Daphne:

> . . . very large, and in it is a white stove with a ledge all round, on it is my Angel of Love by BJ, and the photograph of his portrait of Amy. On the writing table stand all my photographs of those I have most loved in the world. Alas, only you and Hal look at me with living eyes.

Such constant moving 'from place to place' during the busy summer season was very tiring. 'The whole scramble and vulgarity is awful, and above all the noise,' wrote May. However, she then settled at a small hotel in Switzerland, which she found 'quite ideal'. It was only accessible by 'a carriage drawn by carthorses up a road like the side of a house', and the building was 'perched on a precipice that sinks into the lake of Lucerne, looking onto a blue opal sky of peaks. The world looks good, and the only sound is cowbells.' Even in this eagle's nest retreat they received letters twice a day, and May heard from Sir Hugh Clifford, who had returned from Ceylon on leave. He wrote that he would like to see May, as well as Daphne and Frank. A few months after Amy's death, Clifford had remarried. His new wife was a widow whose maiden name had been Bonham, and who was a relative of Amy's husband Lionel. After Amy's death, in the Victorian tradition, Clifford had sent May a framed 'powerful photograph of a sculpture of Death', which she took with her on her travels that summer, arranging it in her room next to the photograph of Burne-Jones's portrait of Amy. In view of something I was soon to discover about Sir Hugh, his gift to May would seem not only rather macabre, but very strange.

Back in England in the autumn, May was staying with her old friend Violet Cecil at Mells, in Somerset, when she received some exciting news from her daughter. Daphne had been getting impatient because, unlike her sister-in-law Dolly, she had not become pregnant during the first weeks of marriage. But now May wrote back: 'My own darling – of all the heavenly bits of news there could be, this is one of the best. I really think it must be a baby.'

May advised her daughter to consult an excellent London doctor she knew of, Dr Playfair, and as soon as she was sure about the baby, to engage a much-recommended nurse. One of Daphne's symptoms was that she was feeling bad tempered, but May told her: 'Don't worry about being cross – thank your stars you are not cross and sick too.' By then May had found a new house in London, 14 Lower Seymour Street; 'I am already thinking of the nursery at No 14 – and that the room shall be finished by next April. What happy daydreams.'

In January 1911, when Daphne was nearly six months pregnant, Hal wrote to her in his typical idiosyncratic style:

I think it is time that I do tell you with respect for decency how glad I am that you are shortly to receive a real live present from some Astral Sphere, and I trust it may be one with short hair and trousers, as I am convinced they do best to start with. It will be great fun for you to bring up, and see it thrive and prosper as I trust it will. I hope it will reproduce the Gaskell nose, which is so delicate in proportion and so fine of line. Tom is doing his best with his proboscis.

In November 1910, May had been seriously ill with pneumonia. When Alfred Milner visited her at Lower Seymour Street on 20 November, she was recuperating on a sofa, but still, as he recorded in his diary, 'very weak'. After Christmas, she told Alfred that for nearly a year now since Amy's death, she had kept almost everything, agonizingly, to herself, implying that there were things that she could not even tell her friend Eda. But as the terrible anniversary of Amy and Lionel's deaths approached, May's sadness intensified, and she felt she must unburden herself. The only person of complete discretion she knew she could turn to was Alfred Milner. As she wrote to him afterwards:

I hesitated for weeks whether it was failure to Amy to tell you the truth and ease the burden of loneliness in this tragedy, which was almost more than I could bear. Then, with added woe at Christmas I felt it was too much, and that Amy would wish me to be helped. Your silence, your understanding sympathy, your intuitive knowledge of her, were some of the most perfect comforts I have ever known, were, are, every day. Nearly every hour of every day. And the isolation and loneliness have gone. Life is easier, and more natural. You have understood her, which is the one thing I feared would be difficult. No, I won't dwell more than I can help on this unfathomable mystery of Life and Death, and will try not to let it detach me from brighter sides of my life.

May explained to Alfred that her grief had made her feel isolated, and that when she was at social occasions, full of 'laughter and merriment', she seemed to be able to join in, but felt 'like a thing apart – as if it was all a play'. Afterwards, this left her exhausted. She continued:

It is a year yesterday that Lionel Bonham died, which was the end of much splendid love, courage and ability. In all the suffering, shame and perplexity I never wished them back ... how it has helped me to unloosen the hands of secrecy and tell the tragic tale to you. I will send you a strange page or two, unfinished, which Amy wrote, and I found the other day in her bag.

I did not find those pages, nor Milner's letters to May, but May's repeated words – 'shame', 'suffering', 'tragic secret' – and the fact that she thought that Milner would 'understand', strengthened my suspicion that Amy had committed suicide, or had possibly been an opium addict.

Together with her long letter to Alfred, May enclosed a poem she had written, simply called 'Amy'. I showed it to a literary friend, who said he thought it rather good, and reminiscent of sonnets by Elizabeth Barrett Browning. It is certainly typically Victorian in style, a sort of hymn to her lost daughter, whom she addressed as 'thou' – 'thou art full of whispers, and of shadows'. Four lines towards the end only add to the mystery of Amy's story:

> *Thy face, remembered, is from other worlds*
> *It has been died for, though I know not when*
> *It had been sung of, though I know not where*
> *It has the strangeness of the burning East*
> *And of sad sea horizons.*

Daphne's first baby was born in London on 4 May 1911, at May's house in Lower Seymour Street. It was a girl, whom she and Frank decided to call Amy. When the baby was three weeks old, Daphne wrote to Frank, who was with his regiment in Yorkshire:

Will she ever grow like Amy? To look at I hope, but not the same nature, for then she wouldn't be happy.

May preferred to call the rosy-cheeked little baby 'Roslein'. The name Amy was still difficult for her:

Amy – I say the word and picture after picture passes before me . . . the golden new born tiny darling, the grave compelling little girl, the rosebud of seventeen, the woman who loved and suffered, the daughter who lost me more tears than all else.

Daphne's low self-esteem was apparent in many of her letters from childhood onwards, and must have been affected by her mother's obvious worship of her elder sister. Even gentle, loving Frank sometimes used to call her, affectionately, 'mad'. She wrote to him:

Tell me, am I often dense and un-understanding? I'm afraid so, and you must miss the quick understanding of Amy. I wish I was more like what you ought to have married. You are so good that I should never know if I hurt you.

Despite the fact that May poured out love to her 'beloved little Daphne' in her letters, her youngest daughter probably knew that for May at least, if not for Frank as well, it was Amy who was the most beautiful, the most talented and, ultimately, the most loved.

It was now that May received a totally unexpected new blow. Her friend Sir Hugh Clifford, who had generously lent his house to Amy in Ceylon, and who had written to May so sympathetically after Amy's death, had just brought out a new book. On 25 May, when Daphne was still recovering from the birth of her little Amy, she wrote to Frank, telling him of a visit from May:

We had a long talk about Hugh Clifford's new book. It has hurt her much. I didn't realise a bit how beastly it was, or how like Amy. It's a vile incomprehensible thing to do. I wonder if he will explain why he did it. Poor darling, it must have hurt you too, and I never realised at all. Forgive me.

What could this mean? I was intrigued, and went straight to the British Library to see if I could identify the book among Clifford's many publications. The only one which was published at exactly the right time, about a month before Daphne wrote her letter, was called *Downfall of the Gods*, a melodramatic novel revolving around the decline of the Khmer dynasty at Angkor in Cambodia. At first glance I did not believe that there could be any connection, but then I noticed a paragraph in the foreword, where Clifford describes his arrival in Angkor, which, I thought, echoed the sentiments Amy might have felt when she arrived in Ceylon:

> I had found that for which I had been seeking. This was the East – the real East – mysterious and very ancient – waiting with her immense and measureless patience to catch the awful whisper that shall reveal the secrets of life, birth and death. For she is ever expectant – the East; never weary, never faithless, waiting, waiting always – for the whisper that does not come.

As I began to read the book, with its flowery prose, I realized that there was only one female character, so this must have been the woman that May had recognized as Amy. It was not difficult to see why she had been upset, and as I read on, I thought she must have been shocked too. The main character is a beautiful boy, just approaching adulthood, 'almost nude, bronze tinted, statuesque, magnificently developed'. His name is Chun, and he is from the casteless masses who have slaved for the last three hundred years building the vast temple of Angkor, in miserable servitude to the Brahmin priests, under their god king. Chun feels that he is different, a demi-god, whose mission must be to liberate his people, the menials.

The female character is a young girl, who was one of the 'temple women' – prostitutes who give their favours only to the priests. One brightly moonlit night, she finds Chun swimming secretly in the forbidden sacred waters of the temple, 'delighting in the strength and beauty of his young manhood'. She steps out of the shadows so that he can see her. She is delicately beautiful and seductive, but with a scornful manner and a 'little, hard laugh'. She tells him that she is the incarnation of the Spirit of Destruction. Chun, seized with a consuming desire he has never felt before, is captivated.

The first descriptions of the mysterious temptress – the 'slight, slender frame' and the 'slim symmetry of her figure' – could easily have been applied to Amy, but to others also. Much more familiar, and recognizable even to me, not only from photographs, but also from

Burne-Jones's famous portrait, were details that followed: the 'small, oval face' with its 'even transparent pallor'; the 'steady gaze' of her 'deep, grave eyes'; the glowing whiteness of her skin; and her chief glory, hair which was 'dry and soft', and 'waved back in two rounded billows from a natural parting on her forehead'. The description did not sound to me like a Cambodian beauty in ancient times; it sounded like Amy.

In Clifford's story the temptress, for she has no name, teases Chun mercilessly; one moment she lets slip the soft silk cloth which is draped across her breasts, and invites Chun to swim naked with her in the moonlit night, awakening even more his 'passionate, wild desire'; the next he hears her 'mocking laughter' as she flees into the shadows once more. Eventually, much later in the story, after endless cruel teasing, she sleeps with the 'intoxicated' Chun, yet continues to deride him constantly for his humble origins. A wise man tells Chun that the Spirit of Destruction is 'insatiable, she craves eternally for the bodies and souls of men. She grinds us to dust . . . she devours us.' No wonder Daphne thought Frank would be hurt too by this unpleasant portrayal of the woman he had loved for so long.

Downfall of the Gods, published by John Murray, was praised by Joseph Conrad and sold well. Years later, Clifford tried to get it made into a film. Like Daphne, I too wondered why Sir Hugh Clifford had chosen to base the character of this cruel temptress so recognizably on the daughter of a friend. Could he himself have tried, unsuccessfully, to seduce Amy, and borne her a grudge, or had he been jealous of her behaviour with other men?

Although May's letters to Daphne after Amy's death were packed with endearments and reassurances of love, she surrounded herself with images of Amy. The photograph of Burne-Jones's portrait, which she took travelling with her, was copied and framed so that she could see her daughter in several rooms of her London house. She also asked Hal to keep Amy's sunny corner room at Kiddington untouched: the bed, a romantic *lit bateau*, with its grand canopy of floral chintz; the elegant dressing table where Amy had sat having her long hair brushed; her pictures on the wall; her clothes, books, photograph albums and Eastern ornaments – all were left as a shrine. Two years later, in May's eulogy to Amy, she declared emotionally: 'The things you have used are sacred, the things you have touched are not as other things.'

To leave Amy's room as it was proved no problem for Hal, as he did not want to change anything at all at Kiddington, and was never to do so, even when it began to decay around him. But May also requested that no one should use or sleep in Amy's room, the best bedroom in the house. When Hal and Dolly's children were growing up, this ghostly room, where everything was eerily draped with dustsheets, intrigued them. My father Tom, my aunt Diana, and little Robin, the youngest, who was born in 1914, would creep in and peep underneath the sheets. This was when they were first told that the aunt they did not remember had died 'of a broken heart'. When their grandmother stayed at Kiddington they often questioned her about why Amy had died but, Diana told me, 'Granny just used to go pink and change the subject.' Dolly did not enlighten the children either; Diana said, 'Mummy was always evasive and secretive about illness and death.' Only when my father was a student, studying architecture, was Amy's room opened up so that he could do his drawings there, with the help of the wonderful light.

May clearly did not want to talk about the circumstances of Amy's death, but Diana remembers that she would often tell her grand-children about her eldest daughter, and in such glowing terms that they became a bit fed up with hearing about her. May would describe Amy as 'beautiful, romantic, clever and wonderful', and 'adored by all'. Now in her mid nineties, Diana, a highly intelligent woman with the most generous nature, remarked recently to me with a touch of old resentment: 'We never heard about anyone else – it was always Amy, Amy, Amy. I think we were meant to think that she was too wonderful to live, and just faded away.'

May wanted not only her family, but everyone to remember Amy as someone wonderful. To this end, a year after Amy's death, she managed to persuade a famous sculptor of the day, Bertram Mackennal, to create a memorial to Amy, which would be placed inside the church at Cranleigh, where she was buried. On an oppressively hot summer day in 1912, May went to see Mackennal at work in his studio on 'my memorial'. She described the visit to Daphne:

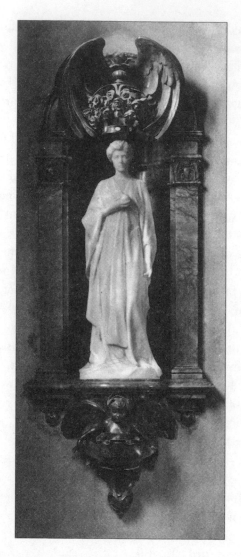

The memorial to Amy in St Nicholas's church, cranleigh in Surrey, by a famous sculptor of the day, Sir Bertram Mackennal.

*It was bitter sweet, but the little appealing figure is most touching, and
has Amy's spirit in it, and the hair, figure and hands are very like.
Mackennal was so excited over it, and by the effect of Amy's opals in the
crown, and the pearls I am giving. He kept working away in sheer delight.
He has made the most delicious sad little Love holding her name in his
baby arms, and lovely thin swanlike wings round him, and a strange little
headdress on his curls, in which we put my fiery opal. Her name is to be
in purple enamel.*

Mackennal was, like Burne-Jones had been, one of the Souls' pet
artists. He was well known for his romantic marble sculptures of
women, mostly nudes, and later for his war sculptures. He had done
a romantic memorial for Lord Curzon's wife in 1906, and he also
created the memorial in St George's Chapel at Windsor to Edward
VII, who died in the same year as Amy. It took Mackennal over two
years to finish Amy's memorial. As the work neared completion, May
wrote to Daphne:

*It has cost my heart drops of blood to force Mackennal to understand her –
if anyone can – but he has insight, real insight, and suddenly it sprang
from the conception of Amy's personality. Oh, I know Amy would like it.*

When, at the beginning of my research for this book, I drove down
to Surrey to visit Holdhurst, the house where Amy died, I also visited
the church at Cranleigh, where I had been told Amy and Lionel were
buried together. I knew then that there was a memorial to Amy in the
church, though not who the artist was. As on the day of her funeral, it
was pouring with rain, and the overhanging branches of the old cedar
tree in the graveyard made everything even darker. The Bonham
family graves are grouped together; small curved headstones in front
of a large stone cross. At the left-hand end is the stone of Major Lionel
Bonham, and Amy, his wife. Grass grows untidily up round the stone.

Once inside the murky church I saw, in the north transept, what I
had really been looking for: Amy's memorial. There it was, a very fine
statuette of Amy, made of white marble. It glowed out of the darkness
in the same way that her face and hands do against the blue-black
background of her portrait by Burne-Jones. Amy's delicate figure

stands within an arched background, with pilasters on either side. In one hand she is holding what looks like an orange, while her other arm hangs loosely. Her dress is classical: long, draped and flowing, rather like many of Burne-Jones's figures. One bare foot peeps out of the hem. The face and particularly the thick, swooped-back hair are recognizably Amy's. A friend of May's who saw the memorial thought it fascinating: 'it has a strange feeling of Amy about it – mystery and beauty. It seems to hold the things that cannot die.'

At the top of the memorial is a single lotus flower in polished bronze, presumably an acknowledgement of Amy's love of the East. Beneath the lotus, the powerful pair of eagle's wings holds a crown topped with a wreath of rosebuds. The crown is set with three very large oval opals, which shine out a lustrous blue and white in the dim light. When May described the memorial to her brother Willie in the Argentine, she called these 'the opals she always wore', but the pearls she had told him would be incorporated do not appear to be there. Under Amy's feet is the little cherub May mentioned, but May's 'fiery opal' is not set in his curls as she had said it was. The cherub holds up an enamel plaque, on which, inscribed in gold, is:

AMY BONHAM 1910

'It is a thing of true beauty,' May wrote. 'It says "This is me", which I know is what Amy would have liked.'

On a marble plaque beneath the memorial, May used a quotation from Sir Thomas Malory's *Morte d'Arthur*. As she chose the words, May must have thought of Burne-Jones, her beloved friend. The quotation was painfully apt for Amy and Lionel's sad end:

I trust I do not displease God for he knoweth my intent. For when I remember of the beauty and of the noblesse that was both with him and with her, so when I saw his corpse and her corpse so lie together my sorrow may never end.

Underneath this, May had added, quite simply:

HER MOTHER February 18th 1910

The quotation refers to the moment when the sorrowful Queen Guinevere, who has broken her marriage vows, is finally left to rest beside the body of her husband, King Arthur. Could May have been implying anything by it? When I was discussing the tragedy, and May's subsequent misery, with my ninety-four-year-old aunt Diana, she said, 'I think that generation rather revelled and made the most of their loneliness and misery, and felt they must leave evidence in letters for all the world to find. Lovely of course for writers like you; and for me, loving dramas as I do!'

At the end of March 1912, May and the faithful Mrs Iles left for the Argentine to visit Willie and his family. On 3 April, aboard the SS *Avon* between Lisbon and Madeira, May wrote to Daphne before she joined the captain's table, 'rather a deadly collection of people', for dinner. On deck couples were 'beginning to be restless, like beasts at the zoo before feeding time'. There were 1,900 passengers, including several of May's acquaintances. But 1,200 of those on board were immigrants going to either Brazil or the Argentine, hoping to make their fortunes. There were several young single Englishmen, who 'paced the deck like dark panthers looking for pretty girls'. And there were heart-breaking scenes too. At Lisbon, May watched a young wife say goodbye to her husband, who was going to Brazil, both of them knowing it could be years before they saw each other again. 'They sat side by side,' she wrote, 'holding hands and never speaking for two hours, staring at the river bank with tears rolling down their cheeks. It was an amazing silence, and it haunted me – the silence and the tears.'

By 19 April they had almost reached Montevideo, on the way to Buenos Aires, where Willie Melville was to meet them. During their voyage they had heard vague rumours that the American liner the *Titanic*, the largest and grandest in the world, had gone down on her maiden voyage. Then, when they stopped at Rio de Janeiro, there were 'so many conflicting reports that even now we are not certain if all on board the *Titanic* are drowned, or all saved, or all at the bottom or the ship gone. But the tragedy is awful.' Their captain was particularly upset, May told Daphne, because Captain Smith of the *Titanic* was a great friend of his. 'There is a feeling of unrest aboard,' said May.

They arrived at Buenos Aires at the end of April. May wrote to Daphne with pride: 'Willie is astonished at my cheerfulness and spirits.' After a short stay in the city, she and Willie, accompanied by Mrs Iles, travelled the 250 miles by train to Drabble station. There, as before, they were met by an open two-horse wagon, which took them to the estancia. They found everything much the same, except that Berry, having broken his leg very badly in a riding accident some months before, was still incapacitated, little Tinito was much bigger, and the garden, which Celestina had designed and planted with real flair, was looking even more lovely. May was reminded of the last time she had been there with Daphne nearly five years previously, and wrote to her:

> I keep on expecting you in your riding habit to come round the corner. Nothing has changed, a high Sirocco wind is blowing and it is very warm. Willie is out looking at colts. Flies abound. You must imagine me lying on the drawing room sofa looking through the open door at Berry and Tinito playing at an aeroplane game I brought, Berry in a chair which he can wheel himself about in, with his bad leg up. But I believe he will soon be able to put it down.

Berry got better every day, and apart from both May and Mrs Iles being attacked 'in hordes' by mosquitoes, life on the estancia was 'pleasant and easy'. Having been in hospital for months, Berry still needed a nurse to look after him. May wrote to Daphne:

> The only little rift is that we fear the nurse, fat, not fair, and forty, is losing her head to the major-domo Mr Talbot, a delightful Irishman. This fatal passion makes her neglect Berry, and leave off her uniform, and do her hair in strange ways, and be capricious in temper . . . Ah me! It seems years since I saw your little face, and kissed Roslein's soft curls and saw Frank's dear, dear face.

Despite the fondness Amy had had for her uncle Willie, I did not find any letters from her either to him or to May while May was staying in the Argentine. I have not discovered one single letter from Amy to her mother throughout all her travelling years, although there must have been hundreds. I looked through every family trunk I could find, but the only letters from Amy were a few to Daphne, and one or two written when she was a child. When May had sorted through Amy's things after her death, and moved what was at Holdhurst back to her room at Kiddington, she took all the correspondence to London, including the mass of letters she had herself written to Amy. In the summer of 1912, after she had returned from the Argentine, May wrote to Daphne one night:

Darling – I was a very wakeful woman tonight and began tearing up bundles of my letters to Amy that I had left to the end. It rather comforted me to see what solid love I gave her. Such love letters they are – she must have cared a little.

Even May had not been certain of Amy's love.

May explained to Daphne that the letters contained 'many little details' of their life together at Beaumont as a family. Some, she said, were happy moments, but she had also been reminded of the summer when she realized that Hal was 'following the same dreary road of depression as his father'. Daphne had now given birth to her second child, a son, whom she and Frank named after their two fathers, Charles Henry. Despite her pleasure at the couple's obvious joy, and even though it was summer, May was finding her grand house in Lower Seymour Street 'quite cold and disappointing', though she was trying to make it pretty in her usual way. 'But I am so tired,' she wrote, 'and the world is dark and wet and sunless.'

While May found the world a sunless place, Daphne and Frank's new world was golden. With two lovely babies and growing love for each other, they seemed euphorically happy. From their letters, you would never have thought that the strange love triangle with Amy, the recent tragedy of her death, and the preceding years of misery had ever happened. Now they were never referred to. Daphne and Frank adored each other: 'I have never loved like this before, life is full of love and health and beauty,' wrote Daphne in her diary. 'Frank and I took the babes out this afternoon and I wanted to stop people in the road and say, "Look at us, we are the happiest people in the world."'

Even Hal, Daphne's brother of few words, told his sister that 'you have truly found yourself a masterpiece of a husband'.

May said that Daphne and Frank's happiness made her life worth living, but she was excluded from their intense relationship. As Amy had pointed out, she and Daphne, while loving each other, had quite different natures, and were often irritated by each other. In London, May was clearly lonely in a house she disliked, but she did not visit Hal and his family much either. 'Kiddington is too full of ghosts for me to be happy there,' she told Daphne.

May's younger brother Beresford Melville, after whom Willie's son Berry was called, had now lost not only his seat as an MP but also his rich wife Sydney, who had died after several years of what must have been Alzheimer's disease. He had had a very difficult time coping with her distressing illness, and now needed a break, and wished to escape the northern winter. He knew that May would also enjoy this, especially as he would be able to finance their journey.

So, in January 1913, Beresford and May prepared to leave 'this damp, dripping country' to find some cheering sun and culture on an Egyptian journey. They were to be accompanied, naturally, by Mrs Iles, and by Beresford's manservant, Robbins. They met at Charing Cross station on the night of 29 January, to take the train to Marseilles, where they boarded a P&O steamer. Before May left, she wrote to Daphne about Hal, who was bad about keeping in touch with his widowed mother, in such stark contrast to the clinging and concerned little mother's boy he used to be. May felt this keenly, and told Daphne she had been surprised to hear from him: 'Hal has actually written me a nice goodbye letter – perhaps because I sent no message to him in mine to Dolly.'

The P&O boat, May reported, was 'awfully stingy' after other liners she had travelled on, such as the Royal Mail and the Orient lines. This vessel 'throbbed horribly', there was very little warm water for washing, 'nasty' early-morning tea, and no electric bells in the cabins for summoning service. 'Mrs Iles is indignant,' wrote May, 'and speaks her mind, comparing it with previous voyages.' By the time they were approaching Port Said they were bored stiff with the monotonous repetition of 'eating, walking, sitting, talking', and, May told Daphne, 'the meals are long and the conversation wearying chaff, but I do my best'. She was tired too of 'the dinner party every evening when one has to curl one's hair, trim one's tongue to talk, and retire tired from silly conversation'.

As she leant over the side of the boat looking at the waves, May wrote, she thought of Daphne and saw 'a happy little mother busy with many things, and Roslein's little golden curls and clear blue eyes'. On board ship, May had noticed a 'mystery' young lady 'who cries a great deal and no one can find out who she is, and where she goes', who reminded her of Amy. And she told Daphne that as she stared further out to sea, towards the 'sad sea horizons', her heart had gone 'further away to another little daughter who wandered so far over these blue seas, and saw with such keen insatiable eyes the wonders of these Eastern lands'.

When they reached Cairo, May began to realize how much things had changed since her previous journey to Egypt twenty years before, in 1891, the year before she met Burne-Jones. Now there were 'swarms of tourists everywhere'. 'Cairo is its beautiful self – but a new Cairo has grown up, a palatial huge white place which is quite an eyesore.' Nevertheless, from the balcony of her room at the Hotel Semiramis, on the banks of the 'world old Nile', May could see the pyramids above a fringe of palm trees on the opposite bank. She wrote:

> Downstairs crowd the idle rich, who dance and eat and flirt, and flourish, and it is all rather beastly, and I am a socialist for the time being. It _is_ luxury and I have the smartest bedroom I have ever slept in. But I don't care for this life much, though I daresay I shall like it better when we are amongst the temples and tombs.

May, travelling as her brother Beresford's guest, found luxury once more in the Winter Palace Hotel at Luxor, but here, among the ancient sites, with a beautiful hotel garden in which to enjoy the warm sunshine, May declared that there was an atmosphere which 'not Paradise itself could wish better'. The hotel guests, who were mostly Americans, changed into evening dress every night for dinner, and danced until the small hours.

While enjoying this comfortable life of pleasure, they were not completely cut off from the rest of the world; notices were put up every day in the hall with news of world events, including a report about Captain Scott's ill-fated expedition to the South Pole. May wrote:

> *Never have I read a more pathetic story than that of Captain Scott. What a hero Oates is – I think when he crawled out into that blizzard to die in the hopes of saving his companions, it was as noble a deed as a man could do. I love to think that at bedrock Englishmen are like that.*

Beresford Melville proved as keen a sightseer as his sister, although they both had their aches; she from her arthritis, and he from the lame leg he had suffered ever since his nurse dropped him in childhood. But it was worth summoning up the energy to see everything. Above all, they found a visit at sunset to the temple of Karnak, 'the biggest building in the world', particularly 'overpowering'. It was just the sort of experience May loved:

> *We wandered between the mighty pillars, and stumbled over acres of stones and arches, and then we saw the sun sink, with an afterglow of amazing beauty which made the stone of the temple turn pale pink. On the other side of the river rose a full moon that from pale, pale gold developed into a young sun for brilliancy.*

Far, far south at Aswan, May and Beresford, accompanied as before by Mrs Iles and Robbins, stayed at the new Savoy Hotel on Elephantine Island, where, May remembered, 'brambles and stones and scorpions flourished twenty years ago when we were here. Now this palace is built, and a lovely garden blooms and shades, and I hear croquet balls too.'

When May had come last with the Waterfords in 1891, there had been no hotel at all, and the town of Aswan had consisted of a few mud houses. Their boat had moored close to the bank of the island for six weeks, and they had scrambled up to explore the wild place. 'This is the first time in my life that I have drifted in such golden ease,' sighed May, obviously no longer in the socialist mood she had experienced in Cairo as she had observed the 'idle rich'.

May used to watch two young girls staying at the Savoy Hotel riding off into the desert early in the mornings, 'and go miles and miles into the shimmering hot immensity'. On 28 February, after she had seen them leave, she thought of Amy and wrote to Daphne:

Ah, Amy would have ridden on and on with her inscrutable eyes, into the far distance that became a golden mist of mystery to her. And today three years ago I left her in the cold earth she hated – but the mystery for her was solved before then, at least she was one step further on the quest – one step nearer to her goal. I am very tired trying to be happy now she is gone.

In July 1913, May went to stay with cousins on the East Sussex downs, near to the gleaming white cliffs known as the Seven Sisters. It was there, with time to kill, that she wrote down her memories of her own family, the Melvilles, and of her childhood at Witley. Separately, she recorded all she knew of several generations of the Gaskell family. Written in her neat handwriting on loose foolscap paper, these documents have been invaluable to me while writing this book, and indeed helped to inspire it. They were, after all, written with 'those who come after' in mind. But at the same time, May was writing her 'eulogy' of Amy, as it came to be known in the family, primarily as a kind of therapy for her own grief.

I want to write of Amy, my eldest born, my lost child. Must she too be forgotten? . . . I am sitting on the side of the downs, looking across the pale calm sea. The cliffs break at my feet – my tired feet, the summer air soothes my heart – my tired heart. Young as she was her heart was tired too.

May went on to describe her daughter with passion:

Gifted with the fatal gifts of beauty and charm she dipped deep into the emotions of body and soul – intensely curious, she was critical of every impulse, wondered at and dissected every passion and emotion. Beauty played on her like wind on a harp. Whatever her little fingers touched they left the print of grace. She cried out for Faith. But doubted the God that could have satisfied her. She read voraciously, and judged the words and thoughts by no criticism but her own. Never was a woman more passionately loved by men and women – she took it as her right. We poured out gifts, and love, and self-sacrifice, and life, and death – they were hers, she was not surprised. At last Fate said 'It is enough, God demands your happiness' – he took it – and she – who could never endure, looked aghast, and lifted up agonised hands for pity – but there was none – and died.

The eulogy only adds more questions as to the real reason for Amy's death. May ended by addressing her daughter directly, overwhelmed by the power of her emotions:

Oh! Amy my beloved, would to God I could have spared you, I would have wept tears of blood all the rest of my life to have spared you. Child of my love and youth, filled with beauty of mind and body. What you are to me only my mother's heart can tell ... From the moment I found you dead, till the moment life is over, it is you, you, you that are with me sleeping and waking. I see you – pictures of you flash into my vision. Always you are here sweetheart. I love you my own, beyond words, and beyond life. Your mother.

At the end of October, Amy still dominated her mother's thoughts. May explained to Daphne that she felt she must go away for a few days:

I have the most profound longing – which is one of those irresistible instincts in my nature, to be alone for a while, you know it has always been one of my failings when things go wrong or are difficult. Nothing now is wrong or difficult – but the past is still too present – and Amy is never out of my mind. I shall go to Rheims to sit in that divine cathedral and come home rested in soul. I do not suppose you can realise the uplifting joy great architecture gives me ... I do not doubt the wisdom of fate or the mercy of God – but it is a tangled world.

As the threat of war drew closer, the world did indeed seem very tangled; many countries were in chaos and conflict, and at home politicians argued over Asquith's attempted Home Rule for Ireland Bill, which almost led to civil war. The suffragettes, in their attempt to secure votes for women, became more and more destructive in their demonstrations, which turned many people against them. Daphne thought their behaviour 'disgraceful but brave'. May often referred to 'my suffragette soul', but I have found no evidence that she joined the movement, although her close friend Sybil, Countess Brassey, was president of the National Union of Women's Suffrage Societies. All in all there was a general feeling that something terrible was bound to happen, but no one quite knew what, or when.

Despite the uncertainties, May set off again on her escapist travels in March 1914, with Mrs Iles at her side. The first few weeks were spent 'taking a cure' at Dr Dengler's Sanatorium in Baden Baden, which was full of friends and acquaintances. The treatment, according to May, seemed to consist mostly of stuffing the inmates with 'huge chunks of meat, dishes of cream, lots of butter – the parlour maids are spies and report to Dr Dengler when any is left'. May was even given a large beef steak for breakfast which, not surprisingly, made her feel sick.

This house is crammed – princes, lords and ladies, millionairesses, Jews, Germans, Americans. Certainly Dengler isn't a snob, everyone takes their turn, and obeys orders from parlour maids equally. Poor Sir Frank Corbett, who is here to get thin, was caught stealing an extra pat of butter from his wife's dish.

At the end of April, as Dr Dengler finally released May from his strict regime, he told her, 'I promise you that before three weeks are over you will feel better than for years – have faith, Mrs Gaskell – the pain will disappear.'

Frank Rose was not the eldest son of the Rose family; but as his two elder brothers had both been killed in the Boer War in 1900, it was Frank who had inherited Hardwick House in April 1913, after his father, Sir Charles Rose, died suddenly, aged sixty-six. His tombstone gives an original cause of death; that he 'died from the effects of an aeroplane flight'. In fact, Sir Charles had been so over-excited by a particularly exhilarating flight in his small aeroplane at Hendon that he had suffered a heart attack immediately afterwards, dropping down dead in the street. Frank's time at Scarborough was at an end, so he and his little family had moved into Hardwick House, now on their own, and spent a blissfully happy Christmas there.

But in the lovely spring of 1914, the order came from the colonel of the Tenth Royal Hussars that Frank was to sail from England for South Africa with his regiment at the beginning of May for a regular overseas tour of duty, which would include squadron and regimental training of young officers. He thought he would be away for at least five months. May wrote to Daphne, speaking of 'the swiftly passing happy days – and lonely days that must come', probably meaning to be sympathetic but only making Daphne dread her husband's departure more. Frank and Daphne decided that with the combination of Frank's absence and the political uncertainties, it would be best to let Hardwick temporarily to the army. They themselves rented Enstone House, a small house near Kiddington, so that Daphne and the 'babes' would be nearer to Hal, Dolly and their children.

On 9 May Daphne went to Southampton to see Frank set sail for South Africa. Afterwards she collected her little Amy and Charles, and motored to their new house. 'Thank God the day is over –' she wrote in her Collins pocket diary, 'the agony is real. Help me.' But Daphne was a strong and active little thing, and she kept busy, though she was often, she admitted, 'very cross'. Writing long letters to Frank and being with her children helped her. As she was so near to her childhood home, she knew many people around. She told Frank about 'the Duke' (the Duke of Marlborough, a near neighbour at Blenheim Palace), who 'was going to have a great Whit Monday fete, but the suffragettes have been frightening him so much, that he's put it off. Apparently Blenheim is one of the places they have on their list to burn.' Daphne added that she thought these 'strident women' were 'most alarming' to men.

Seemingly forever travelling, May was now in Venice, where she had joined her brother Beresford, again as his guest, at the Grand Hotel Britannia on the Grand Canal. May described herself as 'a born tourist'. Her brother left the daily organizing to her, and explained to others in their party, 'My sister is a most determined woman – she always gets her own way in sightseeing.' But, like Alfred Milner, he found May a knowledgeable and enthusiastic companion with whom to look at art and architecture.

May still had time to write to Daphne; she told her that she had seen Amy's old friend Gervy Ker again, and that they had talked of Amy. 'There was no one in the world like Amy,' Mr Ker had observed sadly. May was sympathetic about Frank's departure for South Africa: 'I'm glad the parting is over – partings are the saddest things on earth. Now you must forget loneliness and dream of happiness past, and happiness to come.' But the happiness May envisaged for her daughter was not to come.

May had offered to come and live with Daphne while Frank was away, but then she had written that perhaps it would not be such a good idea after all, as she knew that she was not a good influence on Daphne when she was nervous or unhappy; 'There is something in my personality that rubs you up the wrong way.' This was all too true; later, when May did visit Enstone, Daphne confessed to feeling very irritated, and told Frank in a letter that although she 'felt a beast', she knew there would always be times when she became so annoyed by her mother that she 'felt sick'.

May's time abroad during the first few months of 1914 must, in retrospect, have seemed surreal to her. The possibility of war grew daily greater, yet people back in England could not really believe it would happen. However, the assassination of the Archduke Franz Ferdinand, heir to the Austro-Hungarian throne, on 28 June at Sarajevo finally led to the first-ever global war. May returned to England to find that her friend Herbert Asquith, who had been Liberal Prime Minister since 1908, had now also temporarily been appointed Secretary of State for War. Although acknowledged as a brilliant parliamentarian, he was later criticized as a wartime leader because of his so-called 'laissez faire method of governing'.

On 2 August Daphne wrote in her pocket diary:

Took babes out in the afternoon. A day of suspense. Germany declared war on Russia, invaded France, took Luxemburg. England preparing for war.

The next day, when France had announced war against Germany, and Belgium had also been invaded, Daphne's diary entry was:

*Played in the ladies doubles and we won. Enjoyed it, though couldn't
think of much except war. We are all prepared for war, Navy mobilised,
Army mobilising.*

On 4 August May was staying with friends in the country. Herbert
Asquith was among the distinguished gathering of house guests.
Although everyone knew they were on the brink of war, they tried to
talk of other things at dinner. But there was an unvoiced tension.
When May went to bed, she could not sleep. She recorded later that
she went onto her balcony, where she could smell the scent of jasmine
in the warm air of a perfect summer's night. It was midnight when she
began to hear a distant clatter of hoofbeats on the road beyond the
drive. They became louder until a rider, 'like a horseman of the
Apocalypse', striking firefly sparks in the darkness, galloped up to the
house and shouted, 'Mr Prime Minister! Mr Prime Minister! It is
WAR!'

It was during the sleepless hours which followed this dramatic
news that May took a decision which was to change and broaden her
life, and provide comfort to thousands of soldiers and sailors during
what would prove a far more terrible war than anyone at that time
could imagine. She lay in the darkness thinking of Lionel's words of
gratitude thirteen years before, when she had sent him and his fellow
soldiers books to distract them as they lay wounded in hospital in
South Africa. Alone during that black night, May forgot her own
sorrows and vowed to herself that whatever happened in this war, the
British soldiers would have books and magazines to help ease the pain
and loneliness they would have to endure in hospital. May, now aged
sixty-one, at a time when most women of her class were slipping
gracefully into idle old age, had finally found a purpose in life.

CHAPTER ELEVEN

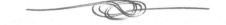

THE TRAGIC WAR

5 AUGUST 1914, THE FIRST DAY OF WAR, WAS WET BUT VERY HOT IN
England. May hurried back to London, and in the evening she wrote
to Daphne. 'Well done about the tennis doubles – I am proud,' was the
first line of the letter. Only then did she go on to tell her daughter
what a strange day it had been in London: 'criers in the street, gravity
– everyone organizing Red Cross committees, work parties, charities'.

There was fervent support for the war from all levels of society.
King George V and Queen Mary came out onto the balcony of
Buckingham Palace again and again, to deafening cheers. But May
was full of apprehension, as she confessed to Daphne:

*I cannot tell you how my whole being shrinks from the concept of more
pain, and the sight of suffering all round. For the first time I should like to
shut my eyes and ears to the future.*

During the morning May called at the Horners' London house to
see if her friend Frances was at home, but she found only the butler,
who said that the Horners' young son Edward was 'mad to go to
war', and had even volunteered to be a valet to one of the officers
on a ship. The butler told May that he felt the same himself: 'I would

go without any wages, in any capacity, if only I could go to the front.'

That night, Alfred Milner came to dine with May alone. The last time he had dined at Lower Seymour Street, in January, the only other guest had been the novelist Henry James. James, now an old man, quite often took May to the theatre. He had known her since the late 1880s, when she had become associated with the Souls, who had adopted James, like Burne-Jones, as one of their cultural heroes.

Henry James greatly admired Burne-Jones's talent, but as the years went by he began to have some reservations about the painter's work being too old-fashioned. However, he always defended his character; he agreed with May that Burne-Jones had been a wonderful friend, who had great charm, and commented that he had grown 'only more lovable, natural and wise' with the passing years. The outbreak of war came as a great shock to Henry James, and finally prompted him to become a British citizen, partly out of loyalty to his adopted country, and partly in protest at America's refusal to enter the war. Sadly he was to die in 1916, a year before the American president, Woodrow Wilson, at last decided to support the allies and declare war on Germany.

During that first fateful night of war, Alfred Milner told May that Sturry, his house in Kent, was to be commandeered as billets for the Kent yeomanry. But he was now occupied with his new London house, 17 Great College Street, near Westminster Abbey, and asked May if she would advise him on decorating and furnishing it. Then, naturally, they spent most of the evening talking of war. May found Alfred's 'calm manner and balanced mind a great refreshment in this welter of anxiety and work – and depression'. As he was leaving, Alfred enquired about Frank and Daphne. May told him that for the moment Daphne was relieved that Frank was safe in South Africa, but he had been away for nearly thirteen weeks now, and she missed him badly. This was true; at the bottom of countless pages in her pocket diary Daphne wrote simply, 'I want him.' Alfred commented, 'May that delightful happiness be spared.'

May had not forgotten her midnight resolve: to form a war library for supplying the sick and wounded armed forces abroad. She had arranged a dinner for a small group of friends to discuss her idea. Her brother Beresford, who had inherited his wife's fortune, 'entered heart and soul into the scheme', and said he would help financially. He also became the library's treasurer. They decided to advertise their cause in the newspapers, asking people to send any books and magazines they could spare. A close friend of May, Lady Battersea, who was one of the principal Souls, owned a palatial mansion, Surrey House, which was currently empty. It was only two doors along from May's old house at Marble Arch. She told May that she would lend it as a depot and offices for the war library. Alfred Milner agreed to be on the committee, as did Constance Battersea and other close friends of May, including Sybil Brassey, who supported the suffragette movement, and Sir Courtauld Thomson, a distinguished colonial administrator. Within a few days Lord Haldane, who was now War Minister, officially approved of the project, and the Admiralty asked if the Navy, 'both sound and sick', could be included in the project as well. In no time at all May's dream became a reality.

Meanwhile, May was also thinking of other ways in which she could contribute to the war effort. On the morning of 7 August, the third day of war, Mrs Iles and another maid, known simply as Black, who was a good seamstress, were set to work. May gave them material and told them it should be 'quickly' made into pyjamas for the forces, and sent off 'at once'. Black then told May that her sister, who lived in a working-class London suburb, had complained about the terrible state her neighbourhood was in, with 'every second man called to fight, businesses shut down and women crying, as the men who are left behind have no work'. May was appalled by the miseries described to her, and tried to think of something she could do to help these unfortunate families. It did not take her long; she wrote to Daphne:

> *I have this morning started a workroom for wives of reservists and territorials, to be paid wages for making ambulance things, which should help them keep the pot boiling.*

From several senior politicians she knew well, such as Milner, Haldane and Balfour, who were in what she called the 'inner circle', May found out all she could about the war. She confided to Daphne:

Kitchener is making the government sit up. He arrived at the War Office, and demanded that his bedroom be prepared at once. They said there was none on the premises. There __must__ be one ready by twelve o'clock was his reply. He then ordered a bathroom to be made __at once__.

The War Office was a large, ornate building near the Foreign Office in Whitehall, which Lord Kitchener, who had been appointed the new Secretary of State for War, made his home as soon as war was declared. Kitchener was a 'strong, silent man', and the hero of the Boer War; his generous moustache and commanding finger are still familiar from reproductions of war-recruitment posters. The first posters, calling for volunteers to form a new army, were put up on 11 August, and had recruited a hundred thousand men within two weeks. Kitchener predicted that the war would last four years, but nobody would believe him, thinking that it would be over within four months. Milner told May that he did not think the war would be long, as there would be such difficulties with the German food supply, but he added that 'the machinery of war is such a doubtful thing that no one can say'. With the outbreak of war, Milner had been brought back into public life to organize coal and food production for Asquith's government. May asked him what 'he thought our chances were', and he replied 'very gravely' and after a pause, 'I think we shall just win – if the Navy can beat them.' But he was right to point out then that no one could predict the time, scale or the unprecedented horrors of this war.

While May set her servants to work for the war effort on 7 August, and London was buzzing with activity, Daphne took her 'babes' out for a walk in the sleepy countryside. It was very hot. In her pocket diary that night she noted, 'Great battle outside Liege – twenty-five thousand German casualties.'

The next day rain freshened the heat, and Daphne bicycled vigorously over to Kiddington to see Dolly. She recorded in her diary that she had enjoyed the visit, and added, 'No troops have sailed yet. Everything being done excellently. He's been gone thirteen weeks and I'm anxious.'

The day after, Daphne heard from May, who had discovered through her high-up sources that Frank's regiment had been ordered to come back from South Africa. This, Daphne realized, meant that he would probably be sent to France before long. 'God help us all,' she wrote in her diary. 'Very miserable – I want Frank more than words can say.'

The next night, she read her Bible as usual, and wrote, 'I read "Be strong, and of good courage, dread not nor be dismayed." And somehow it seemed a message, and comforted.'

The Admiralty and the War Office had reassured May and Beresford that they were ready to accept all the books they could send, and May waited eagerly to see what response their appeal would bring. In the event, as May wrote later in an account of the library's beginnings, 'it was beyond belief'. They had not anticipated the flood of parcels and boxes of books that poured in to Surrey House; everything from 'dirty packets of rubbish from places like Finchley' to an entire library of thirty thousand books sent by one man from his country estate. Then, after advertisements were put in American and Canadian newspapers, books started arriving from all over the world.

May recorded in her account:

Day after day, vans stood unloading at the door of Surrey House, quickly the cases rose far above our heads, crawled up the wide stairs, blocked three immense rooms, invaded passages – and still continued to come.

The vans bringing the books completely blocked the traffic around Marble Arch. May's small team of voluntary helpers worked ceaselessly as 'the torrent poured steadily on'. They had never expected such generosity. But soon they were overwhelmed; they could not cope. May turned to a man she knew to be experienced, capable and kind hearted, Dr Hagberg Wright, the chief librarian of the London Library.

Hagberg Wright was known to be a brilliant scholar and administrator. Fifty-two years old, he was unmarried, tall and handsome, and women found him very attractive. When he arrived at Surrey House and saw the mountains of books, even he was overwhelmed. But he was not to be daunted, and together with five members of his staff, who came voluntarily after-hours and worked late into the nights, they 'brought order to chaos'. Tens of thousands of parish magazines, which they judged would not help to alleviate any suffering, were passed to 'rubbish wagons' outside the building, while rare editions of books were put up for sale to swell the funds. Wonderful gems arrived, such as first editions of Dickens, Thackeray and Charlotte Brontë, and some Indian paper editions of Kipling. Hagberg Wright was to become May's devoted co-organizer of the War Library, and she acknowledged later that his 'wisdom, help and guidance' had been invaluable.

But most of all, perhaps, it was May's determination that made her ambitious project work. This pioneering spirit must surely have been inherited from her father, Canon Melville, who years before at Hatfield College in Durham had started his campaign to make education in England available to the masses. When May had left Kiddington in 1908 to set up on her own in London, she had told Daphne that she had always felt herself to be 'an anomaly' amongst the Gaskells; they retreated into their own world, while May's inclination was to go forward into an ever-wider world. Having experienced an unhappy marriage, tragedy and loss, her strength of character and perseverance now came into their own.

There was a rumour that a ship bringing the Tenth Royal Hussars from South Africa would be back in England in mid-September. Daphne kept on asking May to try to find out, through her friends in the 'inner circle', who included the prime minister Herbert Asquith himself, exactly when the ship would reach Southampton, and what plans there were for the regiment after their return. Lord Haldane, who as War Minister was organizing the British Expeditionary Forces, which Frank would probably join, was another politician who had attended May's pre-war dinner parties. But May was now working long hours every day at Surrey House, and she did not want to harass her distinguished friends. She told her anxious daughter on 14 September:

> *I begin to be shy of getting news for you. I have had a desperate day of work – the hardest yet. The paid packer has enlisted and the new appeal brought in ten thousand more books – I cannot tell you what a rush it has been ... My new cook cannot cook one bit – which is very troublesome –*

and she is a nice young woman. I am too tired to write – so you will
forgive your loving mother won't you – and kiss the babes for me.

'I'm very very lonely,' wrote Daphne in her diary, as she waited for
Frank's return from South Africa. Her feelings reached an almost
unbearable intensity just when she knew it would not be long until she
was reunited with her husband. Two days later, on 19 September,
Frank's ship, the *Balmoral Castle*, docked at Southampton. Daphne
stood outside the entrance to the quay, watching the ship as it steamed
smoothly in. Women were not allowed through the gates, but a Major
Campbell, whom Daphne knew, saw her waiting alone, and let her
slip through to the Embarkation Office. She was the only woman
there. Then on the quay she spotted Frank with his men. 'Wonderful
joy,' Daphne wrote in her diary that night.

But it was to be a strange, brief joy. Frank and Daphne spent their
first night together at the Polygon Hotel in Southampton, and then
Frank had to leave for Ludgershall Camp, near Andover, where he was
to be temporarily stationed while the regiment waited for their horses.
Daphne had arranged that her 'babes', with their nurse, would stay with
May in London, so that she herself could be near Frank. Although May
was working so hard, she loved having her grandchildren with her,
particularly little Amy, whom she now called M'amy:

> *Last night M'amy had tea with me, and was enchanting, her manners so*
> *sedate, her seductions so pronounced. She reminds me of her lost little aunt –*
> *a sort of quiet assumption of her right to things . . . it must be a strange*
> *phantasmagorical life you are leading. God bless you both. The weary*
> *mother.*

Daphne's time with Frank must certainly have seemed unreal. She
moved into lodgings in Ludgershall. She and other Army wives
would walk to the camp to see their loved ones when the soldiers were
free for an hour or two. In two weeks Daphne and Frank only
managed to escape for a few afternoon walks alone, and had two
dinners together at the Prince of Wales Hotel in Ludgershall. But
as a result of that first night at the hotel in Southampton, or
perhaps a secret moment at some secluded spot on one of their

walks, Daphne was pregnant again, although she did not yet know it.

Daphne now knew that Frank's regiment was to leave soon with the British Expeditionary Forces, crossing northern France to Belgium, where the fighting was. But she knew nothing else. May had conflicting reports through her contacts about the exact date of their departure. In the event, it was sooner than they thought. On 3 October, two weeks after his return, Frank was allowed to go up to London for one day with Daphne to see his children. They shopped, and took the 'babes' out to the park. Frank helped Daphne put little Amy and Charles to bed, and told them stories until it was time to catch the train back to Andover.

The next day was 'all confusion and bustle' at the camp, while Daphne packed Frank's things. This was followed by a 'strange and terrible day' of waiting, as Frank had gone ahead with his regiment to Southampton. On 6 October, Daphne drove to Southampton to say goodbye. They had just an hour for lunch at the Dolphin Hotel, and then embraced outside the docks before parting. 'The agony of today has been almost too much,' Daphne wrote in her little diary that evening.

Four days later, Frank wrote cheerfully from Belgium. All was well, he reassured Daphne, there had been no fighting so far, 'though I don't think it will be long before we get at them'. The Hussars had been told that there was a large force of Germans in front of them, and that the Belgians were falling back and would need their support. Frank repeated for the second time, 'everyone cheery and well'. The regiment were not too alarmed by the idea of the Germans, he said, as 'everyone seems to be of the same opinion that the German cavalry are bad. They seldom get off their horses and have never yet faced a charge.' The following day he wrote again to Daphne, telling her that it was 'most probable that we shall take part in a very big move which you may read about in a few days in the papers'.

The Tenth Royal Hussars, as cavalry, were finding the terrain extremely difficult to ride through. The countryside consisted of cultivated areas and woods, criss-crossed by canals and wire fences, with villages every mile or so. It was impossible to avoid the roads. The local people, Frank said, seemed to take the war very calmly, with work and business going on as usual:

. . . everyone is cheery and quite un-apprehensive of any danger. They are
delighted to see us and wherever we go the men are given as many apples,
pears, cigars and cigarettes as they can carry . . . we give our horses plenty
of hay so they are rapidly getting fit.

The optimistic locals also denied what Frank and his men were now
certain of – that Antwerp had fallen. Even his own men, Frank said,
did not 'yet realise the seriousness of war, and are inclined to treat it
rather as a picnic . . . I shall be very careful of myself, so you must not
worry.'

Nearly two weeks later, the picnic was over. Frank confessed that
they had had:

. . . a _very_ hard time lately – in fact harder than anything I have experi-
enced before . . . we have had a good deal of fighting and been under
shellfire for four days. The noise of the shells bursting all round – some-
times five or six at a time – is tremendous, and all we can do is lie still and
wonder where the next one is coming from. I must say it is terrifying.

Because of night attacks, Frank continued, he and his men had only
had about one hour of proper sleep during the last four days.

We have to show ourselves occasionally to prevent the enemy from
advancing and rushing the trenches. Yesterday we soon had eight men
killed and two wounded. A bullet came through the top of the trench
and hit my neck so hard that I thought for a moment I was
wounded.

Nevertheless, Frank reassured Daphne that he was 'quite safe and
well', as he did in every letter. He was just very tired, he said,
and would be grateful if she could send him some chocolate; 'It is
often all we get for the whole day.'

As he finished this long letter, a 'special messenger' was just leaving, so he sent it with him, instead of by the usual post collection.
However, after an unexpected five hours of sleep, thinking that the
letter with the messenger might not reach Daphne, he wrote several
pages more, to be sent in the normal way. This time he admitted that:

The past week has been very hard on men and horses. The Germans are masters at the art of concealing themselves. We used to think the Boers were good – but the Germans are much better.

The forty-eight hours which Frank's regiment had been forced to spend at the bottom of the trenches, just lying there in the damp and cold, under continual deafening shellfire which came 'faster and faster every minute, and rushing within a few feet of us', was something, he told Daphne, they none of them wanted to repeat.

But their marching days were hard too:

We always march before dawn and usually spend sixteen hours in the saddle – one day it was twenty . . . I have not taken my boots off for a week or shaved for five days.

Frank asked Daphne to send him some 'thick khaki shirts with collars and a khaki tie, which will be invaluable in the cold weather'. His next request was for another pair of leather gloves from Gilbert, in Sloane Square, as he had lost his.

We are now at where I imagine the most important fighting is taking place . . . it is impossible to say when this war will end, but let's hope it will be soon. It will be a great day when I see you and the babes again, and then I hope never more shall we be apart. Bless you darling – Frank.

In reality, this was only the beginning of what was to be more than four years of devastating war. And these were Frank Rose's last words to his wife.

Since Frank's departure, Daphne and her children had been staying at May's house in London. In this way Daphne was not alone, and was able to help May with the library, and also to work with Belgian refugees. The fourth of October, when Frank wrote his last letter, was a Saturday. May took Daphne to a Red Cross concert at the Albert Hall, where they sat in a friend's box. The King and Queen were there, and the main performer was the famous soprano Adelina Patti, who 'sang wonderfully'. The following day, Daphne and her friend

Helen Mitford took their children out into Hyde Park. That evening
Helen telephoned to say that her husband Clem, Frank's best friend
and also in his regiment, had been wounded in Belgium. This filled
Daphne with anxiety. She wrote in her diary:

> *Who knows about Frank? God help us wives. Every time I come back to
> the house I know that there may be a telegram. It is becoming a real
> strain, and the longing for him grows and strengthens.*

On 26 October Daphne received Frank's last, very long letter.
Three days later, in exactly the way she had dreaded, she returned to
May's house to find a telegram. The entry in her diary was brief:

> *Got telegram to say Frank killed on 26th. Went to War Office. Shopped
> and went to see Madre. My only wish now is for Death, and God grant it
> may be soon.*

Madre was poor old Lady Rose, Frank's mother, widowed only the
year before, and very frail. She had lost not only her first two sons in
the Boer War, but her fourth and youngest from illness in 1908. Now
she had only a daughter left.

That Daphne could have gone shopping within hours of hearing
that her husband was dead seems unbelievable, unless she felt she had
to buy some mourning clothes immediately. But in fact her diary is
surprisingly full of 'went shopping' entries. This could not have been
household shopping, which the servants would have done, so perhaps
Daphne's frequent shopping expeditions were what we would now
call 'retail therapy'.

On the same day that Daphne received her shattering telegram,
Tommy Bouch, a fellow officer and friend of Frank's, wrote to her
from Zandvoorde, six miles south of Ypres, near where Frank had
been killed:

> *I don't know how to write – I am so terribly sorry for you . . . Poor
> Frankie, he was so well and happy. He was shot stone dead through the
> head, when standing up in the trenches to give his men directions for
> firing. A German sniper had been bothering them a lot, but Frank scorned*

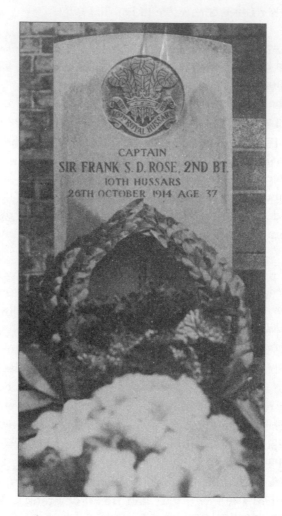

Frank Rose's grave at Zandvoorde, near Ypres.

the obvious danger of exposing himself, and was willing to sacrifice his life
in giving a splendid example to his men. And he died instantaneously,
without any pain at all, or fear, or consciousness of dying. God help you
and all of us – I see no end to the misery of the world.

Daphne was told that Captain Rose and one of his men, Lieutenant Turnor, had been standing together, and were killed at almost exactly the same moment, as they both put their heads over the top of the trench in the late afternoon after a long, bad day of shelling. Frank was looking through his field glasses to try and locate where some of the shots kept coming from. A lance corporal and a private were killed in the same skirmish. Major Shearman, a fellow officer, who saw that the bodies were removed from the front, also wrote to Daphne, full of sympathy and regret at the loss of an officer who had 'such a lovable nature', and was 'one of the kindest, most unselfish of men'. The whole regiment would miss him, he added. Then he reassured Daphne:

I had the bodies brought out at dark. I myself buried them the next
morning in the churchyard at Zandvoorde and placed wooden crosses with
names and dates over each grave so that you will be able later on to visit
the place. I took the ring off his finger, and the Colonel will forward it to
you together with other things I found on him.

As the days went by, more letters of condolence arrived for Daphne, and the reality of her loss began to dawn on her. In her diary, next to recording the daily duties of her war work, household matters and time spent with her children, she entered repeated pleas to God to help her, to soothe her pain or to send death to release her. Her friend Helen Mitford had gone over to Boulogne, to the Allied Forces Base Hospital, where her husband Clem, who had been wounded in the groin, was recovering. She had to tell him about Frank, and knew he would take the news very hard. Clem wrote at once to Daphne:

I am so miserable for you. The fact of losing my oldest friend in the
regiment, and the loss to the regiment, is nothing really to what one feels

for you. Thank God from what one hears it was over at once – you would realise this all the more if you had been in one of these hospitals and seen some of the protracted sufferings.

The whole country, so recently caught up in a fever of support for the war, was beginning to realize that it was not going to be over by Christmas as they had thought, and that the number of lives that might be lost was unimaginable. Another of Frank's fellow officers wrote to Daphne:

Whether it's shrapnel or bullets, a lot of us will keep him company before the war is over, as the beastly trenches to which we return every forty-eight hours are too weakly held for us to do much good at present.

By the end of November 1914, over fifty-four thousand British soldiers who had fought in the first battle of Ypres had lost their lives.

For three weeks after Frank's death, Daphne continued to help May with her War Library every day. May described her daughter's pain as 'so unspeakable that she could only be silent; white, brave and silent'. Only with her oblivious little children, 'dancing and shouting with glee', did Daphne never fail to smile. 'I walk and talk in a dream, the pain is either numbing or terrific, but I smile,' she wrote.

Frank's things were sent back from France, but Daphne could not look at them. Then she found out that she was pregnant again, but instead of joy she felt greater sadness. She also found it increasingly hard to live with her mother, and told May she needed to be alone. Taking her children and their nurse, Daphne left the bustle of London and returned to Hardwick, now vacated by the army.

After a few days May wrote to her daughter with concern and understanding:

Be careful of this coming child – let it too be splendid, and healthy, and beautiful – as worthy of him as the others. But yes, my beloved, I know you are best alone – that instinct is born in us both.

She knew that 'silence, solitude and work' were what would help Daphne, and she added that 'the children will keep you alive'. She did not want to bother her, but she reassured Daphne that her mother's heart would always be with her, and that her love would 'unconsciously shelter' her. Knowing how religious Daphne was, May said she prayed for her daughter constantly, and hoped that her 'incessant' prayers would help her, 'as the spirit of God only reaches one at the darkest hour'. The letter ended: 'Goodbye my child – I shall not write like this again.'

In later years, Daphne became increasingly solitary. The immediate aftermath of Frank's death was probably the beginning of her urge to be alone. But with young children, and live-in servants, it was not always easy. The Hardwick woods became her refuge; whenever she needed to be sure of complete solitude, this is where she would go. Often in her diary she refers to 'anguish' or 'pain' in the woods. It was not until the middle of December that she felt able to unpack Frank's kit. She was unprepared for what she found: 'His belt is stained with his blood. The pain nearly broke me. Oh God of Heaven – have pity and send Death soon.'

On New Year's Eve 1914, Daphne wrote in her diary:

> *And so ends the most miserable year that would be possible to live through. The only consolation is that I have touched the bedrock of agony, and whatever happens in the years to come, I shall never suffer so awfully as I have suffered in 1914.*

But Daphne would not let her suffering go. Each night, from 1915 for nearly ten years, she wrote a letter to Frank telling him everything she had done and felt that day. She never remarried, and she dressed in mourning colours – black, grey, and, with time, a touch of purple – for the rest of her days.

Nowadays, both May and Daphne would probably be offered bereavement counselling for their tragic losses. May's War Library, however, was clearly a sort of therapy for her. There was no time now to mourn for Amy, or to go on one of her protracted 'cures' abroad. Despite the tide of books flooding into Surrey House, more and more were needed as hospitals proliferated and the number of sick and wounded increased at a prodigious rate. At the end of 1914, the Admiralty asked May to supply 'a book a man' to the sailors in the North Sea Fleet and to all the guards round the coasts of the entire British Isles and Ireland. These demands were too overwhelming for the small group at Surrey House to cope with, so branch libraries were formed to send books to the strong and healthy, while May and her team at Surrey House concentrated on the sick and wounded.

As the battlefields extended, the area over which hospitals and hospital ships were supplied with reading matter from this small corner of Marble Arch grew immense; ultimately the books reached as far as France, Italy, Russia, East Africa, Siberia, Australia, New Zealand, Canada, Mesopotamia, Egypt, Malta, Palestine, Greece and India. Constant appeals for both books and funds were needed. It involved a lot of work: not only did the books have to be sorted, catalogued and packed, but many needed repairing before sending out. Later it was estimated that seventeen thousand books were mended each year of the war, and every donor was thanked individually. 'There seemed no end to the demands,' wrote May. But, even though she was sometimes ill, she never gave up.

Cables arrived from distant battlefields with orders such as 'Send twenty-five thousand books at once, light and good print.' Then they heard that typhoid and dysentery patients were so weak they could not hold books at all, but that although they were too ill to read, looking at pictures sometimes comforted them. It was Rudyard Kipling who addressed the problem of how to help the weakest patients. He suggested to May that the general public be encouraged to make scrapbooks, for which he produced specific instructions:

Size about 14" × 11", four sheets. Outside a nice coloured picture. Fill both sides of the paper with attractive pictures, plain and coloured, <u>very</u> short stories, little jokes and anecdotes, short poems. Anything amusing or pretty. Remember the books are for grown men.

These scrapbooks proved even more popular than May had anticipated. She had to admit, 'Rudyard is generally right.'

May's appeals for donations of books pointed out that variety was

important. In order to satisfy all kinds of tastes, she supplied everything from romantic penny novelettes and comics to Shakespeare's
plays, Montaigne's essays and Wordsworth's *Prelude*. The colonials
had an insatiable desire for books of reference; one hospital asked for
the *Encyclopaedia Britannica* in forty volumes. Handbooks were sent
out on anything that could be studied while patients were incapacitated, from oil engines, electricity, artillery, history and
philosophy to chicken farming, gardening, boxing, ferrets, wood-
carving and music. Even then not everyone was satisfied. One soldier
wrote personally to May:

> *Why do you send us such rot to read, Mrs Gaskell? Don't send us stiff
> books, we want the Bull Dog breed series and Nick Carter's detective
> stories – any good murder cases or excitements.*

There were always some places that the books had not yet reached.
From Egypt, May heard from a soldier who pleaded:

> *. . . all we have to read here is a scrap of the advertisement page of the
> Daily Telegraph, which I picked up in the desert. On it we saw that you
> send books to the sick and wounded. Please hurry and send us some.*

For more than a year after the outbreak of war, May ran her War
Library with only the help of her brother Beresford and a group of
friends, who also helped raise funds as the demand for books
increased. The organization required was formidable. And although
people donated generously and publishers supplied new books at
trade price, it became obvious that the War Library was no longer
something which could survive as a private enterprise. 'We were in
despair,' admitted May.

However, help was at hand in the form of the British Red Cross,
which May had approached. In the autumn of 1915 they agreed to
take over the War Library, but for the time being the headquarters
remained at Surrey House, with May and Dr Hagberg Wright as joint
honorary secretaries, and a staff of fifty voluntary workers. The
volunteers could not cope with packing as well as receiving, sorting
and distributing the books, so May had to employ paid packers, but

there were never more than six. There were constant difficulties getting the orders by train or ship to their destinations in every far-flung war zone. But by the end of the war this small, devoted group had distributed over six million books and magazines from Marble Arch to all corners of the world.

The bereaved Gaskell family did have one reason to celebrate the Christmas of 1914. On 10 December Hal's wife Dolly gave birth to her third child, a brother for Tom, who was now eight, and for Diana, who was five. They called the baby Oliver Robin. Although the youngest of the family, Robin, as he was always called, would later inherit Dolly's childhood home, the historic and reputedly haunted Levens Hall, after Dolly's only brother died young. Diana told me that when she was about to be married herself, her mother Dolly – my grandmother – had warned her about sex, saying that she might not like it, as she herself never had. And in her old age, Dolly had talked about her odd marriage. It seems that the eagerness the young Hal had shown when he climbed up the drainpipe at Levens to reach his fiancée's bedroom had not lasted long. The couple, who had married when Dolly was still almost a child, were an ill-matched pair, and with his growing silence, distance and eccentric behaviour, Hal must have been extremely hard to live with. In spite of all these difficulties, however, a sort of understanding survived between them.

Dolly was very pretty indeed; like her mother and her mother-in-law, she was to have admirers all her life, and loved going up to London, where she eventually settled in her old age. One long-standing admirer was Victor Raenaeker, a former curator of the Ashmolean Museum in Oxford, who had been in love with Dolly ever since her early years at Kiddington. When she was over eighty Dolly finally allowed Victor to come and live with her, and I was able to boast to my friends that my grandmother was 'living in sin', based on the fact that she had told her eldest grandson that she and Victor still had 'cuddles'. When I was young I used to enjoy visiting my grandmother; she had a sweet expression, twinkling eyes and a low gentle voice. My uncle Robin wrote in his memoirs that his mother was:

... very funny, usually and apparently by mistake. When her outrageous slips of the tongue were spotted, she would emit one enormous peal of laughter, followed by another at a lower volume ... she had a very good sense of humour, particularly of the ridiculous.

Her lack of tact amused her too. She once gave Robin's fiancée one of her brooches, telling her, 'It will suit you, but it is much too flashy for me.' Realizing immediately the rudeness of what she had said, Dolly had burst out laughing at herself.

Robin became Hal's favourite child; he was clever, with an endearingly impish smile, and far more confident than his older brother Tom. Both boys had inherited the Gaskell eccentricity, but both were also musical, artistic and funny. But the more Robin shone in his father's eyes, the more reserved Tom became. Diana thinks that Hal was an unkind and crushing father to Tom, and she feels he rejected her too as she got older, as he was not interested in young girls. But she excuses her father because she feels he could not cope with life, and suggests that perhaps his silences and neglect of others were a sort of refuge, a defence against the disappointment of his relationship with Dolly, and because he never fulfilled his early dream of becoming a great painter. Diana's first memory of her father is a poignant one of being dangled on Hal's knee, while he was 'happy and laughing'. But she adds, 'Then gloom must have descended.'

By the beginning of 1915, Daphne was feeling no happier about her own pregnancy. She did not want the baby; it was too much of a reminder that Frank was dead. She feared it would only make her even more unhappy. May tried to be understanding and encouraging:

Dear One. Don't be hard on yourself. You will need all the joy and comfort through your time of trial. When you see Charles's expression when he sees the new baby and M'amy's little motherly ways with it (I am sure she will be very motherly) there will be comfort as well as sorrow in Frank's legacy of love.

January had brought the terror of the first German Zeppelin attacks on England. Now it was February, which May always remembered as the black month of Amy's death. These seemed dark days of little hope. Almost every day May heard of the sons of friends who had been wounded or killed in battle. The Cecils' only son George, who had gone off to war with the British Expeditionary Forces in great excitement within days of the outbreak of war, aged only nineteen, had been killed in September 1914, a month before Frank. Violet Cecil's husband Edward was stationed in Egypt, and Violet turned to Alfred Milner for friendship and support even more than before. Although the early predictions that the war would end by Christmas had not been correct, May said that some people were now suggesting it might be over by June, because 'the Germans are in a bad way . . . starvation will do it, not fighting'. But May was apprehensive, and told Daphne: 'I cannot help feeling that a maddened animal is very dangerous.'

In March, the daffodils burst into bloom and May went down to Hardwick to spend a day with Daphne. Mother and daughter got on better than they had for a long time, and afterwards Daphne wrote to May appreciatively. May replied:

I too loved that sunny peaceful day, with the beings I love best in the world – you and your babes – Hardwick is too lovely – but alas, too sad for words. For I see Frank everywhere . . . Yes, dear one, it is work that saves us all, and yours is done nobly and well [Daphne continued to be busy with her refugee work] *– and you are a fine creature, and I am very proud of you. Very. That greedy library swallows me up day and night. Three gone away this week, and work pouring in, so I am very tired. Everyone is terribly strained these days with the bad fighting going on. Even my spirit for music has gone since the war. I think one's notions are so harshly battered that the softer ones have no part to play.*

Tenderly, her letter concluded:

As I came out of Surrey House at the close of a radiant day my thoughts as usual drifted to a lovely red brick house, with the sunlight making shadows in the evening, and two curly heads clamouring for 'Mummy this, Mummy that', and a small black figure going to rest when they are safely in bed. Is it rest? Perhaps merciful sleep as the shadows deepen on the old house. If love and thoughts could help you, mine would – but with grief one enters a Kingdom of loneliness.

During that spring of 1915, the second battle of Ypres started. It brought back, even more painfully, the memory of Frank's death. Now there was the added horror of the first use of poison gas by the Germans, and May began to feel passionately anti-war. With her feminist spirit rising, she wrote to Daphne:

Man and militarism, and ambitions, and pride and jealousy has spoilt it all, and turned the earth to a shambles, and the spring to weeping and tears.

Daphne's tears did not dry when her third baby was born in June. She felt no joy, and none of the comfort her mother had wished for her. Although she had not wanted the baby at all, she had come round to thinking she might be able to bear it if it were a boy, who might be like Frank. It was a girl. To please her mother, Daphne called the baby Briar, thus making her full name Briar Rose, as in the famous series of paintings by Burne-Jones. 'It's all right as long as she doesn't marry a Mr Pipe,' Daphne is reported to have remarked tersely. Nothing was ever to make Daphne really love poor Briar; it was as if her very existence represented the loss of Frank, and for that Briar could never be forgiven.

Daphne did not die until 1966, aged seventy-nine, but she rarely left Hardwick after Frank's death. The country was where she liked to be. Generally referred to as 'a character', she became obsessed in old age by filling in holes in the drive. It was agreed in the family that she was not only eccentric but also had, as she admitted herself in many of her letters, a difficult temperament. Her temper was quick, her manner brisk, and she talked in a clipped, shrill voice. My aunt Diana often used to visit her aunt Daphne at Hardwick after the First World War was over. She was not a 'cosy aunt', Diana told me, in contrast to her grandmother May, who was warm and welcoming and 'always concentrated intensely on whoever she was talking to'. At Hardwick, Diana remembers, 'you always had to toe the line with Daphne, and never be late for meals . . . I can still see her, legs spread, skirt hitched up, warming her behind at the fire for an exact half-hour after meals, as she said it was beneficial for her digestion.'

Daphne's daughter-in-law Phoebe, who was married to her son Charles, was over ninety when I talked to her; she too remembered Daphne as 'a very violent character, with extraordinary ideas'. Daphne's first grandchild Helen, on the other hand, who lived with her grandmother for part of her childhood, loved her without reservation. Daphne would often tell Helen how lucky she was to be pretty; even in old age Daphne still minded about the size of her nose, which despite her nightly prayers never grew any smaller. Daphne's odd ideas extended to her views on bringing up her children. She herself was physically very tough and extremely active; May always called her 'a little Spartan'. This was the way Daphne thought her children should be too, so she took away their shoes in April, whatever the weather, and they had to go barefoot until September.

Helen agrees that Daphne had peculiar ideas, was obsessively religious, and 'tight with money', the old Gaskell trait. Nevertheless she was 'an incredible person', who could be deeply loving to those few who were really close to her. But Daphne's childhood as the ugly little sister, and Frank's death, had left deep scars. In her old age she told another granddaughter that despite Amy's death so many years before, she had never ceased to feel that she lived in the shadow of her beautiful elder sister.

With such an eccentric father and brother, it was not surprising that Daphne was eccentric too. On the positive side, she was full of life and energy, 'an action woman', it was said, and she could be very amusing. She was mad keen on bicycling – her letters are full of it; she would think nothing of bicycling all the way to Kiddington for tea, always with her dog in a basket on the front. When she bicycled into Pangbourne from Hardwick to do her shopping, she would sometimes hook her umbrella to the back of a car and get pulled along. Like her brother Hal, she had odd views about the use of cars; in much the same way that Hal had told his chauffeur not to drive at more than twenty-five miles an hour so as not to wear out the car, Daphne told hers to put away the car if it was wet, to prevent it being spotted with rain. She would then use her bicycle instead.

*

At the beginning of 1917, an old friend of May's, Lady Maud Warrender, already on the committee of the War Library, joined the volunteers working there. She was a forceful individual whom May had known since the 1890s, when they used to meet at house parties on Lord Waterford's estate in Ireland. The supply of books being generated from the library's public appeals was dwindling, and Lady Maud elected to collect a group of friends once a week in order to tour London and the suburbs in a Red Cross ambulance, calling from house to house and asking for unwanted books. Lady Maud found people to be enormously responsive, and always filled the ambulance from floor to roof with books and magazines.

When I read her book, *My First Sixty Years*, Maud Warrender sounded to me like a character straight out of E. F. Benson, and I discovered that she was indeed a friend of his. A larger-than-life personality, Lady Maud was a socialite, whose countless illustrious friends included George V and Ellen Terry. She was also well known as a singer, and there is still today a coveted operatic prize in her name. An early advocate of herbal medicine, Maud Warrender was often consulted by ailing acquaintances on which remedies to take. She particularly recommended 'Count Matte's Electro-Homeopathic Globules', which sound as if they might have done more harm than good. On one occasion Lady Maud raised funds by putting on a concert at Surrey House; the largest reception room was packed with a well-heeled audience, and May had 'streamed the seats with leaflets' appealing for donations. May reported that: 'Maud's concert was a great success, and we made much money. She played everything, and filled the stage in more senses than one.'

One evening in May 1917, Maud Warrender dined with May at Lower Seymour Street. Dr Hagberg Wright was the only other guest. At that time, things were going very badly in France. Hagberg Wright said that he was anxious about the prevalent feeling among the people that the war could not be won with a Royal Family who all had German names. There were even rumours that the King was 'the hidden hand', meaning in cahoots with the enemy. Lady Maud, because of her friendship with the King, decided she must do something about this. She would go and confront His Majesty, she said. Hagberg Wright countered that he 'didn't think she would dare'.

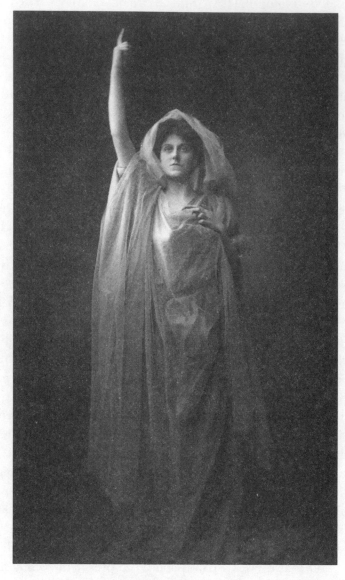

The histrionic Lady Maud Warrender, singer and socialite,
who helped May with the War Library.

Some time later, Maud Warrender sent May an extraordinary document which she had had typed out, though it was never published. She entitled it 'A Day in History'. It consisted of her conversation with George V, typed out like a play, the two characters being 'MW' and 'the King'. In it the King says that he is horrified at the idea that he could be thought of as pro-German. Lady Maud tells the King bluntly that there are too many German names in his family for people to be happy with, now that the country is at war with Germany: 'Three Tecks, six Battenbergs, five Schleswig Holsteins and four Gleichens'. From Maud Warrender's account, we are given to understand that it was ultimately because of her that three weeks later it was announced that King George had decided to give the Royal Family English names, he himself taking the name Windsor instead of Wettin.

May's friendship with Frances Horner also remained close. Over the last twenty-five years they had shared both love and loss together. The war had brought Frances constant anxiety. Her only son Edward, like thousands of young men, had eagerly gone off to fight at the beginning of the war, full of hope. He had been badly wounded three times, but each time had insisted on going back to the Front. Finally, at the end of November 1917, when great heaps of corpses were piling up on the Western Front, he too was killed. Edward Horner had been much loved for his 'sunny nature', and his death added devastatingly to the long list of losses the coterie of the Souls had borne during the war.

Over sixty now, Alfred Milner was still a bachelor, though his friendship with Violet Cecil was closer than ever. But throughout the four gruelling years of war, Alfred saw May regularly too. He would dine with her, often alone, at Lower Seymour Street, or they would meet at his house, 17 Great College Street. At first May would go there to oversee the ongoing decorations; in December 1914 they spent two whole days choosing carpets at Liberty's in Regent Street. In January 1916, May took Alfred to stay with Daphne at Hardwick. There were no other guests, and Alfred met Daphne's curly-headed children: Amy, with her intensely blue eyes, who was now three and a half; Charles, whom Daphne doted on, a year younger; and poor little baby Briar, who did not get much attention. 'Diner a trois and a little talk,' wrote Alfred in his diary. This pleasant interlude of deceptive peace by the quiet river was a distraction from thoughts of the latest Zeppelin raids on Paris, and a battle south of Arras 'in which the Germans seemed to have got the better of it'.

Even though Alfred's re-entry into public life, and his appointment to the War Cabinct when Lloyd George was elected prime minister in December 1916, meant that he was much more busy, he found time to drive down to Cranleigh with May in September 1917 to see Amy's memorial. This was something May had longed for him to do, as she felt he was one of the few people who had 'understood' her eldest daughter. It was a beautiful 'Indian summer' day, and after visiting the church, May and Alfred had tea at an inn near Dorking. They talked of old times, and of Amy, who, they agreed, had at least been spared this war and its miseries.

On 19 April 1918, Milner was appointed Minister of War and saw things through to their dramatic conclusion. On 9 November the Kaiser abdicated. The following day the German Republic was founded. May wrote to Alfred Milner that day, knowing that the following morning would be Armistice Day, and that the fighting was to cease at the eleventh hour of the eleventh day of the eleventh month.

> *My Friend. I must speak to you as the last act of this awful drama is beginning. The crash is stupendous, the death throes of this mighty nation so appalling that I can hardly bear it. They should be veiled in a black cloud of night like a volcanic eruption. This fall of Lucifer, though I have longed for it, prayed for it, is a great final tragedy. I could bear the tension no longer yesterday, and went alone to see that exquisite, passionate, barbaric Russian ballet 'Scheherazade' – brutal but wonderful. Then came a pause – I rose to go – slowly the curtain lifted and 'The Kaiser and King and Crown Prince have abdicated' was clear to read. Ah, but we shouted, and laughed, and clapped, and shouted again. I went straight out into the streets, which were seething with excited moving masses. They did not know, but the electric hearts of men had responded to some mystery in the air. It was wonderful – unforgettable – and you my friend have played a great part in this great end.*

CHAPTER TWELVE

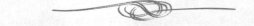

A DETERMINED SPIRIT

AFTER THE WAR, DAPHNE WAS STILL LEARNING HOW TO MANAGE A large house and a much bigger household. May was reassuring, and soon told her daughter that she ran Hardwick exactly as Frank would have wished. But Daphne still turned to her mother for experienced advice. May counselled the little Spartan daughter who was now Lady Rose, mistress of Hardwick:

> *Yes darling, wages are paid to servants when on holiday. Beer and washing are given with board wages. I pay mine for a month before leaving, and when that is over a cheque for the next, and so on. Board wages are not paid when they are on holiday. I should give ten shillings and sixpence to the women, twelve shillings and sixpence for the men, although many pay a little less. At Kiddington they all had milk and vegetables free.*

Daphne's days were busy, and she was distracted by the various demands of the estate, her children, the stud farm, hunting, and local social life. She also continued with the refugee work she had done during the war. It was at night that she still longed for Frank, and wrote her diary as a letter to him, so that she could almost feel he was still alive. On 1 July 1919, she found some keys that fitted two locked

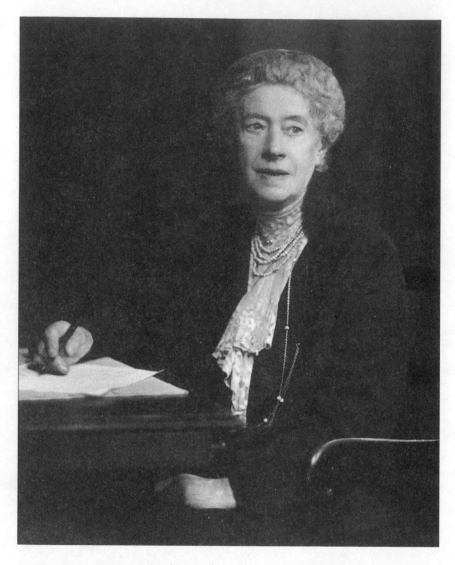

1935; May, quite formidable at eighty-two years old, with,
charasterically, pen and paper. She still looks elegant, with some
of her Irish mother's Waterford lace round her neck.

books that she had noticed in the library soon after her marriage. She had always wondered what they were. As soon as she opened the books she saw that they were diaries, written by Frank in 1906 and 1907, when he was with his regiment in India, and covering the time that Amy was in Ceylon. As always when Daphne wanted to be alone, she went straight up to the woods, taking the diaries with her.

That night she wrote more passionately than ever in her diary:

Beloved, what can I say? That you loved Amy I knew, that you suffered I had guessed, but that your life had been so unutterably lonely and unhappy I had not realised. These gathered thoughts of yours show you to have been just the fine and glorious man I knew you to have been ... But oh Frankie, Frankie, as I read them up in the wood, my heart cried out with pain and love for you – and I asked myself. Did I make up for you in any way, for all the years? Did I satisfy you to the utmost? Did I in some small measure fill the place that Amy held for so long?

Do you remember the day I asked if I should free you? Break off our engagement because Amy was free and on her way home? How you must have longed to then, to have been able to go to her when she came back, with your great love. But you would not hurt me – and she died two days after reaching England. And then we heard of her death at Kineton, I told you when you came in from hunting. We motored straight to Holdhurst. I asked if you would like to see her alone, or should I come up with you – and you said alone. Ah my Beloved how you must have suffered – I never quite realised. Perhaps I was too young. Forgive me, my own, for any pain I gave you.

And now? Is your spirit satisfied? Have you found Amy? Are you two together in perfect happiness? Not the life of this world happiness, but spiritual happiness, above and beyond all this. I wonder? If you are happy with her, then I rejoice my Beloved. She was wonderful – far more wonderful than I could ever be – beautiful – far more beautiful than I could dream of. Perhaps Death was made sweet to you by her presence.

And yet I know you loved me too – gloriously we loved each other – that I know. You made me the happiest woman on earth – I know I too made you content. But my Frank, I want you to know I am not jealous. If Amy can help you now, I want her to. If she can in some way make up for the sorrow she caused you in this life – oh let her. Tell her I forgive her –

if she will do all she may towards your happiness now. When I come,
when the babes come, perhaps we shall all understand. Good night, love of
my life – perhaps you were glad to lay down and sleep.

So, nine years after Amy's death, her strange appeal continued to have its mysterious effect. But even if Daphne was resigned to Amy and Frank joining together 'in perfect happiness' in heaven, what of poor Lionel, by whom May had hoped 'all would be understood' when Amy was reunited with him in death? Was Amy playing the same games with men in the Afterlife as it seemed she had done here on earth?

May's work for the War Library earned her a CBE in the first New Year's honours list after the war. The Red Cross spoke gratefully of Mrs Gaskell's 'untiring labours', and her co-worker Dr Hagberg Wright told her that:

Everyone, and I most of all, knows the great work you did for the world in
the last years; you bore a great burden and have won the love and
affection of many to whom your name will remain a household word.

Although the war was over, May did not stop, or begin to slow down. On 11 November 1918 she had been in Surrey House all day when the telephone call came through to confirm that the Armistice had been signed. May's fellow workers rushed out into the thronged streets to celebrate. May stayed behind in the enormous building. That moment remained vivid to her for the rest of her life:

Outside the crowds shouted and rejoiced. I remember sitting alone that
night amongst the thousands of books and thinking 'Is this all over? Will
the work die? Must the sick lie unemployed and restless?'

Even at that euphoric moment, she realized that books would be just as important to the sick during peacetime.

At the beginning of 1919, the hospitals were full of sick and wounded soldiers, as well as civilians who had been injured in the bombing raids. The lack of stimulus, hospital staff told May, was affecting their patients badly. They sent telegrams and letters to the War Library, begging for 'more supplies than ever'. 'I think it was then that I realised to the full,' wrote May, 'that it wasn't war that made the need for libraries in hospitals, it was suffering.'

So May's campaign began all over again. Once more she placed appeals in the newspapers, to tell people that their generosity was still necessary:

> Literature in hospitals is always needed in war and peace . . . in sending you our grateful thanks for gifts of the past, we ask you to continue to send us your spare books, magazines and illustrated papers.

New premises were found in a smaller house in Lancaster Gate, and the War Library became the Red Cross Hospital Library. May and Hagberg Wright remained as joint honorary secretaries. May found it difficult to persuade the matrons of some civilian hospitals that their patients would benefit from books: 'I remember one visit to a highly praised hospital on the South Coast . . . a starched matron took me through ward after ward of spotless cleanliness and idleness. A few women were knitting – not a magazine, not a book.' May asked the matron why this was so. Her unashamed answer was that she did not allow books in the hospital, as 'they clutter it up so'. May said that surely the patients' friends brought them things to read. The matron replied sharply: 'I take them away at the door.'

May persevered despite much similar resistance. One hospital chaplain accepted supplies of books gratefully, but when May visited his hospital she found five hundred books, still packed up, under his bed. At another hospital, in Aldershot, they assured May that they were already supplied with books, brought by a lady to their patients twice a week. May wondered who this could be, and made a surprise visit to the hospital. There she found 'a dear little lady with apples in the bottom of her basket and religious tracts on top'.

Gradually, however, 'the new idea was in the air', and hospitals began to realize that the books improved patients' spirits, which subsequently made them get better more quickly. Though May returned to a full social life after the war, and was increasingly involved with her grandchildren as they grew older, she remained busy with her library work for the rest of her life.

In 1923, May left the grand elegance of Lower Seymour Street, and moved with Mrs Iles and her most devoted staff to a smaller terraced house in Albion Street, off the Bayswater Road. Her granddaughter Diana, then fourteen, remembers this house well from her visits to May, first when she used to come up to London from Kiddington, and later when she was studying at the Royal College of Music. During the years that May had lived at Kiddington she had given piano and violin lessons to the head gardener's family and other locals in a wooden hut next to the village school, and she was delighted that her first grand-daughter, Diana, seemed to have inherited her musical genes. She took her to concerts whenever she could, and came to hear Diana play the piano and sing in college performances.

'I used to go with Mrs Iles to be received by Granny, sitting up in bed eating her breakfast – quite impressive with a beautiful lace cap on her head,' says Diana today. 'Granny was wonderful to me – I heard Paderewski and Pachmann play, and I saw Karsavina dance, because of Granny. Everyone worshipped Paderewski.' May herself also greatly admired the famous pianist Ignace Paderewski, who had returned to his musical career after being Prime Minister of Poland.* Everyone had wanted to see Tamara Karsavina; she was Diaghilev's greatest ballerina, Diana told me, and 'was on a par with Pavlova, and very intelligent'. But it is the memory of Vladimir de Pachmann, the Ukrainian pianist, that still today makes Diana shriek with laughter like a young girl: 'People used to flock to his concerts because he was so extraordinary. He had this habit of talking to the audience while he played. He was very old when I heard him, and he would suddenly stop in the middle and say things like, "Now just listen to that bit again." Sitting next to Granny, I had to control my giggles.'

* Over thirty years before, Burne-Jones had done a remarkable portrait drawing of Paderewski; he had been walking down a street one day when he noticed a young man in a hansom cab whose wild hair and looks so struck him that he ran after him and asked if he could draw him. The young man was Paderewski, who remarked later that he had felt the painter himself had 'the expression of an apostle'.

May's house in Albion Street was beautifully furnished and decorated. Diana remembers her grandmother as very elegant, and says that her flowing clothes were made of the most luxurious materials. Diana, then an unsophisticated country girl, could not keep her eyes off 'the most beautiful, large diamond-shaped fire opal you ever saw', which May always wore as a ring on her wedding finger. It could be that this was the 'fiery opal' that she had intended for the cherub's curls on Amy's memorial, but then changed her mind. Unfailingly, May would greet her granddaughter warmly, and even though Diana was young, 'and without much conversation', May always made her feel she was interested in everything she said. Diana still remembers vividly the pleasure she felt when she visited her grandmother, and can picture the comfortable drawing room at Albion Street, where she was always given a delicious tea. The walls, as at Kiddington, were covered with William Morris wallpaper, and just above where they sat for tea hung Burne-Jones's dark portrait of Amy, which had moved with May wherever she lived.

'I used to gaze at that painting,' says Diana, 'and wonder about Amy. I've never seen the picture since then, but it is imprinted on my memory.'

Violet Cecil's husband Edward had died of tuberculosis in December 1918, soon after the war had ended, aged fifty-one. At the beginning of March 1921, with the knowledge of only family and close friends, Violet quietly married her friend of three decades, Lord Milner. Still thought of as an eligible bachelor, Alfred Milner was nearly sixty-seven, and Violet was forty-nine. May was one of the few women friends Lord Milner remained close to after his marriage. Shortly before Alfred and Violet formalized their long friendship, May told Alfred once more how much his friendship had meant to her over the years:

There is no one to whom I can talk with such complete freedom, with such certainty of sympathy and patience, and yet no weakness – surely that is real friendship? The essence of friendship is that it carries no strain, like great love, and yet is ready calmly to bear the burdens of love . . . I think, humanly, you have helped me more than anyone or anything through the tragic waters of the past.

But in 1925, Alfred Milner fell ill, after his return from a happy journey back to South Africa with his new wife, Violet. His illness, only diagnosed when he had become partially paralysed, was 'sleeping sickness', the result of a tsetse-fly bite in Africa. He died suddenly at the beginning of May. And May Gaskell lost another valuable friend.

Milner's death created a big gap in May's life, but it is clear from her correspondence that she would always find men to confide in, even if she could not open her heart to them in the same way she had been able to with Alfred. As Diana told me, 'Granny was one of those women who really do prefer men's company.' And the men of her acquaintance, who as May grew older were often much younger than she was, obviously enjoyed hers. In the summer of 1927, when Diana was eighteen and her brother Tom was twenty-one, May took them both on holiday to Switzerland. May was seventy-three, but accompanying her was an attractive, middle-aged man called Sir Guy Marshall. Diana noticed how attentive he was to May. Diana told me with a smile that while she and Tom went up funiculars and on long Alpine walks, 'Granny and Sir Guy had a peaceful time together at a lovely spot on Lake Thun. There's no doubt, even then, Granny had great charisma.'

May believed she could no longer travel as far as the Argentine, and her older brother Willie feared that he would never again see the England to which he still felt he belonged. It saddened him greatly: although he had left it so long ago, Worcestershire remained the place he loved best in the world, and May, the sister he had grown up with there, was still to him the most precious member of his family. Perhaps it was living on the other side of the world that made him feel so strongly. Answering a letter from May in January 1925, Willie, his tall, lean figure slightly bent now, wrote from the veranda of El Clarin, the house he had built on retirement:

> *A charming letter written as of yore in all your inimitable style – Ah darling, say what you like, yours are the letters of the family, for they contain the wisdom of our father, and the charm of our darling little mother. I kissed her this morning, bless her, she looked so smart in a voluminous dress that spread out around her. She sits on a shelf on my dressing table, under the shade of a canopy of fresh flowers that Celestina*

provides for her summer and winter – she knows that her memory is very
precious to me. Goodness only knows how I love my own – my kith and
kin. I love to hear the sound of their voices, and watch their little family
traits handed down from long lost generations – how I love you all,
beloved relations, and how different you are to other beings I ever met.

It was another very sad day for May when, two years later, she
heard that her beloved brother Willie had died of a heart attack. He
was seventy-six years old.

May's own health was erratic, but she worked on for the library
throughout the 1920s, and well into the 1930s. She gave talks, wrote
letters, and made speeches to raise funds. She even pursued Queen
Mary, urging her to donate books on a regular basis. Unfortunately,
although May had encouraged variety, the books sent from
Buckingham Palace were such an eclectic assortment that they were
not always what May considered 'suitable'. Queen Mary was thought
of as imperious, as she appeared stiff and unsmiling in public, but May
believed this was shyness. In 1930, May braved royal displeasure by
writing once more to the Queen, via Lady Cynthia Colville, a lady-in-
waiting who was a friend. Starting with profuse thanks for the
Queen's latest donations, May risked offence by pointing out the
problem concerning the books they received from the palace:

> *The patients in the hospitals are especially interested when they see written*
> *inside 'This is a gift from Her Majesty the Queen', but out of fifty or sixty*
> *books, perhaps twenty or twenty-five are suitable. Reports of society*
> *meetings, catalogues of bulbs, and treatises on manure etc make up the*
> *bulk of what we get from the palace.*

Queen Mary took May's criticism well, and throughout the 1930s
she continued to support the Red Cross Hospital Library with
donations of books, which henceforth she allowed delegates from
the library to hand-pick at the palace. In 1934, when May tackled the
difficult problem of persuading the staff of mental hospitals that their
patients would also benefit from the distraction of books, she
managed to get the Queen, who was 'so glad you are now taking up

that subject', on her side. As May pointed out to the editor of the *Spectator* magazine, the biggest problem in mental hospitals was:

> . . . *the idleness to which patients are condemned. Blank days and nights with nothing to look forward to would cause a sane person to go mad. There is nothing so fatal as condemning an overactive brain to feed on itself or melancholia. Patients deteriorate from the sheer misery of having nothing to do.*

As a result of May's persistence, the British Red Cross and Order of St John Hospital Library, to call it by its full name, now began distributing books to mental hospitals. But May's correspondence with the Queen seems to have had its lighter side too. In one reply to a letter from May, the lady-in-waiting commented:

> *Her Majesty is also much interested to hear further news of the window cleaner! His is indeed a romantic and pleasant story!*

Presumably the window cleaner at the library's offices had taken May into his confidence, not knowing that his private story would be related to the Queen of England. In 1937, Queen Mary finally agreed to become the library's patron.

May, becoming increasingly less mobile, and considering herself 'a useless old crock now as far as activity is concerned', did not stop writing letters, articles and pamphlets. She wrote to anyone she could think of who might be able to give any help, from funding to supplying books to finding premises for new libraries. She appealed to all ages and types. To the Girl Guides she pleaded:

> *Dear Girl Guides, if you have ever been ill you must remember what a comfort a nice magazine or book or picture book was. We want you to help us; the penny novelette you are reading is just what the girl in hospital wants to read and hasn't got; send it to us and she will get it. The storybook you finished on the bus going home from work is just the thing for the girl in the sanatorium.*

*

In 1932, when May was nearly eighty and at home in Albion Street for much of the time, she began re-reading her hundreds of letters from Burne-Jones. It is said that memories of the distant past become sharper with old age, and May needed the past again now. Perhaps too, without Alfred Milner to talk to, she turned back to Burne-Jones's written words because they had comforted, amused and flattered her so many years before. Frail now, her curly hair quite white and her hearing bad, May needed to remind herself of his love, and wanted to laugh again, as he had always made her do.

There had been a night when Burne-Jones had accompanied May to the opera. She had found herself next to an extremely large woman, and Burne-Jones, always hard on obesity in women, had looked downwards and quietly compared the size of May's ankles to those of her neighbour. The next day he sent her the first of many little humorous sketches of the 'fat lady' who had sat next to May at the opera. Burne-Jones often referred admiringly to Samuel Pepys, perhaps feeling a bond with another incurable lover of women. May remembered when she and Burne-Jones had read Pepys's diary together, and the long letter he had written her afterwards in the style of Pepys, telling her, among other things, that he had bought a fine edition of Keats's poems for her:

> . . . that I shall take tomorrow to my Lady in token of my content at her cure for a sore heart I have had for a long time and now, methinks, I can breathe lightly again – so tomorrow betimes I will take coach and to her – for all the ladies that I do know she is the one that hath more grace and sweetness.

It made May think of her old friend Frances Horner, whom Burne-Jones had also loved, and she wrote to her:

> . . . I wonder if you are, as I am, glad that the time left to be sad or glad cannot be long, I am very tired and we have both gelebt and geliebet. Loving May.

Certainly these two women had both lived and loved, but for May, even in old age, life and love had not quite ended yet.

In the mid-1930s, May was shown a beautiful book, *Eros and Psyche*, which contained a long poem by Robert Bridges, with woodcut illustrations after drawings Burne-Jones had made as a young man for his series of Cupid and Psyche. The book had been published by the Gregynog Press, one of the foremost private presses between the wars, which is still in existence today. The director of the Gregynog Press, Loyd Haberly, had taken the Burne-Jones drawings, which were on tracing paper and were so faded and discoloured that direct reproduction would have been impossible, and had made woodblocks from them. Told that Mr Haberly was now a bookbinder, May decided to approach him, to see if he would preserve some of the most precious of her letters from Burne-Jones in bound books. Already, at the request of his trustees, she had promised to leave many others to the British Museum.

Loyd Haberly was an American, from Oregon, who had arrived in England as a young man in the early 1920s on a Rhodes scholarship to Oxford. He became involved with the Arts and Crafts movement first inspired by William Morris. His directorship of the Gregynog Press did not last very long, as his approach was considered 'too pragmatic'. However, with a 'determination to do his own thing', he began a life of printing, bookbinding and tile-making, and wrote a prolific amount of poetry. Haberly built his own kilns and the tiles he designed were medieval in style. Together with Morris, Burne-Jones had long been a hero to him, and remained so even though the popularity of Pre-Raphaelite art had declined dramatically after the turn of the century.

In order to try and find out more, I visited the Victoria and Albert Museum's atmospheric National Art Library, and found one slim volume by Loyd Haberly; a memoir of his printing, tile-making and 'book building' life. I read through it diligently, as it had no index. Then suddenly there was the familiar name: Mrs Gaskell. Over the next four pages I was given a clear image of May in old age, and I learned an extraordinary story. Yet again I had to curb my inclination to noisy excitement in the quiet of a library.

Loyd Haberly first came to see May at 28 Albion Street in mid 1935, when she was eighty-two. A bent old butler opened the door, and showed Loyd into the drawing room where May sat, 'whitened by great age and personal tragedies, but still winterly beautiful and graciously Edwardian in all the best ways'. The house, he found, was

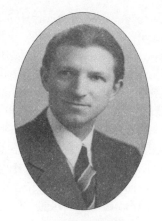

Loyd Haberly, the young American involved in the Arts and Crafts movement and intrigued by the Pre-Raphaelites, who befriended May in her old age.

'a Pre Raphaelitish haven hung with Morris chintzes and Burne-Jones portraits of herself and a beautiful daughter who had died young'.

This first meeting precipitated a close friendship, despite an age gap of over forty years. It lasted for three years, until Haberly finally returned to America. Through May, Loyd felt he was able to enter an era in which he wished he had himself lived; in May's Pre-Raphaelite haven he could see and handle Burne-Jones's writing, and hear about William Morris at first hand. He told May: 'You only, of all my friends

Out of the dark
at birth we bring
a tiny spark
From it may spring
The flame of fame
Or it may glow
awhile & go
back whence it came.

a gloomy thought, which the bright torch of you dispels.
With much love, ME

One of Loyd Haberly's many poems which he included in letters to May

who knew Morris, have given me the true clue through the shadowy mazes of his thousands of printed pages.'

May had an exceptional capacity for friendship, which continued into old age. Within a short time she and Loyd were exchanging frequent affectionate letters, and he was composing countless little poems especially for May, carefully written out in his large, round and rather childish handwriting. I found a fat collection of his letters and poems, carefully labelled by May, in one of the black tin trunks containing her papers. One of the poems she particularly liked was at the end of a letter in which Loyd described a dream he had had. The dream was set 'at the court of Medici and Botticelli', where May sat on a throne. There was much dancing to 'fairylike lute music', but then 'the silence and sadness of autumn evening' fell and May asked Loyd, who was one of the young dancers, to compose a poem to 'match that shadowed mood':

> *The joys we do not taste, the years*
> *Will waste, and neither tears nor prayers*
> *Recall:*
> *Dear we must pay, nor can delay*
> *What Earth demands by night and day*
> *Of all:*
> *So let us now, in Time's despite,*
> *Spend well and wisely on delight.*
> *For soon the night will fall.*

Sometimes Loyd would end his letters 'Affectionately, hopefully, me.' He told May that he had lived for many years in 'poverty, chastity and disobedience'. He had moved between Oxford, Dorset and Wales, and between different groups of people, always busy writing books and poems, printing, binding, tile-making, and animal-keeping. He sent May everything from diagrams of kilns he was constructing for firing his tiles, to almost daily poems. He read hungrily, and discussed the books he read with May. He would make grand statements on literature. 'Nobody but Homer or Chaucer has any business to write long poems,' he once pronounced firmly, even though some of his own were not much shorter.

On his visits to London, Loyd would often stay in May's house for a day or two, but it was not until October 1937 that he came to stay for two weeks to bind May's selection of letters from Burne-Jones. The most private ones, which May was finally to leave to Daphne, she kept aside, slipped into paper folders. Loyd liked May to be there while he worked at the books. Sometimes, when she was out, he would leave a note for her return:

Today was empty without you, I filled it with labour and worked on the books all day. When I can have a whole day with you again I want to tool nice appropriate verses round the back covers to match their fronts.

This was when he skilfully tooled, in gold lettering on the orange-brown morocco leather, 'TIME WILL HASTE AND WASTE, THESE WILL LAST' on one of the volumes, and on another: 'WISE, BEAUTIFUL AND PLAYFUL BITS FROM LETTERS OF SIR EDWARD BURNE-JONES TO HIS FRIEND MAY GASKELL'.

It was from Loyd's memoir that I learnt that in May's youth the Prince of Wales, who had heard May play the piano at a house party, had 'almost persuaded her to give professional concerts so the world could share both her music and her personal beauty of face, form and bearing'.

Music remained one of the most important things in May's life until, according to Loyd, 'her music came to an appalling end'. A few years before, May told Loyd, she had been sound asleep one night when she was woken by loud music. In the darkness she recognized a Brahms symphony that she had heard played in Vienna years before. It sounded as if musicians were playing in her bedroom. When she lit a lamp there was nothing there, nor out in the corridor, yet the symphony played on until its final movement. Then, without a pause, other musicians began playing an overture she remembered hearing at the Berlin Opera. All through 'that terrible night' the music never ceased, and all were individual pieces May had heard in distinct places. She lay on her bed in the lamplight 'in sleepless dread that some strange insanity had taken hold of her mind'.

May went straight to her doctor's consulting rooms in Harley Street the next morning, with music still playing so loudly in her head that she could hardly hear the doctor shouting questions at her. When he had examined her she could see a look of alarm on his face, and he seemed to have no doubt about his prognosis: she was suffering from an illness that usually afflicted only musicians, and she was in mortal danger. The condition, the doctor explained, was 'a strange, inexplicable unblocking of the recording cells of the brain', which unleashed 'from the dark discs of memory' all the music the patient had ever heard, repeating itself over and over again. Unless May underwent 'a difficult and dangerous aural nerve operation', she would be subjected to 'dementing sleepless torments ending in madness and death'.

May was, of course, horrified, but the doctor told her that 'by a fortunate chance' a famous surgeon from Budapest happened to be in London at that moment, who had long experience of treating Hungarian musicians for exactly what May was suffering from. The surgeon had come to London to lecture to a musical society, but was persuaded to operate on May the next day. The operation, Loyd wrote, 'saved her life and reason, but left her almost completely deaf'.

After reading this bizarre story, I immediately consulted a distinguished ear, nose and throat specialist, but all he could tell me was that the music May heard in her head could only have been a hallucination, and she should never have been operated on. The surgeon had probably damaged her hearing, he said. However, he told me that when very musical people feared they were losing their hearing, and were in a high state of anxiety, they sometimes imagined real sounds in their head. There is one other possibility. I knew that in her younger days May took chloral to help her sleep. In the past it had given her extraordinary dreams, and Burne-Jones, some of whose Pre-Raphaelite circle had used drugs with disastrous results, had begged her not to continue taking it. Chloral is now known to be addictive, and the long-term use of it can sometimes cause visual and aural hallucinations. So could this explain the symphonies that May heard so clearly and incessantly that night?

Whatever May's condition, after this operation in 1932 she spent a long period in a nursing home in Broadstairs, Kent, and subsequently began to use a long ear trumpet. Loyd Haberly described how he was able to learn so much from a woman who was 'both an exemplar and encyclopaedia of the late Victorian and the Edwardian', despite her deafness. They would sit on opposite sides of May's drawing-room table, under the painting of Amy. On the table was an ormolu clock. First Loyd would speak slowly and distinctly into the horn of May's ear trumpet for exactly three minutes. Then May would put her ear trumpet down and talk to Loyd, 'in carefully modulated monotone – leading me back and back through manor-garden gates and servant-held doors, opened upon the gilt and gaiety of the British Empire's last throes of vastness and greatness'.

Loyd was apologetic for the amount he charged May for binding the letters – two shillings and sixpence an hour: 'It seems an enormous sum and I am ashamed to take anything and will try to repay you in poems, one for each two shillings and sixpence you pay.'

On some evenings they would read Burne-Jones's letters together. He asked May if she could get him a Hollyer reproduction of Burne-Jones's last lovely drawing of herself, which hung on her stairs at Albion Street: 'You are not only a dear friend but a friend of many years, for I have known you long in BJ's pictures, where this is you and that is you over and over again, perhaps even when he did not know it.'

He also asked May if he could have a photograph of her: 'Can you be photographed in that trailing velvet that you wore last night to delight your Maker and me?' When May had been a troubled wife aged forty, it must have been incredibly flattering to receive Burne-Jones's overwhelming admiration; now that she was in her eighties, to receive similar adulation from this strange young American who lived in the past was a rare bonus to old age.

May still went to Kiddington to open the flower show every summer, an event she always enjoyed. For years, Hal had only visited his mother in London once every six months, combining it with a visit to his dentist, and sometimes the cricket at Lord's. Hal was also very deaf now, and he too had an ear trumpet, a beautiful tortoiseshell one, inlaid with birds and flowers in gold, which he said had belonged to Joshua Reynolds. The complications of two ear trumpets in one conversation must only have increased the lack of communication between mother and son. Although May was upset by Hal's neglect, her daughter-in-law Dolly was more thoughtful, and became much more attentive to May in old age, often coming up to stay with her.

Hal, in his turn, seemed hurt by his mother. His sister Diana told me that one Christmas in the late 1930s Hal received from May a tiny glass birdcage, which he hung on a candlestick on the mantelpiece. Some time later, Dolly asked him if he had thanked his mother for her present. Hal replied gruffly that he had not.

'Oh Hal, you must,' said Dolly. 'It's rude not to.'

Hal turned to her with unusual vehemence: 'It's very rude of her to give it to me.'

Perhaps he knew by now that May had decided to leave all her Burne-Jones paintings, drawings and the most private letters to Daphne. Hal had been very fond of Burne-Jones, and vice versa. He felt, as an artist, that he had learnt much from the great painter; the idea that he would not inherit anything from the large volume of work his mother had been given must have been wounding.

Dolly's frequent visits to London were, particularly during the winter, a way of escaping from the austerity of a crumbling Kiddington and a silent, inattentive husband. Although neighbouring houses now had electric lighting, telephones in several rooms, and some even had oil-fired central-heating, Hal would have none of it. When the roof let in the rain, he would just put a bucket underneath the leak. Over the years the attic rooms became full of them. The kitchen was infested with black beetles, and beetle traps were set at night. There was never any redecoration, except when Tom painted the one bathroom, with its black copper bath, because he could not bear the stained brown walls any longer. Hal would spend nothing on the house and kept Dolly, who never complained, short of money too.

Each day, Hal spent much of the time painting in his room, but was as reluctant as ever to show his work to anyone. His waste-bin was often full of torn-up paintings, and sometimes Dolly would secretly take them away, and if they were only torn in two pieces stick them together, and keep them hidden for the future. On a wall in my house, one of these torn paintings, a charming picture of a woman hanging out washing on a windy day outside her ancient cottage, still gives me great pleasure today.

When Hal was not painting he was out on the estate, walking his dog, or with his beloved flock of rare sheep, with which he seemed better able to communicate than with human beings.

When a neighbour died – the man who had shot Hal in the eye by mistake, and whom Hal considered his worst enemy – Dolly found her husband dressed to go out, and about to set off for the funeral. As Hal rarely left the estate, Dolly was astonished.

'But why are you going? You hated him,' she said.

'Oh,' replied Hal, 'he won't be there.'

Hal saw the occasion as a party, and he could sometimes come to life at parties away from his family. His eccentricity is shown in the story of how one day he appeared in a pair of women's glasses, brightly coloured, Dame Edna style, with flicked-up ends. When Dolly asked him why he was wearing them, he said that he had found them in the drive, and thought they suited him.

But Hal could be cruel. During the 1920s, when Dolly went to London and took the big decision to have her long brown hair cut short in a newly fashionable bob, Hal appeared not to notice any change on her return. But at breakfast next morning, buried in his newspaper, he remarked, without looking up: 'There's a story in the paper of a man who divorced his wife because she had her hair cut in a bob.'

Hal also failed Diana time and again as a father. Her most painful memory is of her wedding day at Kiddington in 1933. Everything had been beautifully organized by Dolly, and the little church was packed with family, relations and many friends, who were waiting for the bride to be brought in by her father. Villagers were lining the path outside. In the house, Diana went downstairs in her wedding dress; she is still elegant now, with miraculously unlined skin, and she must have looked lovely then, with her tall slender figure, dark wavy hair and sparkling eyes. Hal hurried into the hall, but made no comment when he saw her. He picked up his top hat and, with a muttered 'Come on,' marched brusquely ahead of his daughter and round the long terrace towards the church.

Diana hurried after her father, carrying the train of her dress over her arm. As she reached the churchyard, still several steps behind Hal, she saw all the familiar local faces outside the church, and her six little bridesmaids waiting. Since leaving the house, Hal had not looked at or spoken to his daughter, and marched into the church without waiting for her to take his arm. Upset and humiliated, Diana pulled her veil over her face. By the time she had walked up the aisle and reached Gavin, her husband-to-be, she could not hold back the tears. Diana is able to laugh now at the awful memory of the way her father behaved, but at the time she was mortified. The congregation, however, were perhaps so used to Hal's eccentricities that they did not seem surprised when instead of joining May and Dolly in their pew, he spent the service sitting in the pulpit.

When the Tate Gallery was organizing a large Burne-Jones centenary exhibition in 1933, they wanted to borrow the portrait of Amy and other drawings from May. One of the Tate's trustees, Lord Balneil, approached May. They got on immediately, and he remained a friend until her death seven years later. When May met him, Balneil was a striking-looking thirty-three-year-old, happily married with two young sons. He was a busy man, a Member of Parliament, and much involved in all things relating to the arts. But May, through her never-fading charm, very soon managed to persuade him, despite his many commitments, to join her library committee. She could see at once that he would be an asset.

Over the next few years, when he was at his London residence, very near to May in Bryanston Place, David Balneil would often visit her for tea, sometimes accompanied by his wife, Mary. May appreciated these visits, and his friendship. They would talk often about Burne-Jones, and she showed him many of her letters from him, explaining that she had felt she must keep them despite Burne-Jones's view that private letters should be burnt after reading. Balneil commented: 'One day, in the remote future, someone will I suppose find them and give the lie to what Burne-Jones says about old letters by showing that he is among the great letter writers of the world.'

At Christmas 1936, May sent Balneil some of the best of Burne-Jones's illustrated letters, painted in colour, which she had had beautifully bound in vellum in 1905. It was a generous present, but she told him she felt he was someone who would love and care for them.

At the beginning of 1938, May was worrying about political events abroad. She was afraid of another war, and, although old and increasingly frail, she felt that she must put any energy she had left into making renewed appeals for the Red Cross Hospital Library. She thought a letter in *The Times*, directed at young people who had not known war, would be appropriate. In March, she wrote to David

Balneil for his advice. He discouraged her immediate impulse, which he felt would only be right at the imminent outbreak of war:

> *Now I do not believe that these are today's conditions. Europe is, in all conscience, in a terrified and dangerous condition, but I think that the clouds are much lighter than they were ten days ago . . . I feel emphatically that any immediate danger is far less now.*

He thought that the kind of appeal she suggested might be 'over emphatic and alarmist' at that moment. But he reassured May that if, God forbid, war did come, then as a result of the respected organization she had built up, 'volunteers and books would flow in'. He ended his letter by telling May to 'be more happy about the world', and that 'nothing wrong can happen so long as William Morris continues to burst his waistcoat buttons on my mantelpiece', referring to a drawing of Morris by Burne-Jones which May had given him.

But May did not feel happier about the world, and the world did not become more peaceful. At the beginning of summer 1938, May sent an appeal for young library helpers to the editor of *The Times*, Geoffrey Dawson, an acquaintance who was an ardent supporter of Chamberlain's policy of appeasing Germany. She enclosed a heartfelt private note with her appeal:

> *Is it possible dear Mr Geoffrey Dawson, that you can find space for the enclosed in your Times? The thought of those boys – they are such boys, lying in the small outpost air hospitals with nothing to distract and keep fear out of their hearts haunts me. In these bewildering days I feel as if some great irresistible force is driving us whither we would not, and our efforts to stem it are so important. I am very old and very deaf but my mind and feelings keen. Often I wish the strain was over.*

Dawson, who had been a great friend of Lord Milner, was clearly touched by the strength of May's feelings, and agreed to publish her appeal. She addressed it to 'the debutante girls and boys and those young creatures who are waiting on the brink of a gay and happy summer together', and warned them: 'If this horror of war comes it will be sudden. It will be very terrible. The hospitals will overflow.'

*

The uncertainty continued, and it was not until the end of the next summer that England finally declared war on Germany, on 3 September 1939. Even as late as mid-August, Dr Hagberg Wright wrote reassuringly to May, who was having a rest at a seaside hotel:

I am not at all nervous, I don't think we shall have war. Everyone seems more peaceably inclined and there is less talk of trouble . . . My love to you, and I hope you have rest and quiet, blue skies and blue seas.

The card May sent to all her friends at New Year read:

To Hope – Till Hope itself creates the thing it hoped for.

During the preceding year, May, who had been less optimistic than many of her friends, made sure that her Burne-Jones pictures and drawings would be safe in the event of war, lending a large collection of the drawings to the Ashmolean Museum, and depositing the bulk of the letters in the British Museum. She sent Amy's portrait and other pictures to Daphne in the country, but she kept her most private letters from Burne-Jones always by her side.

May herself stayed in London, still with the faithful Mrs Iles for loving care and company. Three weeks after the declaration of war, David Balneil wrote to May on 21 September, two days after the first British casualty list had been published. He was at his country estate, Haigh Hall, near Wigan:

One feels lonely and out of things up here, no news except the wireless (hateful instrument; hateful, breathless gentility of those synthetic announcers) and the papers. One knows nothing unless one is in London but at moments one prefers not to know, and not to think . . . I have the Burne-Jones drawings and letters with me here; it is possible to laugh sometimes, and with Burne-Jones it is easy to laugh and forget everything.

Hal's son Tom, whose passion for fireworks had prompted him to join the Auxiliary Fire Service, visited May in Albion Street and reported to Dolly that he had had 'a sumptuous luncheon at Granny's and found her in very good form, and longing for a crack at the enemy – every conceivable kind of precaution against air raids at No. 28 – gas proofed room – a huge bin of sand, wire netting across windows etc etc.'

Tom's younger brother Robin, who was already married with a child, could not visit May; he was stationed with the Border Regiment at Kendal, near Levens. Soon he was sent out to Dunkirk. On one of his first days, his commanding officer left him on sentry duty up the coast towards Caen, saying he would be back before long to give him further orders. The officer did not return and Robin, after a night spent 'in a wet field of beet', was distracted by an interesting birdcall which he thought came from a hedge on the other side of the field. He walked openly across the field, thinking, in true Gaskell style, only of the bird, and was looking down into the hedge to try and find what the bird was when he saw some grey flannel. The flannel covered the legs of a German soldier, who promptly captured Robin.

Robin spent his entire war as a prisoner at Camp Oflag 7B at Eichstatt, north of Munich, where he was able to get hold of some artists' materials, and passed the time contentedly painting. He drew portraits of the other officers and even a German general, who sent his drawings back to their wives. Before long a group of one hundred art students was formed in the camp, and Robin was asked to lecture them on art and artists. He wrote to his mother Dolly and told her that he was not impressed by the students' work: 'Taste frightful. Tradition despised, slickness is everything, colour violent.'

May's determination to continue working started to tell on her, and she grew very tired; she was eighty-six years old, her heart was weak, her arthritis and rheumatism painful, and she was shy of going out because of her deafness. But, although Mrs Iles and David Balneil urged her to leave London, she was determined to remain at the centre of things, even though just getting through the days was difficult. Her thoughts turned to death. On Christmas Day 1939, Dolly, who was busy with local war work for the Red Cross, as well as with the evacuees she had taken in at Kiddington, wrote affectionately to May:

Darling – your letter came today, Christmas Day, which was so lovely. It was so sweet – and it made me weep. I do understand – that you must long for rest. So for your sake I shall not grieve when the time comes – but

*you will continue to live vividly with all of us as an inspiration and a
wonderful memory of love – and we shall miss you terribly. You have
been my <u>mother</u> I feel – far more than most mothers could be. So I shall be
bound to feel sad – but I only want you to have release of spirit when life is
too weary, and I am sure that in a fuller life you will be very close to us. I
do wish you could see Peace on Earth before you go – when will it come?*

But May was not to see peace on earth again. Only when the Germans
began their night raids at the end of the summer of 1940 did she
reluctantly agree, at her doctor's insistence, to leave London. After
the first raid on London on 7 September, she left for Tunbridge Wells
in Kent. Here she settled in at Cliff Coombe, a nursing home she
knew well from previous visits when she had been ill, or simply tired.
It had recently moved to Tunbridge Wells from Broadstairs, but was
run by the same man, Alick Cater, who had become a friend. On 2
October she heard that 28 Albion Street, her one remaining home, had
been bombed the night before. It was the only house in the street to be
hit. Diana remembers seeing the 'hole' where the house had been,
which looked, she said 'like a gap in a row of teeth'.

May died peacefully in her sleep on 4 November. She had been
writing about the founding of her War Library a few hours earlier.
The next day her body was taken to London for private cremation,
and Daphne came to fetch the ashes, which she took back to
Hardwick. On 8 November Daphne got up early, as May's funeral
service was to take place at twelve noon at Kiddington church. Her
ashes would be buried next to Henry Brooks's grave. The morning
was fine and clear; Daphne, now aged over fifty, insisted that she did
not want to drive over to Kiddington, but that she would bicycle all
the way as she had so often done before. With the casket of ashes
instead of the usual dog in her front basket, she cycled briskly the
whole forty miles. When she arrived at Kiddington she joined Hal,
Dolly and the few other members of the family who were able to get
there. She put the ashes down on a chest in the hall, which stood
where May's Burne-Jones chest had once been.

Rose Iles, who had first come to work for May as a shy young
housemaid with blonde curls almost fifty years before, could perhaps
have been called the chief mourner at the funeral. She had been with

May at every twist and turn of her adult life, and seen all her joys and tragedies. There was no one now who had known May better. She had never married, but mature servants were frequently known as 'Mrs' out of respect. A small figure, Rose stood alone by the graveside as spots of rain began to fall. Thirty years before, she had stood beside May at Amy's funeral. Hal, Dolly and Daphne stood a little apart. There were also several people from the Red Cross Hospital Library. Even in death, May managed to raise funds for the library; as soon as her death was announced, a flood of donations arrived at their headquarters.

I was born near Kiddington three years after my great-grandmother died. Even if she had lived to a hundred I would not have remembered her very well; it is strange to realize that now it is I who must know her better than anyone alive, since I have made discoveries which even her granddaughter Diana says she knew nothing of. Yet how much do I really understand about her now? I have grown to admire her strength of character, her determination, her lively, curious and discerning mind, and her compassion. I would love to have met her, and for her to know me as 'one of those who came after'. Could she have explained the mystery of Amy's character and of her death, I wonder? Could we have discussed the difficulties of her marriage and her attachment to Burne-Jones? Would she have worried, as so many women do, that she had not been a good mother? And would I have been lucky enough to be told the secret of how she attracted devoted male admirers well into her eighties?

May's obituary in *The Times* suggested she could be formidable and daunting – 'a lady of charm and strong character who could at will dominate those around her with a smile or a stern look' – an impression which is borne out in the last photograph I have of her, taken when she was eighty-two. Yet one of her acquaintances, the writer and artist William Rothenstein, who met May in old age, remembered her 'indescribable charm of intellect and person', which he said made her 'beloved by men and women in every walk of life'. Burne-Jones, who had loved the younger May, had found in her qualities that fitted perfectly his fantasy of the ideal woman, and told her that she was 'a calm splendid soul like women of old, straight from heaven'.

To the very end of her long life, it is clear that May often thought back to Burne-Jones, and what he had been to her. Some of his letters never ceased to move her, and probably none more so than the one special letter on which she had pencilled in her old age: 'wonderful magic casement letter'. Written shortly before Burne-Jones's death, it is a long letter, and I imagine that its first sentence must have comforted May as she began to long for final rest:

> I'm glad I have lived – I am glad of all the past – it was worth all the miserable road I have travelled to come to this final home.

But it was a later paragraph that struck May particularly, and she marked it lovingly. As so often in Burne-Jones's letters, it conjures up images from his paintings, but particularly a painting he worked on throughout his last years, 'The Wizard', which portrayed an ageing man, recognizably Burne-Jones himself, showing a young girl a magic mirror, in which you can see ships on a stormy sea. The paragraph my great-grandmother marked seems to me to offer the most perfect promise of love, shelter and protection for May as she looked back on her past sadness and joy, and prepared herself for what now lay ahead.

> . . . you see May, it is these things of the soul that are real, and the only real things in the universe – and the little hidden chamber in my heart where you only can come is more real than your little bedroom – if you can believe it – I will furnish it for you – such a couch for your tired soul to lie on, and music there shall be always, soft and low, and little talks when you are refreshed – news of the outer world – when you are rested and can sit up and stand I'll open a little magic window and you shall choose what land you will see and what time in the world – you shall see Babylon being built if you like – or the Greeks coming into Greece – or the North Sea tossing and full of ships, or the piety of ancient France, plaintive notes of ancient Ireland, kings of Samarcand, Nibelungen terrors – all I have raked with greedy hands into my treasure house since I was a mean wretched looking object of ten till now – into that room with the magical window none has entrance but you.

SELECT BIBLIOGRAPHY

These are some of the books which I have found most informative:

Abdy, Jane and Charlotte Gere, *The Souls*, Sidgwick & Jackson, 1986.

Battersea, Constance, *Reminiscences*, Macmillan, 1992.

Bell, Malcolm, *Sir Edward Burne-Jones – Record and Review*, 1892.

Briggs, Asa, *They Saw It Happen 1897–1940*, 1960.

Briggs, Asa, *Victorian People*, Penguin Books, 1990.

Briggs, Asa, *Victorian Things*, Penguin Books, 1990.

Burne-Jones, Georgiana, *Memorials of Edward Burne-Jones*, 1940.

Cartwright, Julia, *The Life and Work of Sir E. Burne-Jones*, The Art Annual, 1894.

Cecil, David, *Visionary and Dreamer*, Constable, 1969.

Cecil, Hugh and Mirabel, *Imperial Marriage*, John Murray, 2002.

Christian, John, *Edward Burne-Jones*, Metropolitan Museum of Art, 1998.

Clifford, Sir Hugh, *The Downfall of the Gods*, John Murray, 1911.

Dakers, Caroline, *Yours Affectionately, Angelo*, The British Art Journal, 2001.

Fitzgerald, Penelope, *Edward Burne-Jones*, Hamish Hamilton, 1989.

Flanders, Judith, *A Circle of Sisters*, Penguin Books, 2001.

Glendinning, Victoria, *A Suppressed Cry*, Virago, 1995.

Haberly, Loyd, *An American Bookbuilder in England and Wales*, Rota, 1979.

Horner, Francis, *Time Remembered*, Heinemann, 1933.

Lago, Mary, *Burne-Jones Talking: the Conversations with Thomas Rooke 1895–1898*, John Murray, 1982.

Lambert, Angela, *Unquiet Souls*, Macmillan, 1984.

Lasdun, Susan, *Victorians at Home*, Weidenfeld & Nicolson, 1985.

Lycett, Andrew, *Rudyard Kipling*, Weidenfeld & Nicolson, 1999.

Macarthy, Fiona, *William Morris*, Faber & Faber, 1995.

Mackenzie, Jeanne, *The Children of the Souls*, Chatto & Windus, 1996.

Milner, Viscountess, *My Picture Gallery*, John Murray, 1951.

Priestley, J.B., *The Edwardians*, Penguin Books, 2000.

Robertson, W. Graham, *Time Was*, 1931.

Rose, Andrea, *Pre-Raphaelite Portraits*, Oxford Illustrated Press, 1981.

Strachey, Lytton, *Queen Victoria*, Chatto & Windus, 1929.

Thirkell, Angela, *Three Houses*, Moyer Bell, 1998.

Warner, Marina, *The Dragon Empress*, Weidenfeld & Nicolson, 1972.

Warrender, Lady Maud, *My First Sixty Years*, Cassell, 1933.

Waters, Bill, and Harrison, Martin, *Burne-Jones*, Barrie & Jenkins Ltd, 1973.

Wilson, A.N., *The Victorians*, Hutchinson, 2002.

Woolf, Leonard, *Growing – An Autobiography of the Years 1904–1911*, Hogarth Press, 1961.

INDEX